RAND M^cNALLY

D0745396

Historical
Atlas
of the World

HOUGHTON MIFFLIN

Credits

Cartography and Research
Robert K. Argersinger

Gregory Babiak

Barbara Strassheim Benstead

Justin Griffin

Susan Hudson

Felix Lopez

David Simmons

Andrew Skinner

Raymond Tobiaski

Howard Veregin

Editor
Brett R. Gover

Contributing Editors and Consultants
Janet Abu-Lughod, New School of Social Research

Guy Allito, University of Chicago

Ralph Austen, University of Chicago

Joshua Comenetz, University of Florida

George Grantham, Social Studies Liaison

Alan Kolata, University of Chicago

James F. Marran, Chairman Emeritus, Social Studies, New Trier High School

David Northrup, Boston College

R. R. Palmer, Princeton University

John Ruedy, Georgetown University

John Woods, University of Chicago

Design
Rand McNally Design

Map Credits
"The Kingdom of Mali" (page 24), "Trade Routes between Africa and India" (page 24), "The Maya World 300-900 A.D." (page 25), "The Inca Empire" (page 25), and "The Aztec Empire 1463-1532" (page 25) are used with permission of Houghton-Mifflin Company.

The "Afro-Eurasian Trade Circuits" inset map (page 31) is adapted from "Before European Hegemony" by Janet Abu-Lughod. Copyright © 1989 by Oxford University Press, Inc. Used by permission of Oxford University Press, Inc.

The "U.S. Population Movement 1910" map (page 95) is created from data provided by by John S. Adams, William C. Block, Mark Lindberg, Robert McMaster, Steven Ruggles, and Wendy Thomas, National Historical Geographic Information System: Pre-release Version 0.1, Minneapolis: Minnesota Population Center, University of Minnesota, 2004. www.nhgis.org.

Cover Photos
Copyright ©Getty/royalty free

Rand McNally & Company
Skokie, Illinois 60076

10 9 8 7 6 5 4

ISBN: 0-618-84191-1

Table of Contents

Geographic Index of Maps

Map	Page	Africa	Europe	The Middle East	China	Asia	Australia and Oceania	The Americas
Human Emergence on the Changing Face of Earth	6-7	•	•	•	•	•		
The Ancient World in the 7th Century B.C.	8	•	•	•		•		
Classical Greece and the Athenian Empire about 450 B.C.	9		•			•		
Ancient Persia 549 B.C.–651A.D.	10	•	•	•		•		
Han Dynasty 206 B.C.–220 A.D.	11				•	•		
Alexander's Empire 336–323 B.C.	12–13	•	•	•		•		
India 250 B.C. and 400 A.D.	14					•		
China about 100 B.C.	15				•	•		
Roman Republic 31 B.C.	16–17	•	•	•		•		
Roman Empire about 120 A.D.	18–19	•	•	•		•		
Roman Empire about 400 A.D.	20–21	•	•	•		•		
Eastern and Southern Asia about 750 A.D.	22–23			•	•	•		
Trade Routes between Africa and India	24	•		•		•		
The Kingdom of Mali	24	•						
The Maya World 300–900 A.D.	25							•
The Inca Empire 1463–1532	25							•
The Aztec Empire 1519	25							•
Africa circa 900 A.D.	26	•						
Africa circa 1400 A.D.	27	•						
Islamic World 800 A.D. and 1000 A.D.	28–29	•	•	•		•		
International Trade 1350–1450 A.D.	30–31	•	•	•	•	•		
Europe and the Crusader States about 1140	32–33		•	•		•		
Asia at the death of Kublai Khan, 1294	34–35		•	•	•	•		
Europe about 1360	36–37		•	•		•		
European Civilization during the Renaissance	38–39		•					
Europe's Age of Discovery: 15th–17th Centuries	40–41	•	•		•	•		•
Europe about 1560	42		•					
Ottoman Empire 1529–1789	43	•	•	•		•		
The Ottoman, Safavid, and Mughal Empires in 16th and 17th Centuries	44–45	•	•	•		•		
East Asia in the 16th Century	46–47				•	•		
Eastern and Southern Asia about 1775	48–49				•	•		
The Holy Roman Empire 1648	50–51		•					
Europe in 1721	52–53		•					
Native America 1200–1525	54–55							•
Revolutions in the Atlantic World, 1776–1826	56–57		•					•
Latin America about 1790	58–59							•
Latin America 1800–1900	60–61							•
Latin America after Independence: 1821–1929	62–63							•
Canada 1792–1840	64							•
Dominion of Canada 1867	65							•
Industrialization of Europe, 1850	66–67		•					
Expansion of Russia in Europe	68–69		•			•		
Expansion of Russia in Asia	70		•	•		•		
Balkan Peninsula to 1914	71		•	•		•		
Languages of Europe in the 19th Century	72–73		•	•		•		
African Diaspora to 1873	74–75	•	•	•	•	•	•	•
European Partition of Africa: 19th Century	76–77	•						
Resistance to European Colonialism 1870–1917	78–79	•	•	•	•	•	•	
The World About 1900	80–81	•	•	•	•	•	•	•
Asia 1900	82–83	•		•	•	•		
Second World War	84–85	•	•	•	•	•		
Korean War / Vietnam War	86					•		
U.S. Involvement in Central America and the Caribbean 1959–1999	87							•
Political and Military Alliances 2004	88	•	•	•	•	•	•	•
World Economic Alliances 2004	89	•	•	•	•	•	•	•
World Gross Domestic Product 2004	90	•	•	•	•	•	•	•
World Literacy 2004	91	•	•	•	•	•	•	•
World Languages	92	•	•	•	•	•	•	•
World Religions	93	•	•	•	•	•	•	•
World Population Density 1913 and 2000	94	•	•	•	•	•	•	•
U.S. Population Density 1910 and 2000	95							•
Ethnic Diversity in the United States	96							•
Breakup of Yugoslavia	97		•					
Middle East Events, 1945–2006	98-99		•	•		•		
The Extent of Islam	100-101	•	•	•	•	•	•	•
The Islamic World	102-103	•	•	•	•	•		
World Physical Map	104-105	•	•	•	•	•	•	•
World Political Map	106-107	•	•	•	•	•	•	•

Introduction

Information about the past is compiled, stored, and made accessible in a variety of ways. One of these ways is historical maps. Historical maps provide a chronology of important events and show the impact these events had on the places where they occurred. Historical maps support and extend information from primary historical resources such as letters, treaties, and census data. Historical maps are summaries of past events in graphic form.

The maps in the Rand McNally *Historical Atlas of the World* portray the rich panoply of the world's history from preliterate times to the present. They show how cultures and civilization were linked and how they interacted. The maps make it clear that history is not static. Rather, it is about change and movement across time. The maps show change by presenting the dynamics of expansion, cooperation, and conflict.

Benefits of Using the Rand McNally *Historical Atlas of the World*

Events gain fuller meaning.

Knowing where events took place gives them fuller meaning and often explains causes and effects. For example, the map showing Russia's expansion in Europe clearly illustrates that a major goal of the czars was to access warm-water ports that would connect their realm to the world's seas and oceans.

Connections among events are clarified.

Through the visual power of historical maps, the links between and among events become clearer. The maps showing diffusion of languages and religions are good illustrations of this, as is the map of Native Americans that details the rise and fall of indigenous peoples of North and South America.

Similarities and differences become apparent.

The maps in this historical atlas provide the opportunity to compare and contrast places over time. For example, the series of Roman Empire maps present snapshots of the empire at three different points in time.

The influence of sense of place is conveyed.

Maps in this atlas can convey a people's sense of place at a particular time in history. The map of Europe's Age of Discovery is a good illustration. The cartographer has deliberately centered the continent so that the map's projection reflects the extent and ambition of Europe's exploration at the end of the Renaissance.

Trends emerge.

Another benefit of using this historical atlas is that trends become apparent. Maps of the westward expansion of the United States show how the nation was settled, what technologies were used, who was displaced, and in what sequence. In another example, the inset map of the Mogul Empire in India under Aurangzeb reveals how a dynasty can become powerfully established in little more than a century.

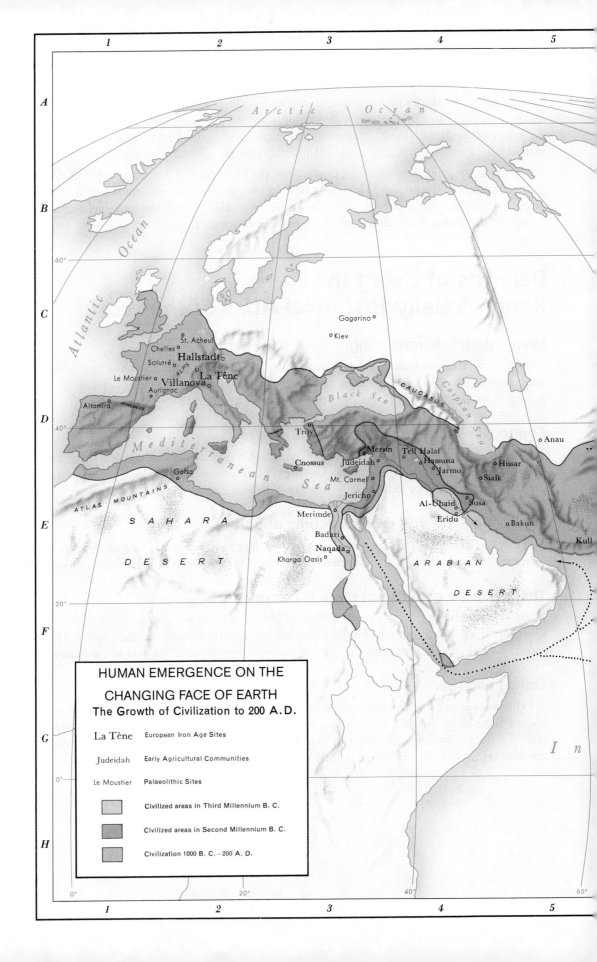

HUMAN EMERGENCE ON THE
CHANGING FACE OF EARTH
The Growth of Civilization to 200 A.D.

La Tène   European Iron Age Sites

Judeidah   Early Agricultural Communities

Le Moustier Palaeolithic Sites

Civilized areas in Third Millennium B. C.

Civilized areas in Second Millennium B. C.

Civilization 1000 B. C. — 200 A. D.

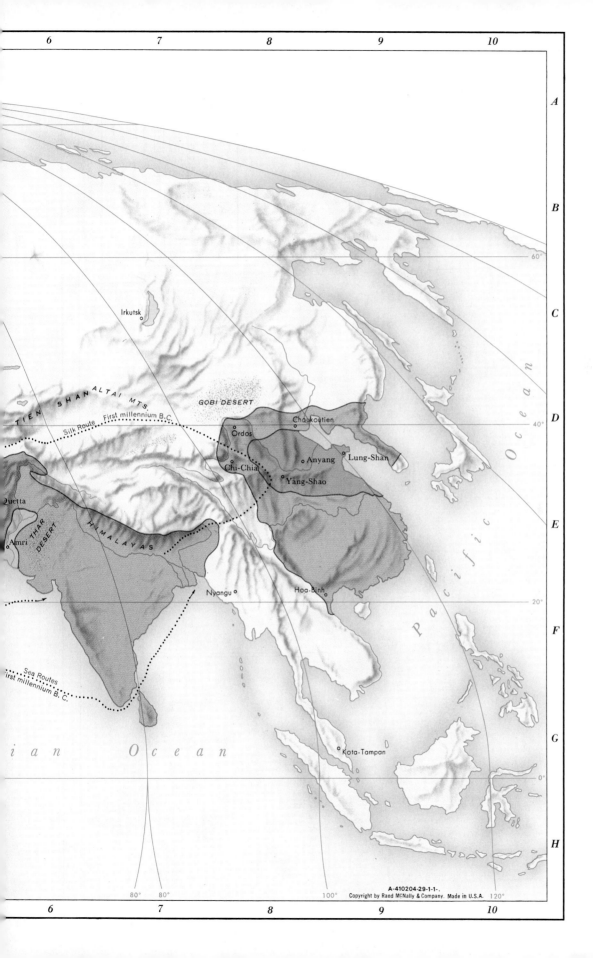

6   7   8   9   10

A

B

60°

C

Irkutsk

TIEN SHAN ALTAI MTS.

GOBI DESERT

D   40°

Silk Route   First millennium B.C.

Ordos

Chaukoutien

Anyang   Lung-Shan

Chi-Chia

Yang-Shao

Quetta

E   20°

THAR DESERT

Amri   HIMALAYAS

Nyangu

Hoa-Binh

F

Sea Routes

irst millennium B. C.

Pacific Ocean

G

Kota-Tampan

ian   Ocean

0°

H

80°   80°   100°   120°

A-410204-29-1-1-.

Copyright by Rand McNally & Company. Made in U.S.A.

6   7   8   9   10

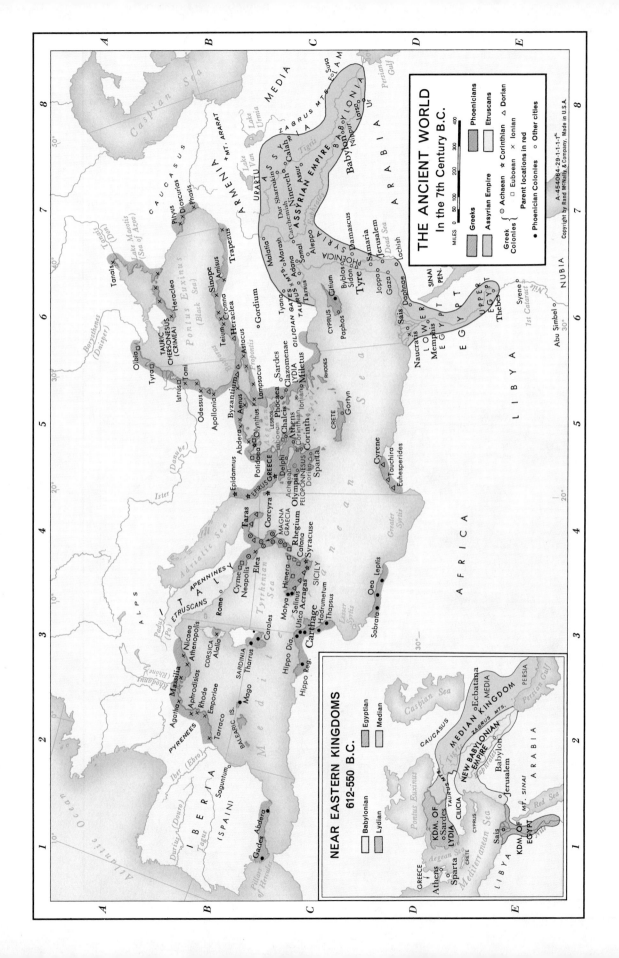

THE ANCIENT WORLD
In the 7th Century B.C.

MILES 0 50 100 200 300 400

Greeks
Assyrian Empire
Phoenicians
Etruscans

Greek Colonies:
○ Achaean   ☆ Corinthian   △ Dorian
□ Euboean   × Ionian

Parent locations in red
● Phoenician Colonies   ○ Other cities

A-454064-29-1-1-1″
Copyright by Rand McNally & Company. Made in U.S.A.

NEAR EASTERN KINGDOMS
612-550 B.C.

Babylonian
Lydian
Egyptian
Median

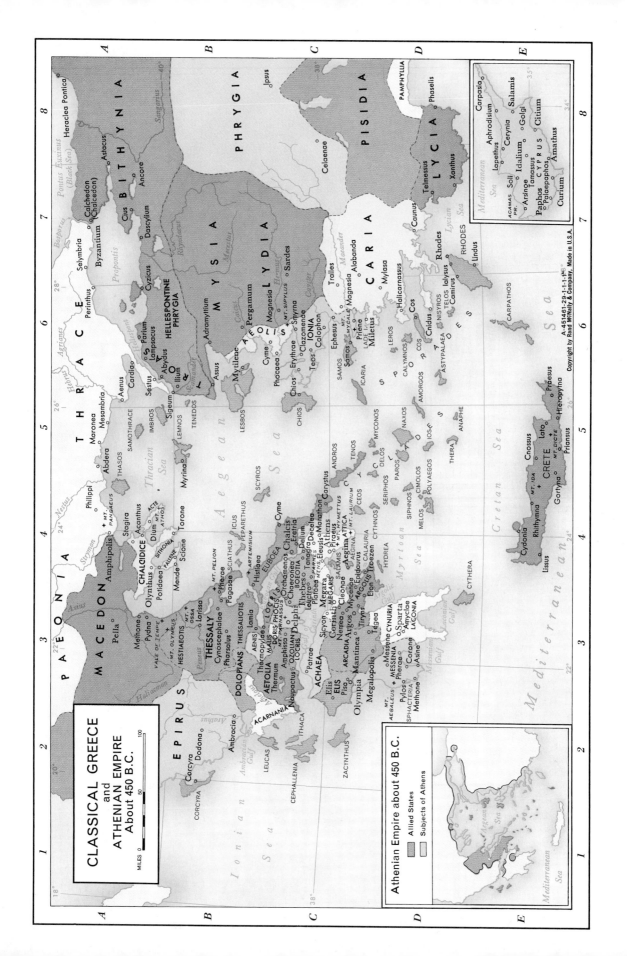

CLASSICAL GREECE and ATHENIAN EMPIRE About 450 B.C.

MILES 0   50   100

Athenian Empire about 450 B.C.

Allied States
Subjects of Athens

Copyright by Rand McNally & Company, Made in U.S.A.
A-451461-29-1-1-1-1

9

ANCIENT PERSIA 549 B.C. – 651 A.D.

SASANIAN EMPIRE 224 – 651 A.D.

Christian Centers:
◇ Nestorian
◇ Monophysite
□ Zoroastrian Center
■ Buddhist Center
● Capital City
Area of Irrigation

MILES
KILOMETRES

Disputed Area along the Frontier of the Empire
Trade Route
Sasanian Campaigns
Invasion by the Byzantines
Invasion by the Hephthalites

PARTHIAN EMPIRE 141 B.C. – 224 A.D.

Greatest Extent of the Empire
Royal Road
Disputed Area along the Frontier
Trade Center
Invasion by the Romans
Christian City
Invasion by the Saka Tribes
Capital City

MILES
KILOMETRES

ACHAEMENID EMPIRE 549 – 330 B.C.

Greatest Extent of the Empire
Disputed Area along the Frontier of the Empire
Royal Road
Route of the 10,000 (401 B.C.)
Darius I Expedition into Scythia
The 20 Satrapies of Herodotus
Trade Route
XX
Administrative Center

MILES
KILOMETRES

10

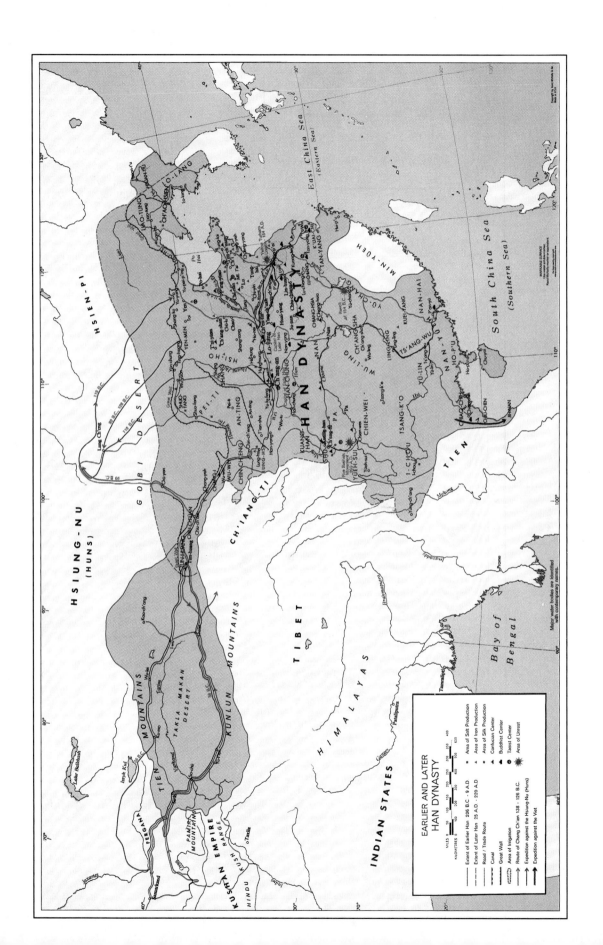

EARLIER AND LATER
HAN DYNASTY

Extent of Earlier Han 206 B.C. - 9 A.D.	✴ Area of Salt Production
Extent of Later Han 25 A.D. - 220 A.D.	⬥ Area of Iron Production
Road / Trade Route	▲ Area of Silk Production
Canal	⬤ Confucian Center
Great Wall	◆ Buddhist Center
Area of Irrigation	☯ Taoist Center
Route of Chang Ch'ien 138 - 126 B.C.	✸ Area of Unrest
Expedition against the Hsiung-Nu (Huns)	
Expedition against the Viet	

MILES 0   50   100   150   200   250   300   350   400
KILOMETRES 0   100   200   300   400   500   600

11

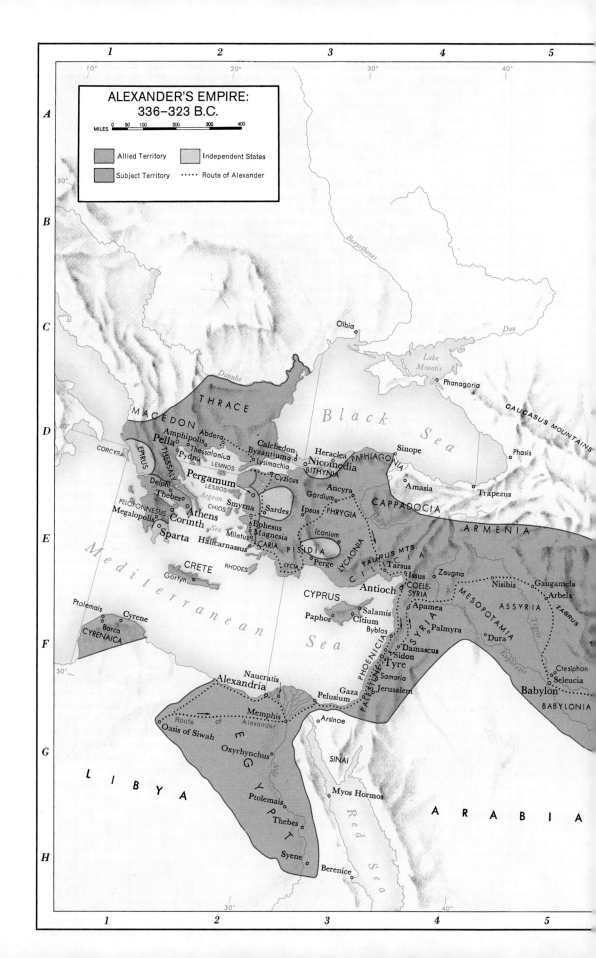

ALEXANDER'S EMPIRE:
336–323 B.C.

MILES 0 50 100 200 300 400

Allied Territory
Subject Territory
Independent States
Route of Alexander

Black Sea

Olbia

Lake Maeotis

Phanagoria

Don

CAUCASUS MOUNTAINS

Phasis

Borysthenes

Danube

THRACE

MACEDON

Abdera

Amphipolis
Pella
Thessalonica
Pydna

Calchedon
Byzantium
Lysimachia

Heraclea

Nicomedia
BITHYNIA

PAPHLAGONIA

Sinope

Amasia

Trapezus

EPIRUS
THESSALY

Delphi
Thebes

Pergamum
LESBOS

LEMNOS

Cyzicus

Ancyra
Gordium

PHRYGIA

Ipsus

CAPPADOCIA

ARMENIA

CORCYRA

Aegean Sea

Smyrna
CHIOS

Sardes

PELOPONNESUS
Megalopolis

Athens
Corinth

Ephesus
Miletus
Magnesia
CARIA

Iconium

LYCAONIA

TAURUS MTS.

C I L I C I A

Sparta

Halicarnassus

PISIDIA

Perge

Tarsus

Issus

Zeugma

Gaugamela

Nisibis
Arbela

CRETE
Gortyn

RHODES

LYCIA

Antioch
COELE-
SYRIA

Apamea

MESOPOTAMIA

ASSYRIA

ZAGRUS

CYPRUS

Paphos

Salamis
Citium
Byblos

Palmyra

Dura

Tigris

Ptolemais
Cyrene
Barca
CYRENAICA

Mediterranean

Sea

PHOENICIA

Damascus
Sidon
Tyre

SYRIA

Euphrates

Ctesiphon
Seleucia

Babylon

BABYLONIA

Naucratis

Alexandria

Gaza
Pelusium

Samaria
Jerusalem

PALESTINE

Memphis

Arsinoe

Route of Alexander

Oasis of Siwah

E
G
Y
P
T

Oxyrhynchus

Nile

SINAI

L I B Y A

Ptolemais

Thebes

Myos Hormos

Red Sea

A R A B I A

Syene

Berenice

10°   20°   30°   40°

50°

40°

30°

30°   40°

1   2   3   4   5

A   B   C   D   E   F   G   H

12

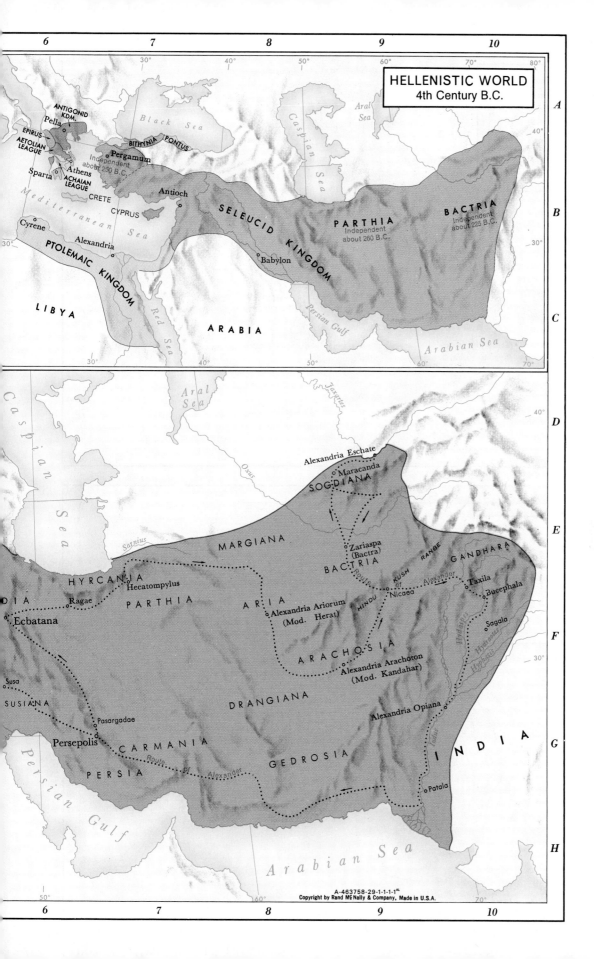

6   7   8   9   10

30°   40°   50°   60°   70°   80°

HELLENISTIC WORLD
4th Century B.C.

A

Aral Sea

40°

Black Sea

ANTIGONID KDM.
Pella
EPIRUS
AETOLIAN LEAGUE

BITHYNIA   **PONTUS**

Caspian Sea

B

Pergamum
Independent about 250 B.C.

Sparta
Athens
ACHAIAN LEAGUE

CRETE

Antioch

CYPRUS

SELEUCID KINGDOM

PARTHIA
Independent about 260 B.C.

BACTRIA
Independent about 225 B.C.

40°

30°

Cyrene

Mediterranean Sea

Alexandria

PTOLEMAIC KINGDOM

Babylon

30°

LIBYA

Red Sea

ARABIA

Persian Gulf

Arabian Sea

C

70°

Aral Sea

Jaxartes

40°

D

Alexandria Eschate

Caspian Sea

Oxus

Maracanda
SOGDIANA

MARGIANA

Sarnius

Zariaspa
(Bactra)
BACTRIA

RANGE

GANDHARA

E

40°

HYRCANIA
Hecatompylus

KUSH

Nicaea

Taxila

Bucephala

DIA
Ragae

PARTHIA

ARIA

Alexandria Ariorum
(Mod. Herat)

HINDU

Alexander

Hydaspes

Ecbatana

ARACHOSIA

Sagala

F

30°

Susa

SUSIANA

Alexandria Arachoton
(Mod. Kandahar)

Hydraotis

Hyphasis

Pasargadae

DRANGIANA

Alexandria Opiana

Indus

I N D I A

Persepolis

CARMANIA

Route of Alexander

GEDROSIA

G

Persian Gulf

PERSIA

Patala

H

Arabian Sea

50°   60°   70°

A-463758-29-1-1-1-1^AC
Copyright by Rand McNally & Company, Made in U.S.A.

6   7   8   9   10

INDIA 250 B.C. AND 400 A.D.

MAURYAN EMPIRE
under Asoka
about 250 B.C.

MILES 0 50 100 200 300

Mauryan Empire
+ Archaeological sites

Birthplace of
Gautama Buddha
563? B.C.

SOGDIANA
BACTRIA
(HINDU KUSH)
ARIA-
PAROPANISADAI
ARACHOSIA
GEDROSIA
KASHMIR
GANDHARA
Taxila
(KARAKORAM MTS.)
(KHYBER PASS)
+ Harappa Site
Location of early
Indo-Aryan
Civilization
Mohenjo-
Daro site +
Pattala
SAUVIRA
(THAR DESERT)
(Indus)
Sindhu
SURASHTRA
Bharukaccha
Surparaka
(Soparai)
MAHARASHTRA
AVANTI
Ujjain
Indraprastha
Mathura
Kausombi
Prayaga
Kosi
Ayodhya
Sravasti
KOSALA
Kapilavastu
Paton
Vaisali
MAGADHA
Rajagriha
Pataliputra
PUNDRA-
VARDHANA
Champa
TAMALITTI
Tamralipti
VANGA
SAMATATA
KALINGA
Tosali
ANDHRA
Godavari
Krishna
Mahanadi
Ganga
(Ganges)
Yamuna
(HIMALAYA M'T'S.)
Ganga
Sanchi
KERALA
SATIYA
CHOLA
PANDYA
Kanchi
Anuradhapura
TAMRAPARNI
(CEYLON)
(A r a b i a n   S e a)
(B a y   o f   B e n g a l)
Oxus

Copyright by Rand McNally & Company. Made in U.S.A.

GUPTA EMPIRE
under Chandragupta II
about 400 A.D.

MILES 0 50 100 200 300

Gupta Empire
States tributary to Empire

(HINDU KUSH)
(KARAKORAM MTS.)
Remnant of
KUSHAN
EMPIRE
Purushapura
(Indus)
Sindhu
Oxus
ABHIRA
SURASHTRA
Valabhi
Surparaka
(Soparai)
Bharukaccha
(Barygaza)
KONKAN
Muziris
CHERA
PANDYA
Madura
GANGA
Kanchi
CHOLA
PALLAVA
KADAMBA
Bonavasi
Nosik
Pratishhana
(Paithan)
KONKAN
MALAVA
Ujjain
Padmavati
Mathura
EMPIRE
GUPTA
(Indraprastha)
Sakala
KARTRIPURA
MADRA
YAUDHEYA
ARJUNAYANA
(THAR DESERT)
Kanyakubja
Kausombi
Eran
Bharhut
Sanchi
Prayaga
Kosi
Sravasti
Ayodhya
Vaisali
Pataliputra
Nalanda
Bodh Gaya
Champa
Tamralipti
SAMATATA
KAMARUPA
NEPAL
(HIMALAYA M'T'S.)
Ganges
Jumna
NAHAKOSALA
VAKATAKA
DEVA RASHTRA
Amaravati
VENGI
Godavari
Krishna
Mahanadi
Narbada
Anuradhapura
SIMHALA
(CEYLON)
(A r a b i a n   S e a)
(B a y   o f   B e n g a l)

Copyright by Rand McNally & Company, Made in U.S.A.

14

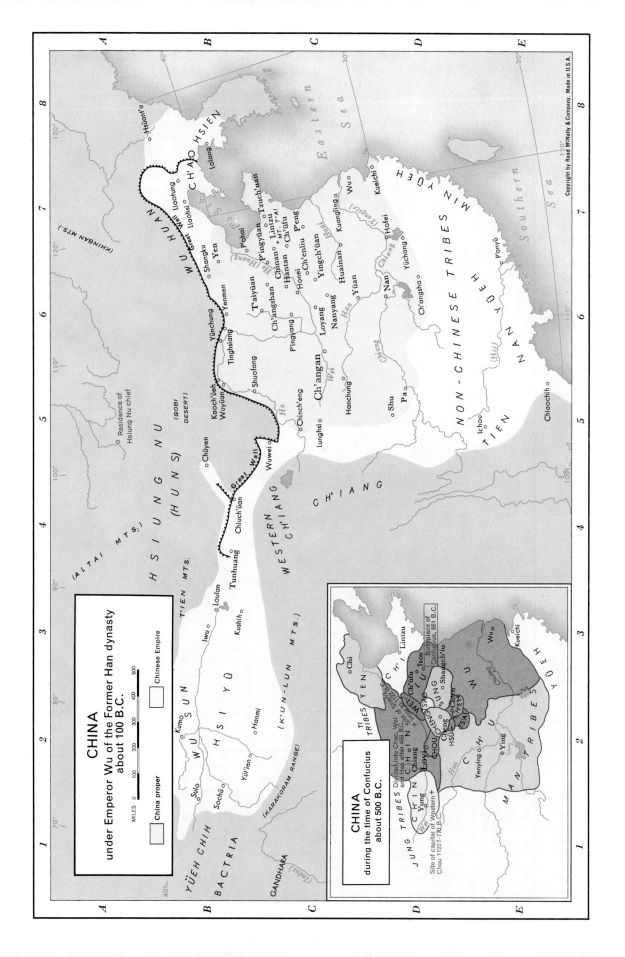

CHINA
under Emperor Wu of the Former Han dynasty about 100 B.C.

MILES
0   100   200   300   400   500

China proper

Chinese Empire

(KHINGAN MTS.)

(ALTAI MTS.)

Residence of
Hsiung Nu chief

HSIUNG NU
(HUNS)

(GOBI DESERT)

TIEN MTS.

YÜEH CHIH

BACTRIA

GANDHARA

Indus

Solo
Sochü
Yütien

(KUN-LUN MTS.)

(KARAKORAM RANGE)

Kumo
WU SUN
HSI YÜ
Hanmi
Kushih
Loulan
Iwu

HSÜ

Hsüan?u

Wall
Liaotung
Great
Liaohsi

CH'AO HSIEN

Lolang

WU HUA
HUA

Shangku
Yen

Pohai

Shuofang
Wuyüan
Kaoch'üeh

Chüyen

Great Wall

Chiuch'üan

Tunhuang

WESTERN CH'IANG

CH'IANG

Lunghsi

Chinch'eng

Hanchung

Shu

Pa

Ichou

TIEN

Ho

Wei

Wuwei

Yünchung
Yenmen
Tinghsiang

T'aiyüan
Ch'angshan
P'ingyang
P'ingyüan
Chinan
Hantan
Honei
Loyang
Nanyang
Yingch'uan

Lintzu
Tzuch'üan
MT. T'AI
Ch'ufu
P'eng
Ch'enliu

Ho (Huang)

Eastern Sea

Wu
Kueichi

Kuangling

Huainan
Nan
Yüan
Ch'ang

Hofei

Yüchang

Han
Chiang
Hsi

Chiang (Yangtze)

NON-CHINESE TRIBES
HU NAN

MIN YÜEH

NAN YÜEH

Ch'angsha

Chiaochih

Panyü

Southern Sea

Copyright by Rand McNally & Company. Made in U.S.A.

CHINA
during the time of Confucius about 500 B.C.

JUNG TRIBES

TI TRIBES

YEN
Chi
Lintzu

CH'I

CH'IN
Yung

Wu

CHOU
Loyi

CH'IN

SUNG
Tsou
Birthplace of Confucius, 551 B.C.

Shangch'iu

CHENG
HSÜ

Divided into Chao, Wei and Han after 456 B.C.

WU
Kueichi

TS'AO

HSÜ
CHEN
YEN

Ch'en
Ying

Chiang

Yenying

MAN TRIBES

YÜEH

Han

Wu = Western +

Site of capital of Western + Chou 1122?-770 B.C.

15

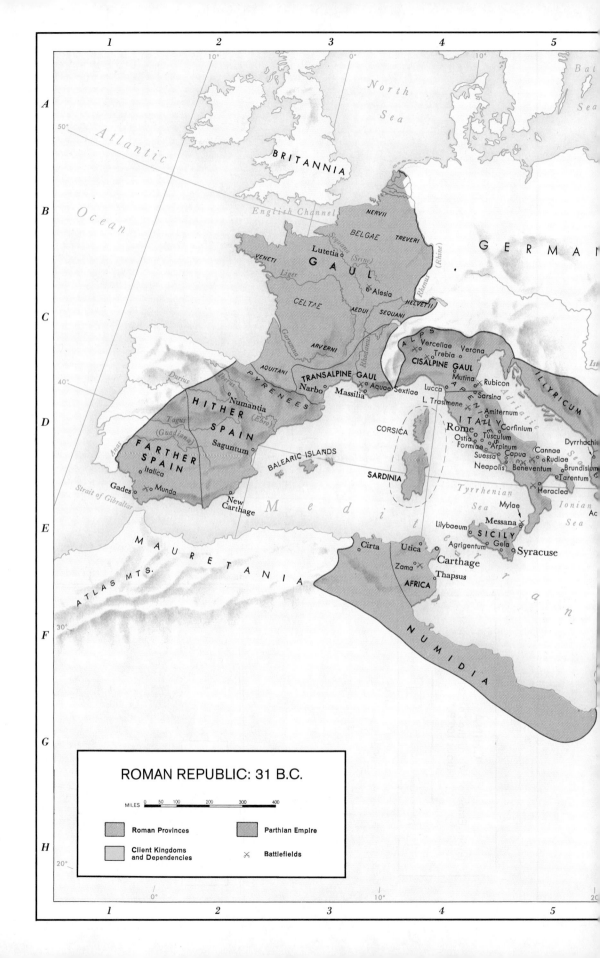

ROMAN REPUBLIC: 31 B.C.

MILES 0 50 100   200   300   400

| | Roman Provinces | | Parthian Empire |
| | Client Kingdoms and Dependencies | ✗ | Battlefields |

16

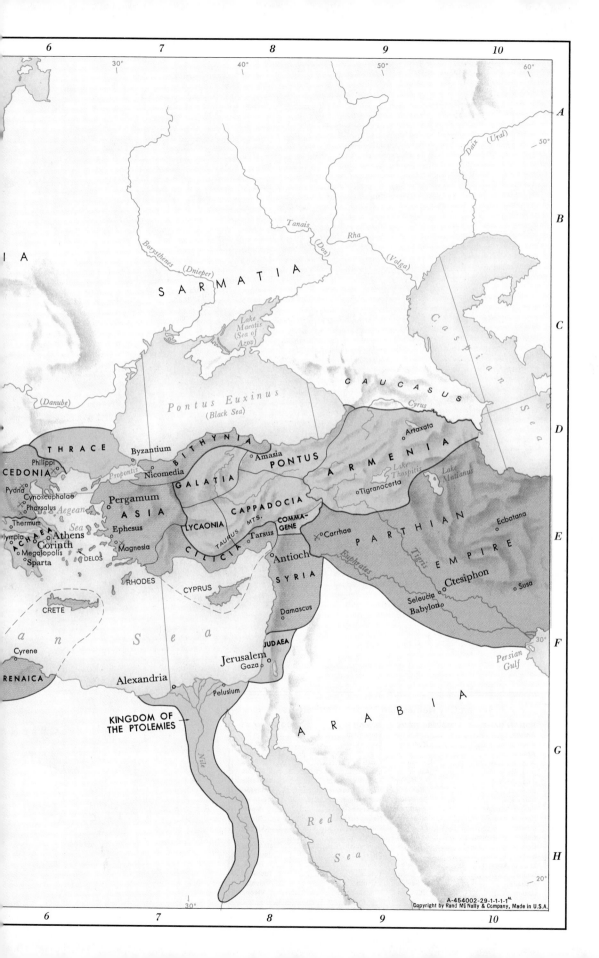

6   7   8   9   10

30°   40°   50°   60°

A

50°

B

S A R M A T I A

Tanais (Don)

Borysthenes (Dnieper)

Rha (Volga)

Daix (Ural)

C

Lake Maeotis (Sea of Azov)

Caspian Sea

Pontus Euxinus (Black Sea)

C A U C A S U S

Cyrus

D

(Danube)

THRACE

Philippi

CEDONIA

Byzantium

BITHYNIA

Nicomedia

Propontis

GALATIA

Amasia

PONTUS

A R M E N I A

Artaxata

Lake Thospitis

Lake Matianus

Pydna
Cynoscephalae
Pharsalus
Thermum

Pergamum

ASIA

Ephesus

LYCAONIA

CAPPADOCIA

Tigranocerta

P A R T H I A N

Ecbatana

E

Aegean Sea

Olympia
ACHAEA
Athens
Corinth
Megalopolis
Sparta

DELOS

Magnesia

TAURUS MTS.

CILICIA

Tarsus

COMMA-
GENE

Carrhae

Euphrates

E M P I R E

Tigris

Susa

RHODES

CYPRUS

Antioch

SYRIA

Ctesiphon

Seleucia
Babylon

CRETE

Damascus

F

30°

a n   *S e a*

Cyrene

JUDAEA

Jerusalem

Gaza

Persian Gulf

RENAICA

Alexandria

Pelusium

A R A B I A

G

KINGDOM OF
THE PTOLEMIES

Nile

Red

H

20°

Sea

A-454002-29-1-1-1-1^AL
Copyright by Rand McNally & Company, Made in U.S.A.

6   7   8   9   10

30°

North Sea

Atlantic Ocean

Baltic Sea

IRELAND

BRITAIN
Wall of Antoninus
Wall of Hadrian
Eburacum
Deva
Lindum
BRITAIN
Camulodunum
Londinium

English Channel

Elbe
GERMANY
(Lost in 9 A D)
Colonia Agrippina

Vistula

LOWER GERMANY
Lugdunum Batavorum
Moguntiacum

Augusta Treverorum
BELGICA
Lutetia
LUGDUNENSIS
GAUL
Argentoratum

Cantabrian Sea
Liger

CARPATHIANS

Augustodunum
UPPER GERMANY
Vindonissa
Augusta Vindelicorum
Vindobona
Carnuntum
Aquincum
NORICUM
PANNONIA

Burdigala
AQUITANIA
Lugdunum

Rhine

Sarmizegetusa
(Colonia Ulpia Trajana)

Bracara Augusta
Portus Cale
Douro
Asturica
TARRACONENSIS
PYRENNES
Numantia
SPAIN
Caesar Augusta
Ilerda
Tolosa
NARBONENSIS
ALPINE PROVS.
Nemausus
Arelate
Narbo
Comum
Mediolanum
Verona
Aquileia
Genua
ILLYRICUM
Siscia
Sirmium
DACIA
Vindobona
Vindelicorum
DALMATIA
Vimiliacium
Naissus
MOESIA

Salmantica
LUSITANIA
Emerita Augusta
Olisipo
Ebro
Tagus
Toletum
Valentia
Tarraco
Massilia
Ligurian Sea
Florentia
Ancona
Salonae
Narona
Serdica
Philippopol

Guadiana
Corduba
BAETICA
Hispalis
Castulo
BALEARIC IS.
CORSICA AND SARDINIA
ITALY
Rome
Ostia
Adriatic Sea
Dyrrhachium
MACEDONIA
Thessalonic

Munda
Gades
Malaca
New Carthage
Carales
Tyrrhenian Sea
Capua
Pompeii
Tarentum
Brundisium
CORCYRA
EPIRUS
Demetr

Tingis
MAURETANIA
Hippo Diarrhytus
Hippo Regius
Sitifis
Utica
Messana
Rhegium
Ionian Sea
Corinth
ACHAIA
Athe
Sparta

ATLAS MTS.
GAETULIA
Lambaesis
Cirta
Theveste
Carthage
Agrigentum
SICILY
Syracuse

Thamugadi
AFRICA
Hadrumetum
Thapsus
Mediterranean

Lesser Syrtis
NUMIDIA
Oea
Leptis
Greater Syrtis
CRETE AND
Gorty

Cyrene
CYRENA
AFRICA

Roman City Names and Modern Equivalents

ROMAN NAME	MODERN NAME	ROMAN NAME	MODERN NAME
Ancyra	Ankara	Londinium	London
Aquincum	Budapest	Lugdunum	Lyon
Arelate	Arles	Lugdunum Batavorum	Leiden
Augusta Treverorum	Trier, Treves	Lutetia	Paris
Augusta Vindelicorum	Augsburg	Malaca	Malaga
Augustodunum	Autun	Massilia	Marseille
Bononia	Bologna	Mazaca Caesarea	Kayseri
Burdigala	Bordeaux	Mediolanum	Milan
Caesar Augusta	Saragossa	Moguntiacum	Mainz
Camulodunum	Colchester	Nemausus	Nimes
Carales	Cagliari	Olisipo	Lisbon
Colonia Agrippina	Cologne	Patavium	Padua
Deva	Chester	Salmantica	Salamanca
Eburacum	York	Thessalonica	Salonika
Emerita Augusta	Merida	Toletum	Toledo
Gades	Cadiz	Tolosa	Toulouse
Hispalis	Seville	Valentia	Valencia
Lindum	Lincoln	Vindobona	Vienna

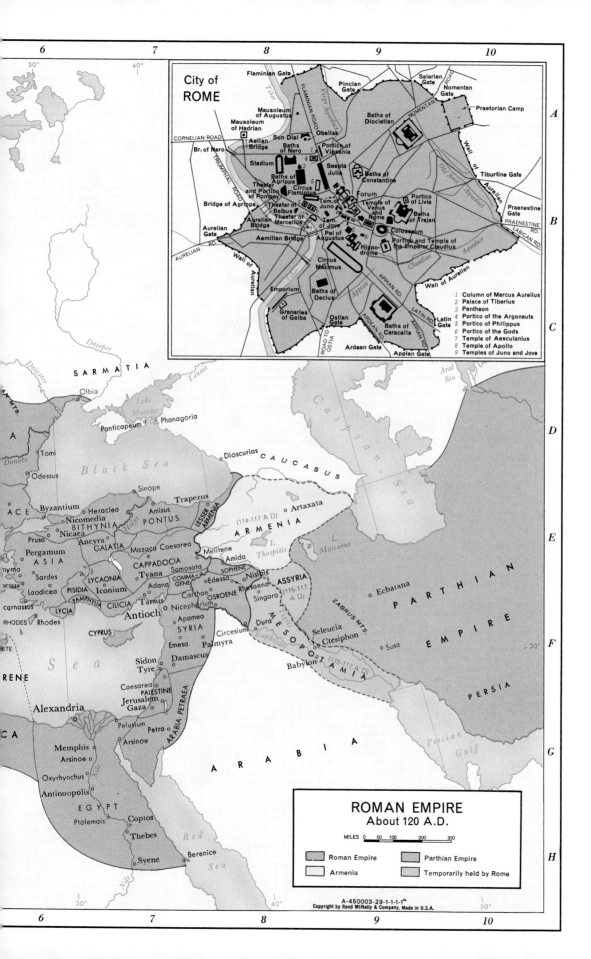

City of
ROME

Flaminian Gate
Pincian Gate
Salarian Gate
Nomentan Gate
Praetorian Camp
Mausoleum of Augustus
Mausoleum of Hadrian
Sun Dial
Obelisk
Baths of Diocletian
CORNELIAN ROAD
Aelian Bridge
Baths of Nero
Portico of Vipsania
Br. of Nero
Stadium
Saepta Julia
Tiburtine Gate
Baths of Agrippa
Baths of Constantine
Theater and Portico of Pompey
Circus Flaminius
Temple of Juno
Forum
Temple of Venus and Rome
Portico of Livia
Aurelian Aqueduct
Praenestine Gate
Bridge of Agrippa
Theater of Balbus
Theater of Marcellus
Baths of Trajan
PRAENESTINE RD.
Aurelian Bridge
Tem. of Jove
Colosseum
LABICAN RD.
Aurelian Gate
Pal. of Augustus
Portico and Temple of the Emperor Claudius
Aemilian Bridge
Hippo-drome
Wall of Aurelian
Circus Maximus
Emporium
Baths of Decius
Aqueduct
Granaries of Galba
Ostian Gate
Baths of Caracalla
Ardean Gate
Appian Gate

ROAD TO OSTIA

1 Column of Marcus Aurelius
2 Palace of Tiberius
3 Pantheon
4 Portico of the Argonauts
5 Portico of Philippus
6 Portico of the Gods
7 Temple of Aesculanius
8 Temple of Apollo
9 Temples of Juno and Jove

SARMATIA
Olbia
Dnieper
Dniester
Tanais
Aral Sea
Lake Maeotis
Panticapeum
Phanagoria
Caspian Sea
Black Sea
Dioscurias
CAUCASUS
Tomi
Danube
Odessus
Sinope
Trapezus
Artaxata
Byzantium
Heraclea
Amisus
LESSER ARMENIA
(114-117 A.D.)
ARMENIA
Nicomedia
PONTUS
Nicaea
BITHYNIA
Ancyra
GALATIA
Melitene
L. Thospitis
L. Matianus
Pergamum
ASIA
Mazaca Caesarea
Amida
Prusa
CAPPADOCIA
Ecbatana
Sardes
Tyana
Samosata
SOPHENE
Laodicea
LYCAONIA
Iconium
COMMA-GENE
Edessa
Nisibis
ASSYRIA
(115-117 A.D.)
PARTHIAN
PISIDIA
Adana
Carrhae
Rhesaena
EMPIRE
PAMPHYLIA
CILICIA
Tarsus
OSROENE
Singara
ZAGRUS MTS.
RHODES
Nicephorium
Susa
Rhodes
LYCIA
Apamea
Dura
Seleucia
Antioch
SYRIA
Ctesiphon
MESOPOTAMIA
PERSIA
CYPRUS
Emesa
Palmyra
Circesium
Euphrates
Sidon
Damascus
Babylon
(115-117 A.D.)
Tyre
Caesarea
PALESTINE
Jerusalem
ARABIA PETRAEA
Gaza
Persian Gulf
Alexandria
Pelusium
Petra
Memphis
Arsinoe
ARABIA
Oxyrhynchus
Antinoopolis
EGYPT
Ptolemais
Coptos
Thebes
Red Sea
Syene
Berenice
Nile

ROMAN EMPIRE
About 120 A.D.

MILES 0 50 100 200 300

Roman Empire   Parthian Empire
Armenia   Temporarily held by Rome

A-450003-29-1-1-1-1
Copyright by Rand McNally & Company, Made in U.S.A.

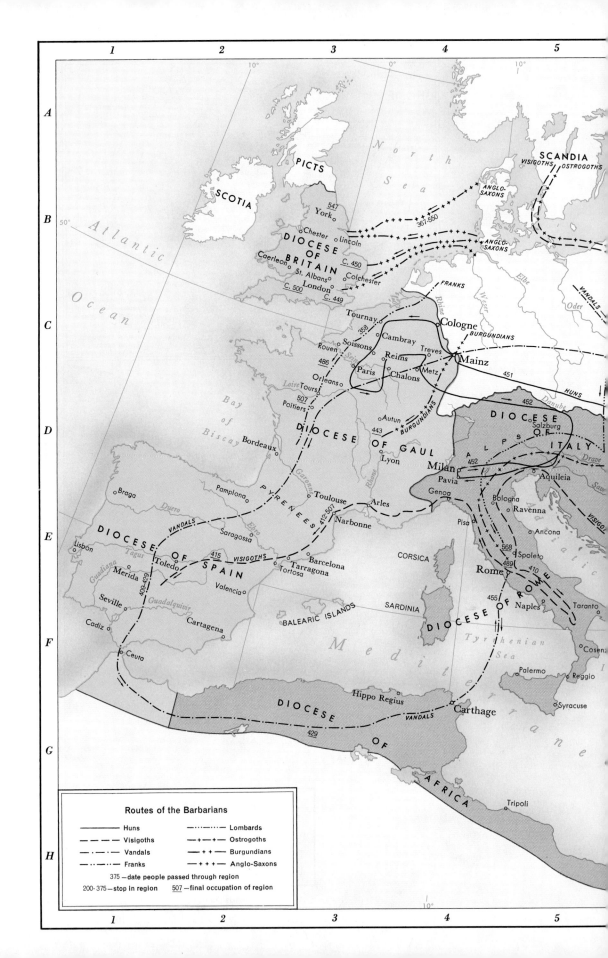

Routes of the Barbarians

———— Huns	———·———·——— Lombards
— — — Visigoths	—+—+—+— Ostrogoths
—·—·—·— Vandals	+ + + Burgundians
—··—··— Franks	+ + + Anglo-Saxons

375 —date people passed through region

200- 375 —stop in region   507 —final occupation of region

PICTS

SCOTIA

SCANDIA

VISIGOTHS OSTROGOTHS

ANGLO-SAXONS

361-550

ANGLO-SAXONS

VANDALS

547
York

Chester Lincoln

DIOCESE
OF
BRITAIN

C. 450

Caerleon St. Albans
London Colchester
C. 500 C. 449

North Sea

FRANKS

Rhine Weser Elbe Oder

Tournay
358
Cambray Cologne
Soissons Treves BURGUNDIANS
Rouen Reims Mainz
486 Paris Metz
Orleans Chalons 451 HUNS
Tours
507 Poitiers
Autun 452 Danube
443 BURGUNDIANS
DIOCESE OF GAUL
Lyon DIOCESE Salzburg
OF
ITALY
Milan 452 Aquileia
Pavia Drave
Bordeaux Genoa Bologna Save
Ravenna
Braga Pamplona Pisa VISIGO.
PYRENEES Toulouse Arles Ancona
Saragossa Narbonne 568 Spoleto
Duero Ebro 412-507 489 410 Rome
VANDALS 455 Naples Taranto
Lisbon 415 VISIGOTHS CORSICA
Toledo Barcelona Tortosa Cosenza
DIOCESE OF Tarragona SARDINIA DIOCESE OF ROME Palermo Reggio
Merida SPAIN Valencia BALEARIC ISLANDS Syracuse
409-429
Seville Cartagena
Cadiz Tyrrhenian
Ceuta Sea
Mediterranean
Hippo Regius Carthage
DIOCESE VANDALS
429 OF
AFRICA Tripoli

Atlantic Ocean

Bay of Biscay

Seine Loire Garonne Rhone Tagus Guadiana Guadalquivir

ALPS

10° 0° 10°

50°

A B C D E F G H

1 2 3 4 5

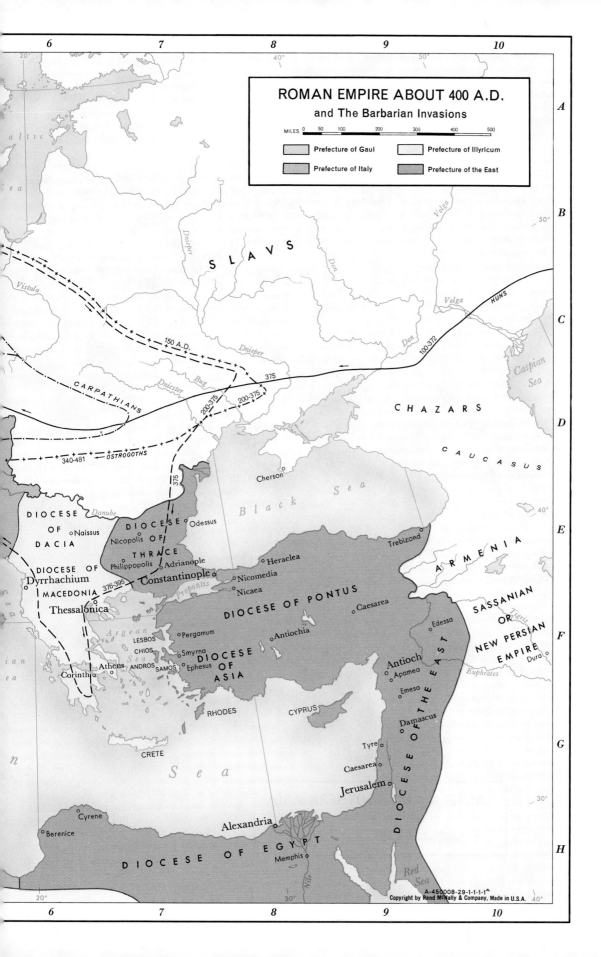

ROMAN EMPIRE ABOUT 400 A.D.
and The Barbarian Invasions

MILES 0 50 100 200 300 400 500

Prefecture of Gaul   Prefecture of Illyricum

Prefecture of Italy   Prefecture of the East

SLAVS

Baltic Sea

Vistula

Dnieper

Don

Volga

HUNS

Caspian Sea

150 A.D.

Dnieper

375

Dniester

Bug

200-375

200-375

CARPATHIANS

340-481   OSTROGOTHS

100-372

CHAZARS

CAUCASUS

375

Cherson

Black Sea

ARMENIA

DIOCESE OF DACIA

Danube

○ Naissus

DIOCESE OF THRACE

Nicopolis ○

○ Odessus

Trebizond

SASSANIAN OR NEW PERSIAN EMPIRE

Philippopolis ○

○ Adrianople

Heraclea ●

DIOCESE OF MACEDONIA

DIOCESE OF Dyrrhachium

376-395

Constantinople ●

○ Nicomedia

○ Nicaea

Propontis

DIOCESE OF PONTUS

○ Caesarea

○ Edessa

Tigris

Euphrates

Dura ○

Thessalonica ●

Pergamum ○

Antiochia ○

Antioch ○ Apamea

Aegean Sea

LESBOS

CHIOS

○ Smyrna

DIOCESE OF ASIA

Emesa ○

Athens ● ANDROS SAMOS ○ Ephesus

Corinth ○

RHODES

CYPRUS

Damascus ○

DIOCESE OF THE EAST

Tyre ○

Caesarea ○

CRETE

Sea

Jerusalem ●

Ionian Sea

Mediterranean Sea

Cyrene ○

Alexandria ●

Berenice ○

DIOCESE OF EGYPT

Memphis ○

Nile

Red Sea

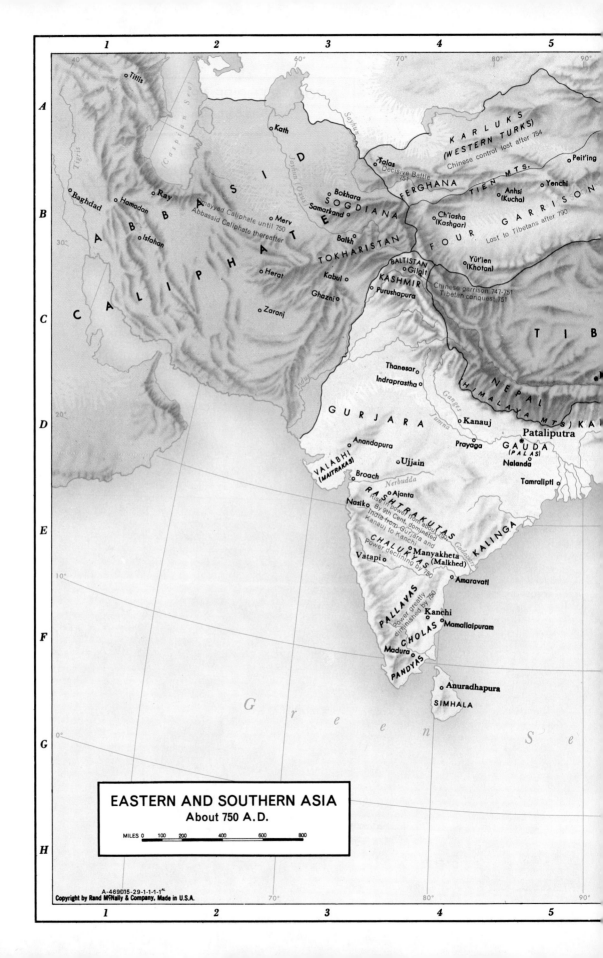

EASTERN AND SOUTHERN ASIA

About 750 A.D.

MILES 0   100   200   400   600   800

A-469015-29-1-1-1-1^AL
Copyright by Rand McNally & Company, Made in U.S.A.

Tiflis

Kath

KARLUKS
(WESTERN TURKS)
Chinese control lost after 754

Talas
Decisive Battle
751

Peit'ing

FERGHANA

TIEN MTS.

Anhsi
(Kucha)

Yenchi

Baghdad

Ray

Hamadan

Isfahan

Bokhara

Samarkand

SOGDIANA

FOUR GARRISON

Ch'iasha
(Kashgar)

Lost to Tibetans after 790

Merv

Balkh

TOKHARISTAN

Yüt'ien
(Khotan)

Herat

Kabul

Ghazni

Zaranj

BALTISTAN
Gilgit

KASHMIR

Purushapura

Chinese garrison 747-751
Tibetan conquest 751

T I B

Thanesar

Indraprastha

NEPAL

Kanauj

GURJARA

Prayaga

Pataliputra

GAUDA
(PALAS)

Anandapura

Nalanda

VALABHI
(MAITRAKAS)

Ujjain

Broach

Nerbudda

Tamralipti

RASHTRAKUTAS
Rise of power from about 750. By 9th Cent. dominated
India from Gurjara and
Kanauj to Kanchi

Ajanta

Nasik

KALINGA

CHALUKYAS
Power declining by 750

Manyakheta
(Malkhed)

Vatapi

Amaravati

PALLAVAS
Power greatly
diminished by 750

Kanchi

Mamallaipuram

CHOLAS

Madura

PANDYAS

Anuradhapura

SIMHALA

G r e e n   S e

A B B A S I D   C A L I P H A T E
Umayyad Caliphate until 750
Abbassid Caliphate thereafter

Caspian Sea

Tigris

Jaxartes

Jayhun (Oxus)

Indus

Ganges

Jumna

Godavari

HIMALAYA MTS.

HIMALAYA MTS.

6   **7**   **8**   **9**   **10**

100°   110°   120°   130°   140°

A

Uighur⊛ Capital

UIGHURS
(EASTERN TURKS)
(GOBI DESERT)

Capital ⊛

KHITANS

P'O HAI

Liaofung ○

SILLA

Capital from 734

Hanchow ○

Heian ⊛ ● Nara
Capital from 710-784

⊛ Capital

J A P A N

B

30°

○ Tunhuang

L U N G Y U

Great Wall

L I A O T U N G

Taiyüan ●

HOPEI

Weichow ●

Yün ●

Eastern

Sea

TUYÜHUNS

Shan ●

KUANNEI

Huang

CHINGCHI

Loyang ● Pien ○ Sung ●

HONAN

Yangchow ○

○ Soochow

C

20°

T U C H I

Ch'angan ⊛

TÜCHI

HUAINAN

Hsüan ○

○ Yüeh

CHIENNAN

SHANNAN
HSI

SHANNAN
TUNG

Chiangling ●

Hangchow ○

Ch'engtu ●

C H I N A

CHIANGNAN
HSI

CHIANGNAN
TUNG

Yangtze

asa

CH'IENCHUNG

○ Ch'üanchow

D

URA

● Tali

LINGNAN

Kwangchow ●

Southern

ahmaputra

NAN CHAO
(T'AI)

ANNAM

Chiaochow ●

Sea

E

10°

Halin ○

P Y U

UPPER
(ILAND)

(HAINAN)

ikshetra

M O N S

Thaton ●

CHENLA

CHAMPA

Amaravati ●

F

DVARAVATI

LOWER
(MARITIME)

Mekong

KAUTHARA

● Virapura

CHENLA

PANDURANGA

G

TAMBRALINGA

LANGKASUKA

(B O R N E O)

KEDAH

H

10°

(S U M A T R A)

Malayu ○

BANKA

The Srivijayan Empire,
perhaps under a Sailendran ruler,
probably included more of Sumatra
and Java and even portions of the
Malay peninsula and Borneo by
the end of the 8th Century

S R I V I J A Y A ● Srivijaya

(J A V A)

SAILENDRAS

TARUMA

Borobodur
Built 772?

MATARAM

100°

6   **7**   **8**   **9**   **10**

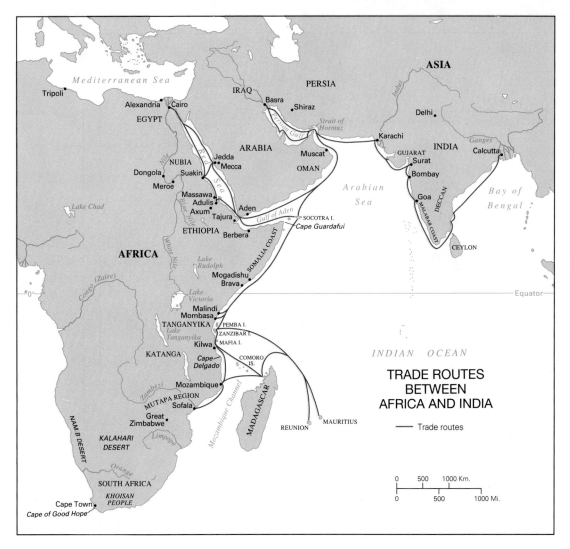

TRADE ROUTES BETWEEN AFRICA AND INDIA

—— Trade routes

Mediterranean Sea

Tripoli
Alexandria • Cairo
EGYPT
PERSIA
IRAQ
Basra • Shiraz
ASIA

Delhi

ARABIA
Jedda
NUBIA
Mecca
Dongola •
Suakin •
Meroe •
Massawa •
Adulis •
Axum • Tajura
ETHIOPIA
Berbera •

Muscat
OMAN
Strait of Hormuz
Karachi
GUJARAT
Surat
Bombay
INDIA
Ganges
Calcutta

Lake Chad

AFRICA

Nile
Red Sea
Blue Nile
White Nile

Aden
Gulf of Aden
SOCOTRA I.
Cape Guardafui

Arabian Sea

Goa
DECCAN
MALABAR COAST

Bay of Bengal

CEYLON

Lake Rudolph
Lake Victoria
SOMALIA COAST
Mogadishu •
Brava •

Equator

Malindi
Mombasa •
TANGANYIKA
Lake Tanganyika
Kilwa •
KATANGA
Cape Delgado
PEMBA I.
ZANZIBAR I.
MAFIA I.
COMORO IS.

INDIAN OCEAN

Mozambique •
MUTAPA REGION
Sofala •
Zambezi
Great Zimbabwe •
Limpopo
MADAGASCAR
Mozambique Channel

REUNION • MAURITIUS

NAM B DESERT
KALAHARI DESERT
Orange
SOUTH AFRICA
KHOISAN PEOPLE
Cape Town •
Cape of Good Hope

| 0 | 500 | 1000 Km. |
| 0 | 500 | 1000 Mi. |

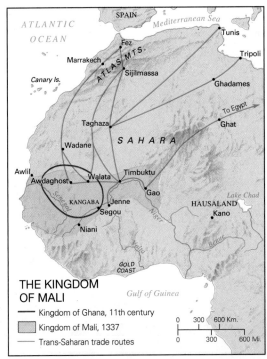

THE KINGDOM OF MALI

—— Kingdom of Ghana, 11th century
▨ Kingdom of Mali, 1337
—— Trans-Saharan trade routes

ATLANTIC OCEAN
SPAIN
Mediterranean Sea
Tunis
Fez
Marrakech
ATLAS MTS.
Tripoli
Sijilmassa
Ghadames
Canary Is.
To Egypt
Taghaza
SAHARA
Ghat
Wadane
Awlil •
Walata
Timbuktu
Awdaghost •
Senegal
KANGABA
Jenne
Gao
HAUSALAND
Kano
Lake Chad
Segou
Niger
Niani
Benue
GOLD COAST
Gulf of Guinea

| 0 | 300 | 600 Km. |
| 0 | 300 | 600 Mi. |

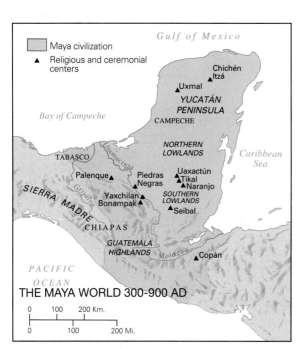

Maya civilization

▲ Religious and ceremonial centers

Gulf of Mexico

Chichén Itzá ▲

▲ Uxmal

YUCATÁN PENINSULA

CAMPECHE

Bay of Campeche

NORTHERN LOWLANDS

Caribbean Sea

TABASCO

Palenque ▲   ▲ Piedras Negras   ▲ Uaxactún
                ▲ Tikal
                ▲ Naranjo

SIERRA MADRE

Yaxchilan ▲
Bonampak ▲

SOUTHERN LOWLANDS

▲ Seibal

CHIAPAS

GUATEMALA HIGHLANDS

▲ Copán

PACIFIC OCEAN

THE MAYA WORLD 300-900 AD

0   100   200 Km.

0   100   200 Mi.

Caribbean Sea

ISTHMUS OF PANAMA

Orinoco

ATLANTIC OCEAN

Tumbes

Cajamarca

HUAYLAS VALLEY

Lima

SOUTH AMERICA

Cuzco

CUZCO VALLEY
TITICACA VALLEY

BRAZILIAN HIGHLANDS

PACIFIC OCEAN

Maule

THE INCA EMPIRE 1463-1532

Inca Empire in 1532

— Network of Inca roads

0   600   1200 Km.

0   600   1200 Mi.

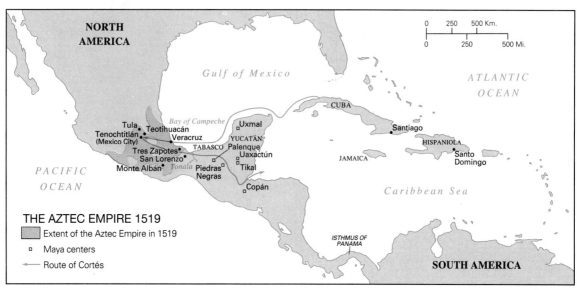

NORTH AMERICA

Gulf of Mexico

ATLANTIC OCEAN

CUBA

Tula ●
Tenochtitlán ● ● Teotihuacán
(Mexico City)   Veracruz ●

□ Uxmal

YUCATÁN

Santiago ●

Tres Zapotes ●   TABASCO   Palenque □
San Lorenzo ●   Uaxactún □
Monte Albán ●   *Tonala*   Piedras
                            Negras □   Tikal □

HISPANIOLA

JAMAICA

Santo Domingo

PACIFIC OCEAN

□ Copán

Caribbean Sea

THE AZTEC EMPIRE 1519

Extent of the Aztec Empire in 1519

□ Maya centers

← Route of Cortés

ISTHMUS OF PANAMA

SOUTH AMERICA

0   250   500 Km.

0   250   500 Mi.

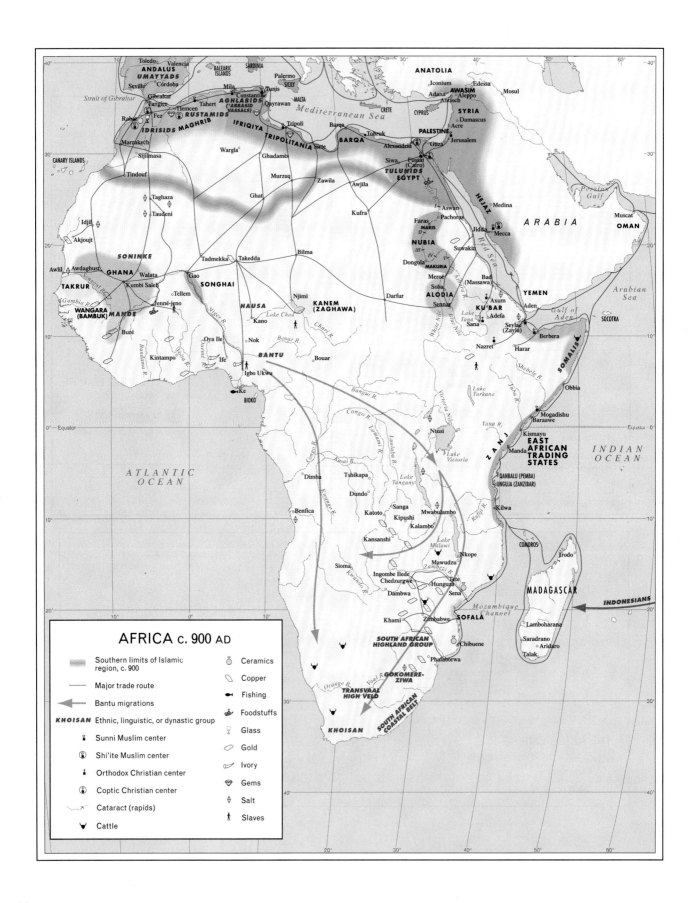

AFRICA c. 900 AD

Southern limits of Islamic region, c. 900

—— Major trade route

← Bantu migrations

KHOISAN Ethnic, linguistic, or dynastic group

⚑ Sunni Muslim center

☪ Shi'ite Muslim center

☦ Orthodox Christian center

✝ Coptic Christian center

Cataract (rapids)

🐂 Cattle

⚱ Ceramics

Copper

🐟 Fishing

Foodstuffs

⟁ Glass

Gold

Ivory

◈ Gems

Salt

Slaves

Map labels

ANDALUS
UMAYYADS
Toledo Valencia
BALEARIC ISLANDS
SARDINIA
Seville Córdoba
Palermo
SICILY
ANATOLIA
Iconium Edessa
Adana Antioch Aleppo Mosul
AWASIM
SYRIA
Damascus Acre
CYPRUS
Strait of Gibraltar
Gibraltar Mila Tunis
Constantine Qayrawan
AGHLABIDS ('ABBASID VASSALS)
Tangier Tlemcen
Tahert
Mediterranean Sea
CRETE
MALTA
PALESTINE
Jerusalem
Gaza
Rabat Fez
IDRISIDS MAGHRIB
RUSTAMIDS
IFRIQIYA
Tripoli Barqa Tobruk
TRIPOLITANIA Sirte
BARQA
Marrakech
CANARY ISLANDS
Sijilmasa
Wargla
Ghadamès
Alexandria
Siwa Fustat (Cairo)
EGYPT
TULUNIDS
Persian Gulf
Tindouf
Murzuq
Zawila
Awjila
Kufra
ARABIA
Medina
Muscat
OMAN
Taghaza
Ghat
Aswan Pachoras
Jidda Mecca
Taudeni
Idjil
Akjoujt
NUBIA
Faras MARIS
Dongola MAKURIA
Suwakin
Bad (Massawa)
Red Sea
Arabian Sea
SONINKE
Tadmekka Takedda
Bilma
Meroë Soba
ALODIA
Axum
YEMEN
Awlil Awdaghust
GHANA Walata
Gao
Kumbi Saleh
SONGHAI
Darfur
Sennar
KU'BAR
Adefa
Aden
Lake Tana Sana
Seylac (Zayla)
SOCOTRA
Gulf of Aden
Berbera
TAKRUR
Tellem
HAUSA
Njimi
KANEM (ZAGHAWA)
Nazret
Harar
MANDE
Jenné-jeno
Kano
Lake Chad
SOMALIS
WANGARA (BAMBUK)
Buré
Oya Ile
Nok
Benue R.
Bouar
Chari R.
Shebele R.
Kintampo
Ife
BANTU
Igbo Ukwu
Ke
BIOKO
Congo R.
Bangui R.
Lomami R.
Lake Turkana
Juba R.
Obbia
Tana R.
Lake Victoria
Victoria Nile
Mogadishu
Baraawe
EQUATOR
Equator
ATLANTIC OCEAN
Ntusi
ZANJ
Kismayu
Manda
EAST AFRICAN TRADING STATES
INDIAN OCEAN
Dimba
Tshikapa
Lake Tanganyika
DANBALU (PEMBA)
UNGUJA (ZANZIBAR)
Dundo
Benfica
Sanga
Katoto Kipushi
Mwabulambo
Kalambo
Kilwa
Kansanshi
Lake Malawi
Nkope
COMOROS
Irodo
Sioma
Mawudzu
Ingombe Ilede
Chedzurgwe
Hunguza
Sena
MADAGASCAR
Dambwa
Tete
Zambesi R.
Khami
Zimbabwe
SOFALA
Chibuene
Lamboharana
SOUTH AFRICAN HIGHLAND GROUP
Phalaborwa
Saradrano
Aridaro
Talak
Mozambique Channel
GOKOMERE-ZIWA
TRANSVAAL HIGH VELD
Orange R.
Vaal R.
KHOISAN
SOUTH AFRICAN COASTAL BELT
INDONESIANS
Senegal R.
Gambia R.
Niger R.
Bandama R.
Volta R.
Kwango R.
Kasai R.
Lualaba R.
Kwando R.
Limpopo R.

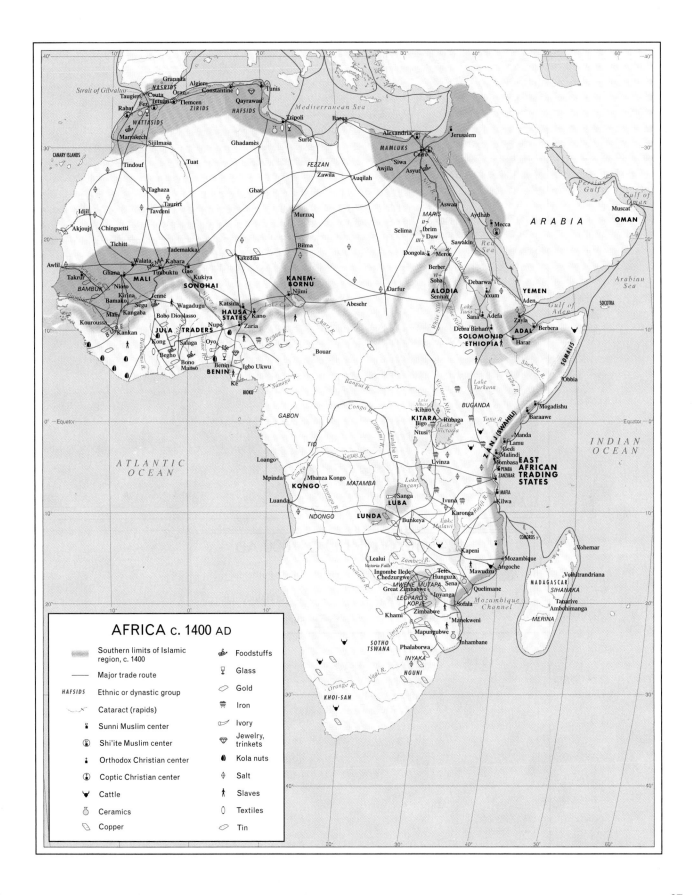

AFRICA c. 1400 AD

Legend:

- Southern limits of Islamic region, c. 1400
- Major trade route
- *HAFSIDS* — Ethnic or dynastic group
- Cataract (rapids)
- Sunni Muslim center
- Shi'ite Muslim center
- Orthodox Christian center
- Coptic Christian center
- Cattle
- Ceramics
- Copper
- Foodstuffs
- Glass
- Gold
- Iron
- Ivory
- Jewelry, trinkets
- Kola nuts
- Salt
- Slaves
- Textiles
- Tin

Map labels:

Strait of Gibraltar, Granada, *NASRIDS*, Algiers, Constantine, Tunis, Taugiers, Ceuta, Oran, Qayrawan, Tetuan, Tlemcen, Rabat, Fez, *ZIRIDS*, *HAFSIDS*, Tripoli, Barqa, *Mediterranean Sea*, Surte, Alexandria, Jerusalem, *WATTASIDS*, Marrakech, Sijilmasa, Ghadamès, *MAMLUKS*, Cairo, *CANARY ISLANDS*, Tindouf, Tuat, *FEZZAN*, Siwa, Awjila, Asyut, *ARABIA*, Taghaza, Ghat, Zawila, Murzuq, Auqilah, Aswan, *OMAN*, Tauriri, Tavdeni, Idjil, *MARIS*, Selima, Ibrim, Daw, Mecca, Muscat, Akjoujt, Chinguetti, Tademakka, Bilma, *Red Sea*, *Persian Gulf*, *Gulf of Oman*, Tichitt, Takedda, Dongola, Meroe, Sawakin, *Arabian Sea*, Walata, Kabara, Awlil, Takrur, Ghana, Tinbuktu, Gao, Kukiya, *KANEM-BORNU*, Darfur, Berber, Soba, Debarwa, Axum, *YEMEN*, Aden, SOCOTRA, *BAMBUK*, Nioro, *MALI*, *SONGHAI*, Njimi, *ALODIA*, Sennar, Sana, Adefa, Berbera, Kirina, Jenné, Lake Chad, Abesehr, *SOLOMONID ETHIOPIA*, Zayla, *ADAL*, Bamako, Segu, Wagadugu, Katsina, Kano, Debra Birhan, Harar, Kangaba, Bobo Dioulasso, *HAUSA STATES*, Zaria, *SOMALIS*, Kouroussa, *JULA TRADERS*, Nupe, Obbia, Kankan, Kong, Salaga, Oyo, Ife, Bouar, Mogadishu, Baraawe, Begho, Bono Manso, Benin, Igbo Ukwu, *BENIN*, *GABON*, *BUGANDA*, Manda, Ké, BIOKO, Lake Turkana, Kibiro, *KITARA*, Bigo, Ruhaga, Lamu, Gedi, Malindi, *TIO*, Ntusi, Lake Victoria, *ZANJ (SWAHILI)*, Mombasa, PEMBA, *EAST AFRICAN TRADING STATES*, Loango, *Congo R.*, Uvinza, ZANZIBAR, MAFIA, *ATLANTIC OCEAN*, Mpinda, Mbanza Kongo, *MATAMBA*, Ivuna, Kilwa, *INDIAN OCEAN*, Luanda, *KONGO*, *LUBA*, Sanga, Karonga, *NDONGO*, *LUNDA*, Bunkeya, Lake Malawi, COMOROS, Vohemar, Kapeni, Mozambique, Lealui, *Victoria Falls*, *Zambezi R.*, Angoche, Volotrandriana, Ingombe Ilede, Chedzurgwe, Tete, Hunguza, Mawudzu, Quelimane, *MADAGASCAR*, *SIHANAKA*, *MWENE MUTAPA*, Sena, Great Zimbabwe, Inyanga, *MERINA*, Tanarive, Ambohimanga, *LEOPARD'S KOPJE*, Zimbabwe, Sofala, *Mozambique Channel*, Khami, Manekweni, Mapungubwe, Inhambane, *SOTHO TSWANA*, Phalaborwa, *INYAKA*, *NGUNI*, *KHOI-SAN*, *Orange R.*, *Vaal R.*, *Limpopo R.*

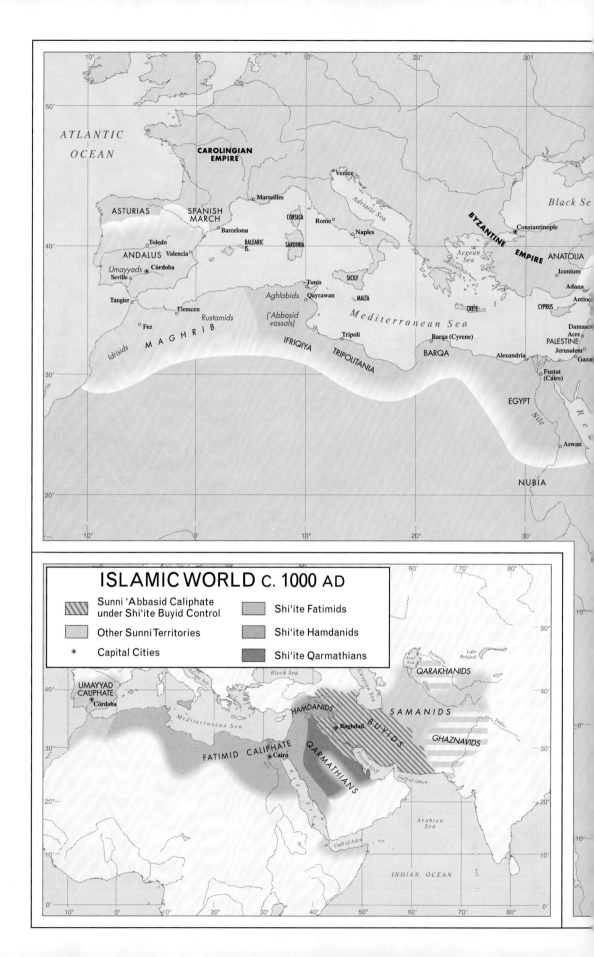

ATLANTIC
OCEAN

**CAROLINGIAN
EMPIRE**

Venice

Marseilles

Adriatic Sea

ASTURIAS SPANISH
MARCH

CORSICA
Rome
Naples

BYZANTINE
Constantinople

Black Se

Barcelona

BALEARIC
IS.

SARDINIA

*Aegean
Sea*

EMPIRE ANATOLIA

Toledo

ANDALUS Valencia

40°

SICILY

Iconium

Umayyads Córdoba

Seville

Tunis

Adana

Tangier

Aghlabids Qayrawan

MALTA

CRETE

CYPRUS

Antioc

Tlemcen

Rustamids

('Abbasid
vassals)

Mediterranean Sea

Damasc
Acre

Fez

Idrisids

MAGHRIB

Tripoli

IFRIQIYA

TRIPOLITANIA

Barqa (Cyrene)

BARQA

PALESTINE
Jerusalem
Gaza

Alexandria

Fustat
(Cairo)

EGYPT

Nile

Re

Aswan

NUBIA

30°

ISLAMIC WORLD c. 1000 AD

Sunni 'Abbasid Caliphate
under Shi'ite Buyid Control

Shi'ite Fatimids

Other Sunni Territories

Shi'ite Hamdanids

Capital Cities

Shi'ite Qarmathians

60° 70° 80°

QARAKHANIDS

*Lake
Balqash*

UMAYYAD
CALIPHATE

Black Sea

HAMDANIDS

SAMANIDS

Córdoba

Mediterranean Sea

Baghdad

B U Y I D S

GHAZNAVIDS

FATIMID CALIPHATE

Cairo

QARMATHIANS

Persian Gulf

Gulf of Oman

Red Sea

*Arabian
Sea*

Gulf of Aden

INDIAN OCEAN

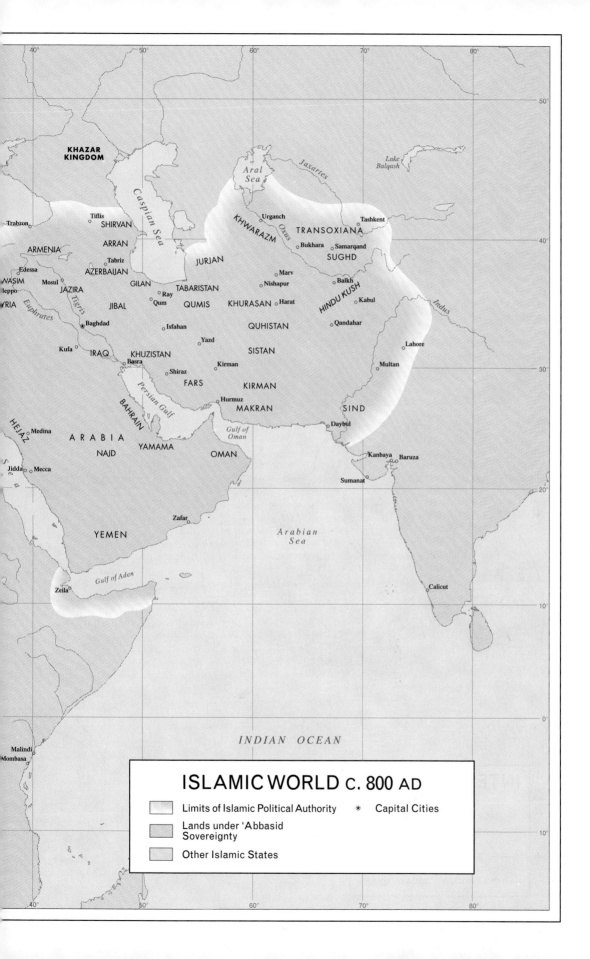

KHAZAR
KINGDOM

Caspian Sea

Aral Sea

Jaxartes

Lake Balqash

Trabzon

Tiflis
SHIRVAN

Urganch

Tashkent

KHWARAZM

TRANSOXIANA

ARMENIA

ARRAN

Oxus

Bukhara

Samarqand

Tabriz

SUGHD

Edessa

AZERBAIJAN

JURJAN

WASIM

Mosul

GILAN

Marv

Balkh

Aleppo

JAZIRA

Ray

Nishapur

Tigris

RIA

Euphrates

JIBAL

Qum

TABARISTAN

KHURASAN

Harat

HINDU KUSH

Kabul

Indus

Baghdad

Isfahan

QUMIS

QUHISTAN

Qandahar

Kufa

Yazd

IRAQ

KHUZISTAN

Basra

SISTAN

Lahore

Shiraz

Kirman

Multan

Persian Gulf

FARS

KIRMAN

BAHRAIN

Hurmuz

KIRMAN

SIND

HEJAZ

Medina

ARABIA

MAKRAN

Daybul

Gulf of Oman

Sea

NAJD

YAMAMA

OMAN

Kanbaya

Baruza

Jidda

Mecca

Sumanat

Zafar

YEMEN

Arabian Sea

Gulf of Aden

Zeila

Calicut

INDIAN OCEAN

Malindi

Mombasa

ISLAMIC WORLD C. 800 AD

Limits of Islamic Political Authority   ✸   Capital Cities

Lands under 'Abbasid Sovereignty

Other Islamic States

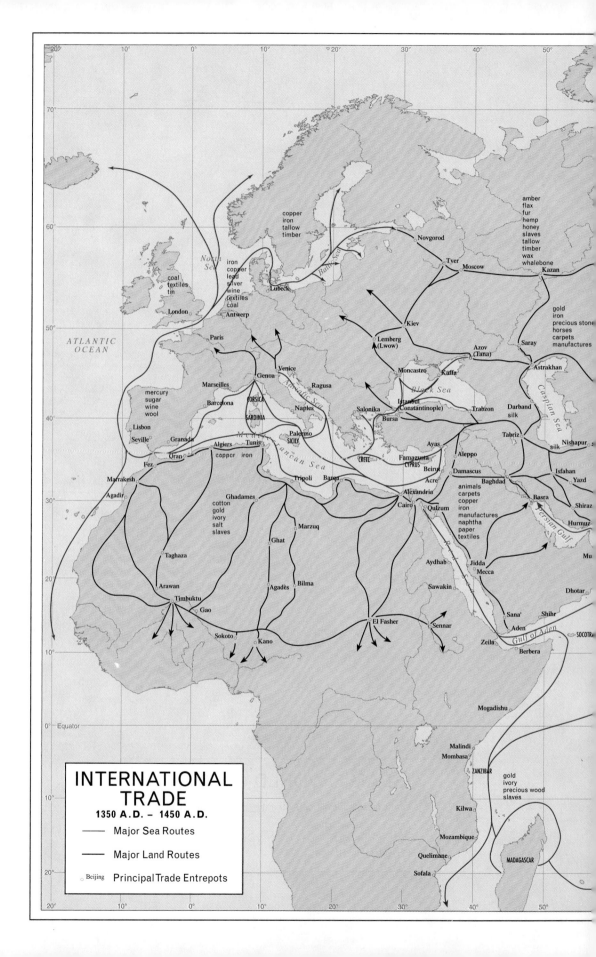

INTERNATIONAL TRADE
1350 A.D. – 1450 A.D.

— Major Sea Routes

— Major Land Routes

○ Beijing   Principal Trade Entrepots

copper
iron
tallow
timber

iron
copper
lead
silver
wine
textiles
coal

coal
textiles
tin

amber
flax
fur
hemp
honey
slaves
tallow
timber
wax
whalebone

gold
iron
precious stones
horses
carpets
manufactures

silk

silk

mercury
sugar
wine
wool

copper   iron

cotton
gold
ivory
salt
slaves

animals
carpets
copper
iron
manufactures
naphtha
paper
textiles

gold
ivory
precious wood
slaves

Novgorod
Tver
Moscow
Kazan
Kiev
Lemberg
(Lwow)
Azov
(Tana)
Saray
Astrakhan
Moncastro
Kaffa
Salonika
Istanbul
(Constantinople)
Bursa
Trabzon
Darband
Tabriz
Nishapur
Ayas
Aleppo
Isfahan
Yazd
Beirut
Damascus
Baghdad
Basra
Shiraz
Hurmuz
Acre
Alexandria
Cairo
Quizum
Mu
Aydhab
Jidda
Mecca
Sawakin
Dhotar
Sana'
Shihr
El Fasher
Sennar
Zeila
Aden
Berbera
Mogadishu
Malindi
Mombasa
ZANZIBAR
Kilwa
Mozambique
Quelimane
Sofala

North Sea
Baltic Sea
ATLANTIC OCEAN
London
Antwerp
Paris
Lubeck
Venice
Genoa
Marseilles
Barcelona
CORSICA
SARDINIA
Naples
Palermo
SICILY
Ragusa
Adriatic Sea
Black Sea
Caspian Sea
Mediterranean Sea
CRETE
Famagusta
CYPRUS
Tripoli
Barqa
Lisbon
Seville
Granada
Algiers
Tunis
Oran
Fez
Marrakesh
Agadir
Ghadames
Marzuq
Ghat
Taghaza
Arawan
Timbuktu
Gao
Sokoto
Kano
Agadès
Bilma
Persian Gulf
Gulf of Aden
SOCOTRA
MADAGASCAR
Equator

30

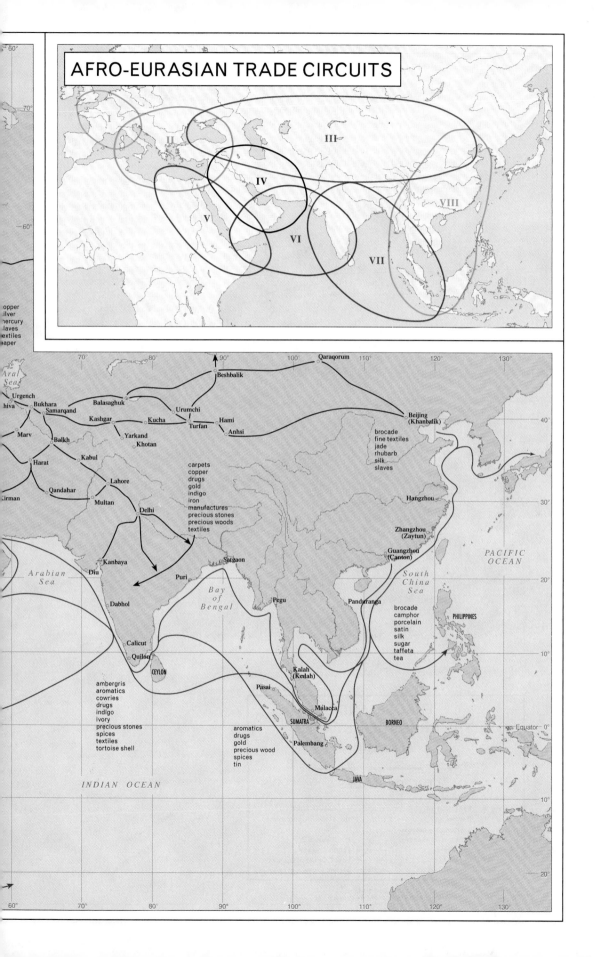

AFRO-EURASIAN TRADE CIRCUITS

I
II
III
IV
V
VI
VII
VIII

opper
iercury
laves
extiles
aper

Aral
Sea

Urgench
hiva
Bukhara
Samarqand
Marv
Balkh
Harat
Kabul
Kirman
Qandahar
Lahore
Multan
Delhi
Kanbaya
Diu

Balasaghuk
Kashgar
Kucha
Urumchi
Yarkand
Turfan
Hami
Khotan
Anhsi

Beshbalik
Qaraqorum
Beijing
(Khanbalik)

brocade
fine textiles
jade
rhubarb
silk
slaves

Hangzhou

Zhangzhou
(Zaytun)

Guangzhou
(Canton)

PACIFIC
OCEAN

carpets
copper
drugs
gold
indigo
iron
manufactures
precious stones
precious woods
textiles

Saigaon
Puri

Bay
of
Bengal

Pegu

Panduranga

South
China
Sea

brocade
camphor
porcelain
satin
silk
sugar
taffeta
tea

PHILIPPINES

Dabhol

Calicut
Quilon
CEYLON

Kalah
(Kedah)

Pasai

Malacca

SUMATRA

BORNEO

Equator 0°

ambergris
aromatics
cowries
drugs
indigo
ivory
precious stones
spices
textiles
tortoise shell

aromatics
drugs
gold
precious wood
spices
tin

Palembang

JAVA

INDIAN OCEAN

Arabian
Sea

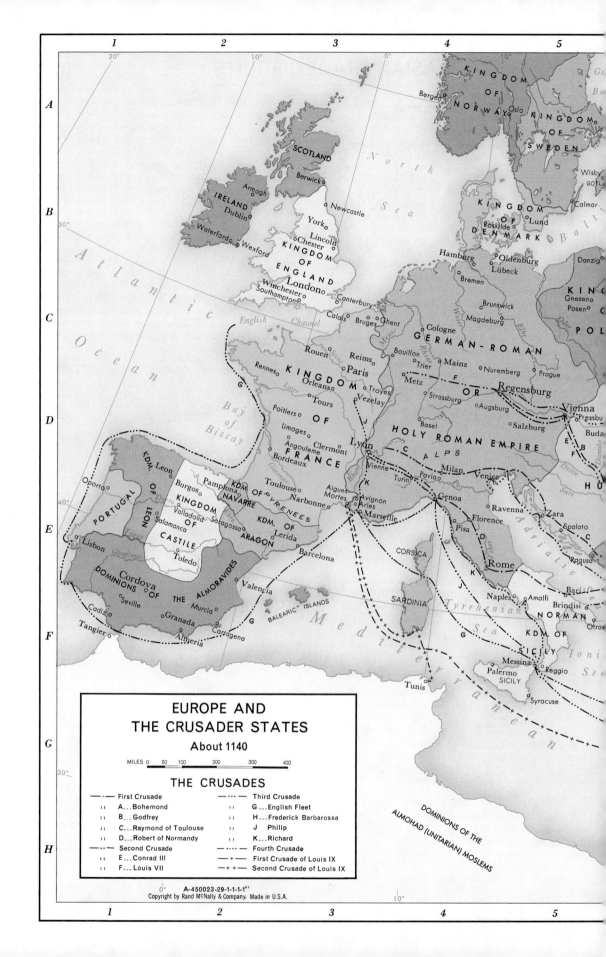

EUROPE AND
THE CRUSADER STATES

About 1140

MILES 0   50   100   200   300   400

THE CRUSADES

—·—·— First Crusade	—··—··— Third Crusade
A...Bohemond	G...English Fleet
B...Godfrey	H...Frederick Barbarossa
C...Raymond of Toulouse	J...Philip
D...Robert of Normandy	K...Richard
——— Second Crusade	—····— Fourth Crusade
E...Conrad III	—+—+— First Crusade of Louis IX
F...Louis VII	—+—+— Second Crusade of Louis IX

A-450023-29-1-1-1-1ᴬᴸ
Copyright by Rand McNally & Company. Made in U.S.A.

32

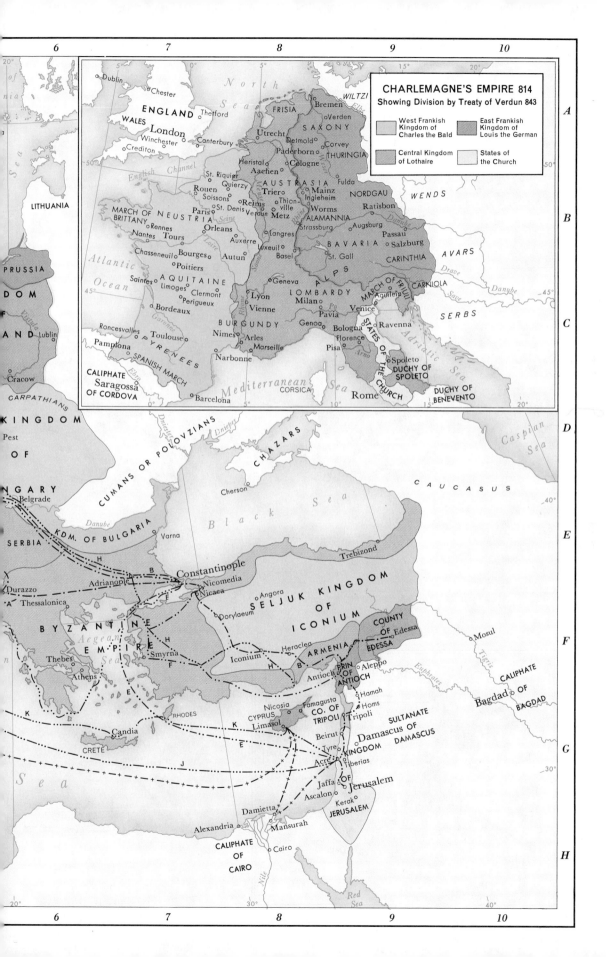

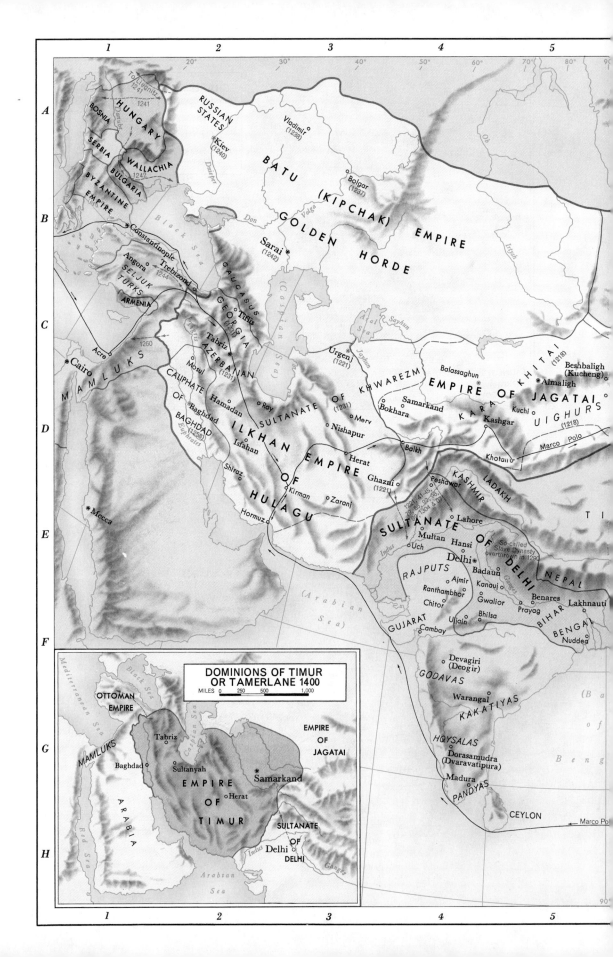

DOMINIONS OF TIMUR
OR TAMERLANE 1400

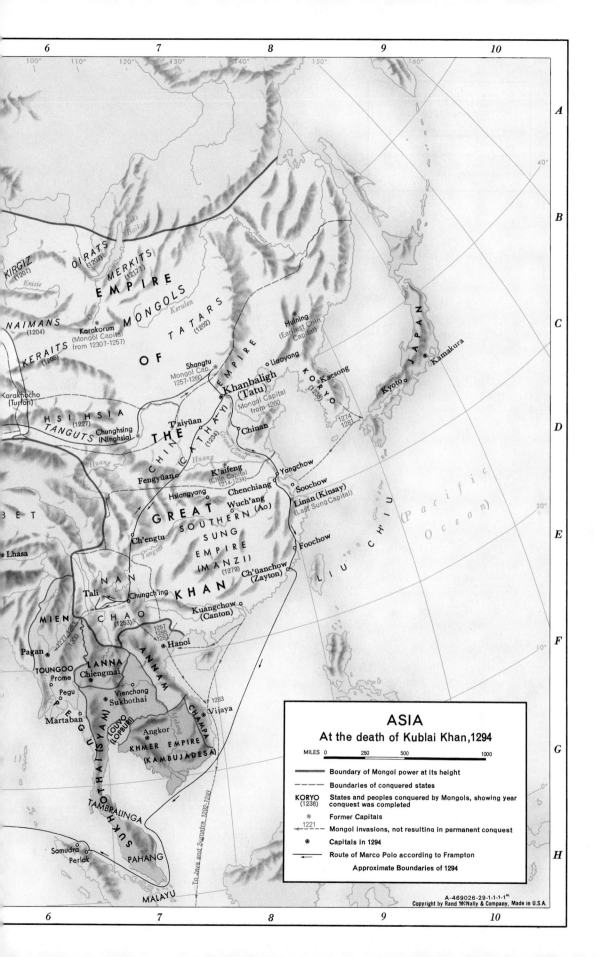

ASIA
At the death of Kublai Khan, 1294

EUROPE
About 1360

MILES 0   50 100   200   300

——— Boundary of Holy Roman Empire
‑ ‑ ‑ Boundary of France

NORWAY

FAEROES

SHETLAND ISLANDS
Bergen

ORKNEY ISLANDS
HEBRIDES

Oslo

S W

Upsala

North Sea

DENMARK
Calmar

SCOTLAND ○ Aberdeen
Bannockburn
Falkirk ○ Edinburgh
○ Berwick
○ Carlisle

Copenhagen

IRELAND
Armagh
○ Dublin

York ○
Lincoln ○
Chester ○

Lubeck ○   ○ Stralsund
POMERANIA
Hamburg

Gnesen ○
Posen ○

WALES
ENGLAND
Thames

Norwich ○

HOLLAND

Bremen ○

Magdeburg ○   BRANDENBURG

S I L E S I A

Atlantic
○ Wexford
Cork ○

London

Bruges

English Channel   Calais
Agincourt   ○

Ghent
BRABANT

Rhine

Cologne ○

H O L Y

BOHEMIA

Prague

Harfleur ○   Crecy
○ Rouen
Caen ○

HAINAUT

LUXEMBURG

Trier ○   ○ Frankfurt
Mainz

R O M A N

Regensburg   MORAVIA

Reims
Compiegne
Vaucouleurs ○

BRITTANY
Rennes ○   Bretigny
FRANCE

Paris

Domremy

Ocean

Nantes ○
Loire

Orleans ○

Troyes ○

Dijon ○

Chinon ○
Poitiers ○

LORRAINE

Strassburg ○

Basel ○

PALATINATE

Besancon ○
SWISS CONFED.

BAVARIA
Munich ○

E M P I R E

Vienna
Salzburg ○

Budau

Bay of Biscay

Limoges ○

Bordeaux

AQUITAINE

BURGUNDY
Garonne

Lyon ○

Constance ○

Danube

A U S T R I A

Drave

Turin ○
LANDS OF THE VISCONTI

Milan ○

SAVOY

Po

Trieste ○

Ferrara ○

REPUBLIC

Bayonne ○
Toulouse ○
Pau ○

NAVARRE

Avignon ○
Narbonne ○

DAUPHINY

Marseille ○

PROVENCE

Genoa ○

Venice

B O S N I

OF

Florence ○   Bologna ○

PAPAL STATES

VENICE

Ragusa ○

Adriatic Sea

PORTUGAL
Santiago ○
Leon ○

Ebro

Saragossa ○

ARAGON

Barcelona ○

CORSICA
(To Genoa)

Rome ○

KINGDOM

Salamanca ○
Toledo ○
Tagus

CASTILE

Duero

Valencia ○

BALEARIC ISLANDS

SARDINIA
(To Aragon)

OF

Lisbon ○
Guadiana

(To Aragon)

Naples ○

NAPLES

Tarant

Seville ○   Cordova ○
Guadalquivir

○ Granada
GRANADA

Gibraltar ○

Cadiz ○

M e d i t e r r a n e a n

Palermo ○   ○ Messina

KINGDOM OF SICILY

Reggio ○

M A R I N D S

M O S L E M   S T A T E S

Algiers ○

Tunis ○

MALTA

Z I A N I D S

H A F S I D S

A-450028-29-1-1-1-1^AL
Copyright by Rand McNally & Company. Made in U.S.A.

20°   10°   0°   10°

50°

40°

0°   10°

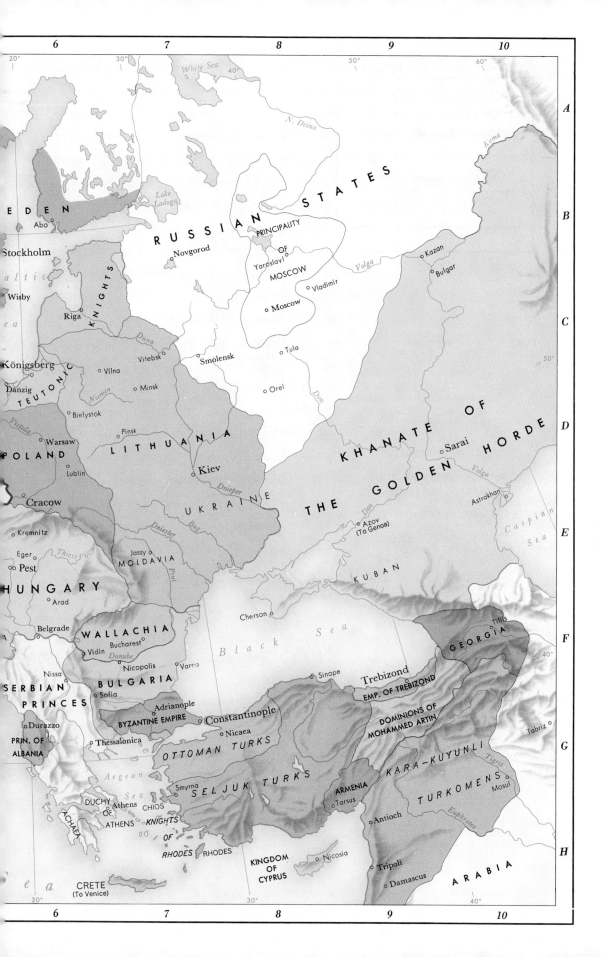

20° 30° *White Sea* 40° 50° 60°

A

N. Dvina

Kama

S W

E D E N

R U S S I A N   S T A T E S

Lake Ladoga

B

Abo

Stockholm

PRINCIPALITY

○ Novgorod

OF

○ Kazan

Wisby

Yaroslavl

○ Bulgar

altic

MOSCOW

Volga

○ Vladimir

Riga

K N I G H T S

○ Moscow

C

Duna

Königsberg

Vitebsk

Smolensk

○ Tula

50°

T E U T O N I C

Niemen

○ Vilna

○ Minsk

○ Orel

Danzig

Don

○ Bielystok

D

Vistula

Warsaw

○ Pinsk

L I T H U A N I A

K H A N A T E   O F

○ Sarai

POLAND

Lublin

Kiev

Volga

Cracow

Dnieper

U K R A I N E

T H E   G O L D E N   H O R D E

Kremnitz

Dniester

Bug

Astrakhan

Thiess

Eger

Jassy

Don

Azov

○ Pest

M O L D A V I A

Prut

(To Genoa)

E

Caspian Sea

H U N G A R Y

K U B A N

Arad

Belgrade

W A L L A C H I A

Cherson

Black   Sea

Tflis

F

Vidin

Bucharest

G E O R G I A

40°

Danube

Nicopolis

Varna

Nissa

B U L G A R I A

Sinope

Trebizond

S E R B I A N

Sofia

EMP. OF TREBIZOND

P R I N C E S

Adrianople

Durazzo

BYZANTINE EMPIRE

Constantinople

DOMINIONS OF

MOHAMMED ARTIN

Tabriz

PRIN. OF

Thessalonica

Nicaea

G

ALBANIA

O T T O M A N   T U R K S

K A R A – K U Y U N L I

Aegean

Smyrna

S E L J U K   T U R K S

ARMENIA

T U R K O M E N S

Tigris

DUCHY

Athens

CHIOS

Tarsus

Mosul

A C H A E A

Sea

OF

Antioch

Euphrates

ATHENS

K N I G H T S

OF

R H O D E S   RHODES

KINGDOM

Nicosia

H

OF

Tripoli

e a

CRETE

CYPRUS

A R A B I A

(To Venice)

Damascus

20° 30° 40°

EUROPEAN CIVILIZATION
During The Renaissance

MILES 0 50 100   200   300

——————— Boundaries of approximately 1470

Location of
School of Art ————➤   Early printing
                            press
Important church ————➤   Library
council

• Birthplace outside city

<u>Florence</u> Location of important Renaissance
building

NORWAY

DENMARK

North Sea

SCOTLAND
Edinburgh
John Knox,
1505

IRELAND
Dublin

Coverdale,
1488

WALES
Cranmer,
1489
ENGLAND
Tyndale,
1490
Malory,
15th Cent.
More, 1478 Oxford   Colet, 1466
Hampton Court London Rotterdam Leiden Erasmus, 1466
Wyatt,
1503   Caxton, 1422 Canterbury Bruges Bruegel, 1520 Van der Wyden Van Eyck, 1381
Linacre, 1480 Van Eyck, 1400 Louvain
Le Fevre d'Étaples, DOMAINS Massys, 1460
1455 Commes, Gossart, 1470
1445   Noyon
Chartier, 1392 Calvin, 1509 Nicholas of Trier
Paris Cusa, 1401
Pare, 1510 NATIONAL LIBRARY DUKES
Fontainebleau COLLEGE OF FRANCE, 1530
Boccaccio, 1313
Blois Charles of Orleans, 1391
Rabelais, 1490 Villon, 1431 OF
Azay-le-Rideau Chambord Dijon Basel
Amboise Zurich
Tours BURGUNDY
Jean Fouquet, Moulins Paracelsus,
1415 1493 Geneva

Lübeck

HOLY

Agricola, Bremen
1443
Wittenberg
Cologne Luther, •
1483
Erfurt
Behaim, 14
Ulrich Regiomontanus, 1
von Hutten, Mainz Dürer, 1471
1488 Gutenberg, Nuremberg
1397
Melanchthon, ROM
1497
Reuchlin, Regensburg
1455 Altdorfer, 1480
Augsburg
Holbein, 1497
Constance
Zwingli, 1484 EMPIR

Trent

AGE OF HUMANISM

RENAISSANCE PAINTING
AND SCULPTURE

CLASSICAL AND BIBLICAL STUDIES

FIRST PRINTED BOOKS

Bay of

Biscay

FRANCE

Bordeaux

Angoulême
Marguerite de Navarre,
1492

Loyola, 1493
Servetus, 1511 <u>Pau</u>
NAVARRE PYRENEES

PORTUGAL

Lisbon

Vasco da Gama,
1450

Magellan,
1480 *Duero*
Ximenes,
1438
Madrid *Tagus*
CASTILE

Seville *Guadalquivir*
Las Casas,
1474 *Guadiana*

GRANADA

Rhone

Milan

Po
Genoa Venice

Bologna Ferrara
Pisa Florence PAPAL
Siena
Perugia
STATES

Avignon

Marseille

ARAGON

Barcelona

CORSICA
(Genoa)

SARDINIA
(Aragon)

Rome
VATICAN LIBRARY
c. 1450
SOCIETY OF JESUS
1540

Tyrrhen

Sea

Palermo

BALEARIC ISLANDS
(Aragon)

Mediterran

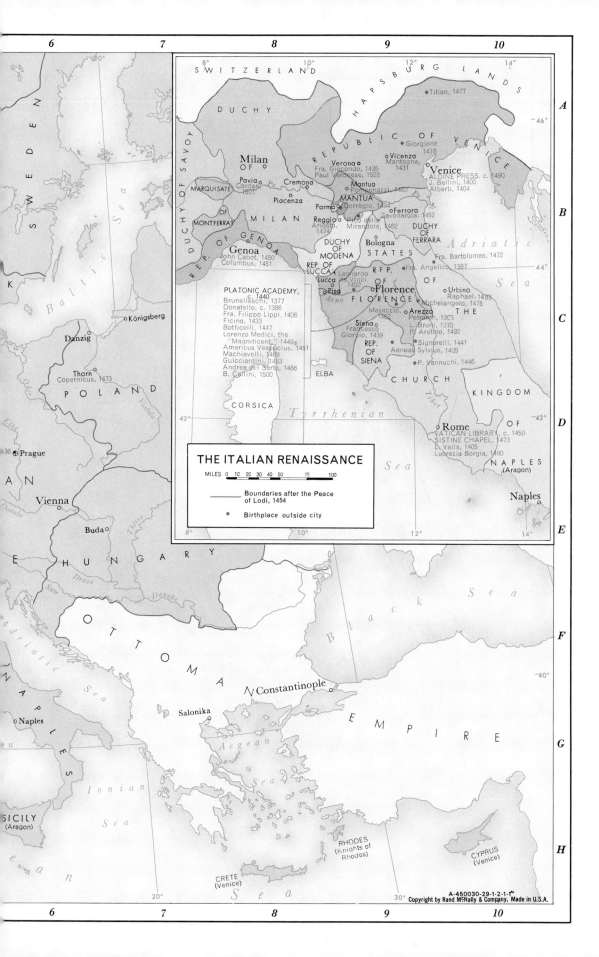

Map grid references (top): 6 7 8 9 10

8° 10° 12° 14°

SWITZERLAND

HAPSBURG LANDS

DUCHY
•Titian, 1477

A
—46°

REPUBLIC OF VENICE
•Giorgione
1478

Milan
OF

•Vicenza
Mantegna,
1431

Verona
•Fra. Giocondo, 1435
Paul Veronese, 1528

Venice
ALDINE PRESS. c. 1490
J. Bellini, 1400
Alberti, 1404

DUCHY OF SAVOY

MARQUISATE

Pavia
Cardan,
1501

Cremona

Piacenza

Po

Mantua
MANTUA
Pomponazzi, 1462

OF

MILAN

Parma•Correggio, 1494

B

OF
MONTFERRAT

REP. OF GENOA

Genoa
John Cabot, 1450
Columbus, 1451

Reggio
Ariosto,
1474

DUCHY
OF
MODENA

Pico della
Mirandola, 1462

Ferrara
Savonarola, 1452

DUCHY
OF
FERRARA

Adriatic

REP. OF
LUCCA

Lucca

Bologna
STATES

R.F.P.

Fra. Bartolomeo, 1472

Sea
—44°

PLATONIC ACADEMY,
1440
Brunelleschi, 1377
Donatello, c. 1386
Fra. Filippo Lippi, 1406
Ficino, 1433
Botticelli, 1447
Lorenzo Medici, the
"Magnificent," 1449
Americus Vespucius, 1451
Machiavelli, 1469
Guicciardini, 1483
Andrea del Sarto, 1486
B. Cellini, 1500

Leonardo
da Vinci,
1452

Pisa

Arno

OF
FLORENCE

Masaccio,
1402

Siena
Francesco
Giorgio, 1439

Florence

Arezzo

Petrarch, 1303

Fra. Angelico, 1387

Urbino
Raphael, 1483
Michelangelo, 1475

THE

L. Bruni, 1370
P. Aretino, 1492

C

REP.
OF
SIENA

•Signorelli, 1441

Aeneas Sylvius, 1405

•P. Vannuchi, 1446

CORSICA

ELBA

Tyrrhenian
—42°

CHURCH

Tiber

KINGDOM

42°

D

THE ITALIAN RENAISSANCE

MILES 0 10 20 30 40 50   75   100

——— Boundaries after the Peace
of Lodi, 1454

• Birthplace outside city

Sea

Rome
VATICAN LIBRARY, c. 1450
SISTINE CHAPEL, 1473
L. Valla, 1405
Lucrezia Borgia, 1480

OF
—42°

NAPLES
(Aragon)

Naples

E

8° 10° 12° 14°

Map grid references outside inset:

20°

SWEDEN

Baltic Sea

•Königsberg

K

Danzig

Thorn
Copernicus, 1473

POLAND

Vistula

Elbe

36 •Prague

AN

Vienna

Danube

Buda

HUNGARY

Thiss

Drave

Danube

Save

E

OTTOMAN

F

Adriatic Sea

N
APLES

•Naples

•Salonika

N Constantinople

EMPIRE
—40°

Black Sea

G

Aegean Sea

Ionian Sea

SICILY
(Aragon)

RHODES
(Knights of
Rhodes)

CYPRUS
(Venice)

H

CRETE
(Venice)

Sea

20°   30°

A-450030-29-1-2-1-1
Copyright by Rand McNally & Company, Made in U.S.A.

6 7 8 9 10

39

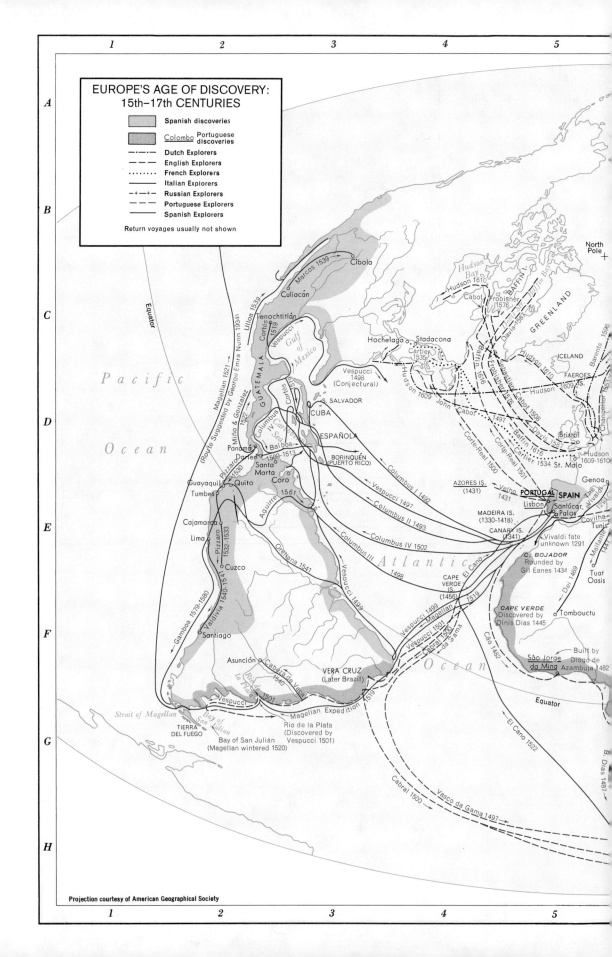

EUROPE'S AGE OF DISCOVERY:
15th–17th CENTURIES

Spanish discoveries

Colombo Portuguese discoveries

— · — · — Dutch Explorers

— — — English Explorers

· · · · · · French Explorers

———— Italian Explorers

— + — + Russian Explorers

— — — — Portuguese Explorers

———— Spanish Explorers

Return voyages usually not shown

Pacific Ocean

Equator

(Route Suggested by George Emra Nunn 1934)

Magellan 1521

Miño & Gonzalez 1522

Ulloa 1539

Marcos 1539

Cibola

Culiacán

Tenochtitlán

Cortés 1519

Vespucci 1519

Gulf of Mexico

Cortés 1519

Hochelaga

Stadacona

Cartier 1535

Vespucci 1498 (Conjectural)

S. SALVADOR

CUBA

Columbus IV Cortés 1519

ESPAÑOLA

Panamá

Darien

Balboa 1509-1513

Santa Marta

Coro

BORINQUÉN (PUERTO RICO)

Columbus I 1492

Guayaquil

Quito

Tumbes

Pizarro 1531-1550

Aguirre 1561

Columbus II 1493

Cajamarca

Lima

Pizarro 1532-1533

Orellana 1541

Columbus IV 1502

Vespucci 1497

Vespucci 1499

Columbus III 1498

Cuzco

Gamboa 1579-1580

Valdivia 1540-1541

Santiago

Asunción

Cabeza de Vaca 1540

Río de la Plata

VERA CRUZ (Later Brazil)

Vespucci 1501

Strait of Magellan

TIERRA DEL FUEGO

Bay of San Julián

Bay of San Julián (Magellan wintered 1520)

Río de la Plata (Discovered by Vespucci 1501)

Vespucci

Magellan Expedition

Atlantic Ocean

North Pole

Hudson Bay

Hudson 1610

BAFFIN I.

Cabot

Frobisher 1576

GREENLAND

Davis 1587

Hudson 1610

ICELAND

FAEROES IS.

Barents 1596

Chancellor 1553

Sebastian Cabot 1508

Hudson 1609

Hudson 1609

John Cabot 1497

Corte-Real 1500

Corte-Real 1501

Cartier 1534

Baffin 1616

Davis 1587

Bristol

Hudson 1609-1610

St. Malo

Genoa

AZORES IS. (1431)

Velho 1431

PORTUGAL

SPAIN

Lisbon

Santúcar

Palos

MADEIRA IS. (1330-1418)

CANARY IS. (1341)

Vivaldi fate unknown 1291

C. BOJADOR Rounded by Gil Eanes 1434

Genoa

The Vivaldi 1291

Covilhã

Tunis

Malfante 1447

Tuat Oasis

CAPE VERDE IS. (1456)

El Cano 1519

CAPE VERDE Discovered by Dinis Dias 1445

Dei 1469

Tombouctu

São Jorge da Mina

Built by Diogo de Azambuja 1482

Cão 1482

Vespucci 1499

Magellan 1501

Vespucci 1501

Cabral da Gama

Equator

Cabral 1500

Vasco da Gama 1497

El Cano 1522

B. Dias 1487

Projection courtesy of American Geographical Society

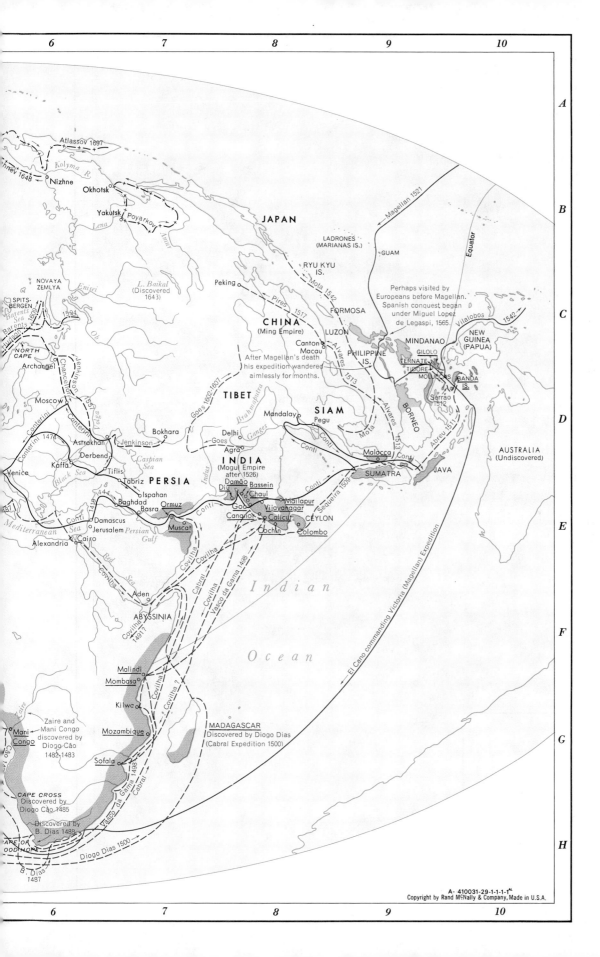

A

B

C

D

E

F

G

H

Atlassov 1697

hnev 1648   Nizhne

Okhotsk

Yakutsk   Poyarkov

NOVAYA
ZEMLYA

SPITS-
BERGEN

Barents
Sea 1596

Hudson

NORTH
CAPE

Archangel

Moscow

Conterini 1476

Astrakhan

Derbend

Kaffa

Venice

Tabriz

Tiflis

PERSIA

Ispahan

Baghdad

Basra

Damascus

Jerusalem

Cairo

Alexandria

Aden

ABYSSINIA
Covilha
1491?

Malindi

Mombasa

Kilwa

Mani
Congo

Zaire and
Mani Congo
discovered by
Diogo Cão
1482-1483

Mozambique

Sofala

CAPE CROSS
Discovered by
Diogo Cão 1485

Discovered by
B. Dias 1488

APE OF
OOD HOPE

B. Dias
1487

JAPAN

LADRONES
(MARIANAS IS.)

GUAM

Magellan 1521

Equator

RYU KYU
IS.

Mota 1542

FORMOSA

Peking

Pires
1517

CHINA
(Ming Empire)

LUZON

Canton
Macau

Alvares

PHILIPPINE
IS.

MINDANAO

GILOLO
TERNATE
TIDORE
MOLUCCAS

BANDA
IS.

Serrão
1512

Perhaps visited by
Europeans before Magellan.
Spanish conquest began
under Miguel Lopez
de Legaspi, 1565.

Villalobos

NEW
GUINEA
(PAPUA)

1542

After Magellan's death
his expedition wandered
aimlessly for months.

TIBET

Goes 1602-1607

Brahmaputra

Mandalay

SIAM

Pegu

Delhi
Goes

Agra

Ganges

Conti

Conti

Mota

BORNEO

Alvares

1513

Abreu 1511

Conti

AUSTRALIA
(Undiscovered)

INDIA
(Mogul Empire
after 1526)

Bokhara

Jenkinson

Caspian
Sea

Indus

Damão
Diu
Goa
Cananor

Bassein
Chaul

Vijayanagar
Calicut

Cochin

Mailapur

CEYLON

Colombo

Malacca

Conti

SUMATRA

Sequeira 1509

JAVA

Ormuz

Conti

Muscat

Covilha

Covilha

Cabral

Covilha

Vasco da Gama 1498

Covilha

Red
Sea

Persian
Gulf

Mediterranean
Sea

Black Sea

1444

Conti 1444

Conti

El Cano commanding Victoria (Magellan) Expedition

Indian

Ocean

MADAGASCAR
Discovered by Diogo Dias
(Cabral Expedition 1500)

Vasco da Gama 1498

Cabral

Diogo Dias 1500

L. Baikal
(Discovered
1643)

Enisei

Ob

Lena

Amur

Kolyma R.

Jenkinson 1559

Conterini

Jenkinson

Covilha?

Covilha?

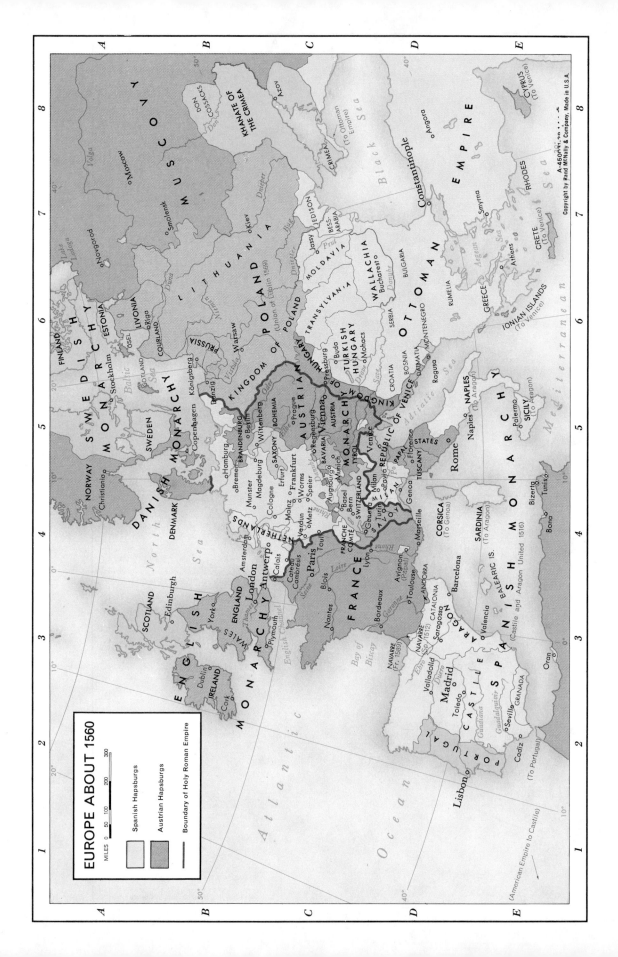

EUROPE ABOUT 1560

MILES 0 50 100 200 300

Spanish Hapsburgs

Austrian Hapsburgs

Boundary of Holy Roman Empire

MUSCOVY

NORWAY

SWEDISH MONARCHY

FINLAND

SWEDEN

DENMARK

DANISH MONARCHY

ENGLISH MONARCHY

SCOTLAND

ENGLAND

WALES

IRELAND

Dublin
Cork
Edinburgh
York
London
Plymouth

NETHERLANDS

Amsterdam
Antwerp
Calais
Cateau Cambrésis

FRANCE

Paris
Blois
Nantes
Bordeaux
Toulouse
Lyon
Marseille
Toul
Metz
Verdun

FRANCHE COMTÉ
LORRAINE
SAVOY
SWITZERLAND
Basel
Bern
Geneva

BRANDENBURG
Berlin
Hamburg
Bremen
Münster
Magdeburg
Cologne
Mainz
Frankfurt
Erfurt
Worms
Speier
Wittenberg
SAXONY
BOHEMIA
Prague
Regensburg
Augsburg
Munich
BAVARIA

KINGDOM OF POLAND

Danzig
Königsberg
PRUSSIA
Warsaw

LITHUANIA

ESTONIA
LIVONIA
Riga
COURLAND
OSEL

Moscow
Novgorod
Smolensk
Kiev

DON COSSACKS

KHANATE OF THE CRIMEA

CRIMEA

AUSTRIAN MONARCHY

AUSTRIA
Vienna
Pressburg
Buda
Mohács
TYROL
HUNGARY
KINGDOM OF HUNGARY

TURKISH HUNGARY

TRANSYLVANIA

MOLDAVIA
Jassy
WALLACHIA
Bucharest
SERBIA
BOSNIA
CROATIA
DALMATIA
Ragusa
MONTENEGRO
BULGARIA

OTTOMAN EMPIRE

Constantinople
Angora
Smyrna
RHODES

RUMELIA
GREECE
Athens

IONIAN ISLANDS (To Venice)

CRETE (To Venice)

CYPRUS (To Venice)

REPUBLIC OF VENICE

Venice
Milan
Turin
Genoa
PAPAL STATES
Florence
TUSCANY
Rome
Naples
NAPLES (To Aragon)

CORSICA (To Genoa)

SARDINIA (To Aragon)

SICILY (To Aragon)
Palermo

Bizerta
Tunis
Bona

SPANISH MONARCHY

Madrid
Valladolid
Toledo
Seville
Cadiz
Granada
GRANADA
CASTILE
Oran

PORTUGAL
Lisbon

ARAGON
Barcelona
Valencia
Saragossa
CATALONIA
ANDORRA
NAVARRE (Fr. 1589)
NAVARRE (Sp. 1512)

BALEARIC IS.

(Castile and Aragon United 1516)

Avignon (Papal)

Rhône
Loire
Seine
Garonne

Volga
Don
Dnieper
Dniester
Dvina
Danube
Vistula
Oder
Elbe
Rhine
Ebro
Duero
Guadiana
Guadalquivir
Tagus
Save
Drave
Prut
Bug

North Sea
Baltic Sea
Black Sea
Adriatic Sea
Aegean Sea
Ionian Sea
Mediterranean Sea
English Channel
Bay of Biscay
Atlantic Ocean
Lake Ladoga

Christiania
Stockholm
Copenhagen

(American Empire to Castile)

(To Portugal)

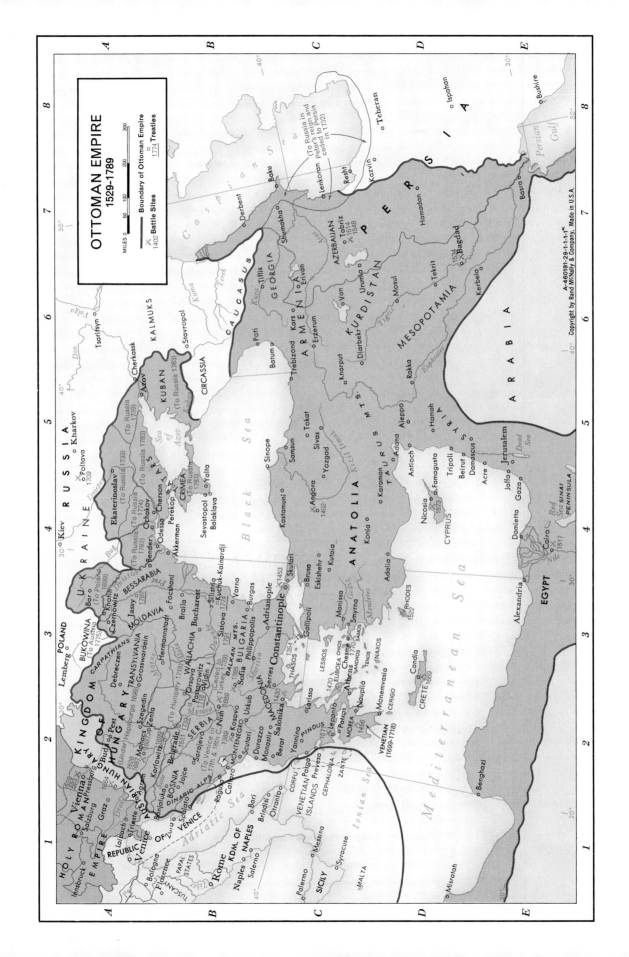

OTTOMAN EMPIRE
1529-1789

MILES 0 50 100 200 300

▬▬ Boundary of Ottoman Empire

✕ Battle Sites
1402

□ Treaties
1774

43

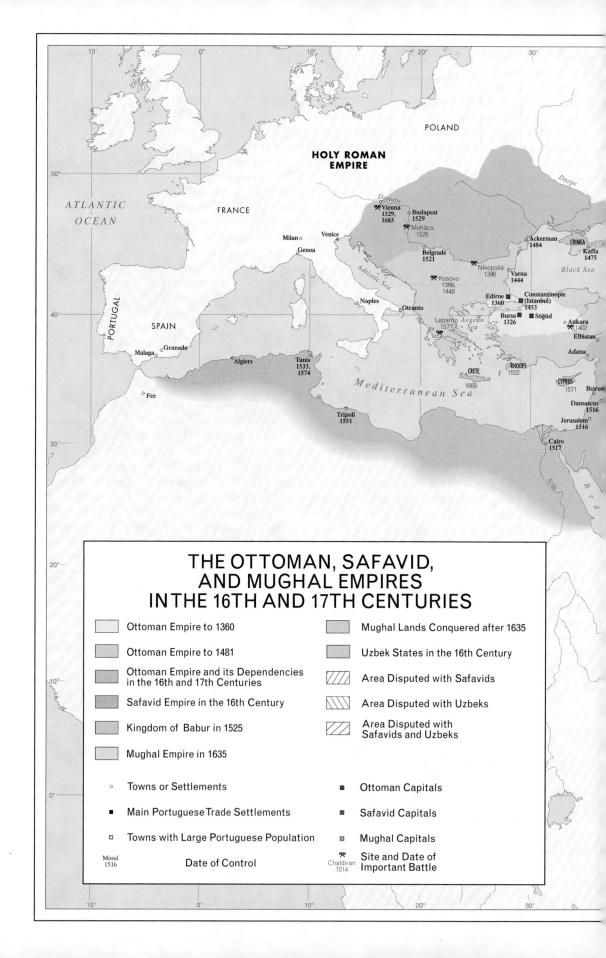

THE OTTOMAN, SAFAVID, AND MUGHAL EMPIRES IN THE 16TH AND 17TH CENTURIES

☐ Ottoman Empire to 1360		☐ Mughal Lands Conquered after 1635
☐ Ottoman Empire to 1481		☐ Uzbek States in the 16th Century
☐ Ottoman Empire and its Dependencies in the 16th and 17th Centuries		▨ Area Disputed with Safavids
☐ Safavid Empire in the 16th Century		▨ Area Disputed with Uzbeks
☐ Kingdom of Babur in 1525		▨ Area Disputed with Safavids and Uzbeks
☐ Mughal Empire in 1635		

○	Towns or Settlements	■	Ottoman Capitals
■	Main Portuguese Trade Settlements	■	Safavid Capitals
☐	Towns with Large Portuguese Population	■	Mughal Capitals
Mosul 1516	Date of Control	Chaldiran 1514 ✖	Site and Date of Important Battle

44

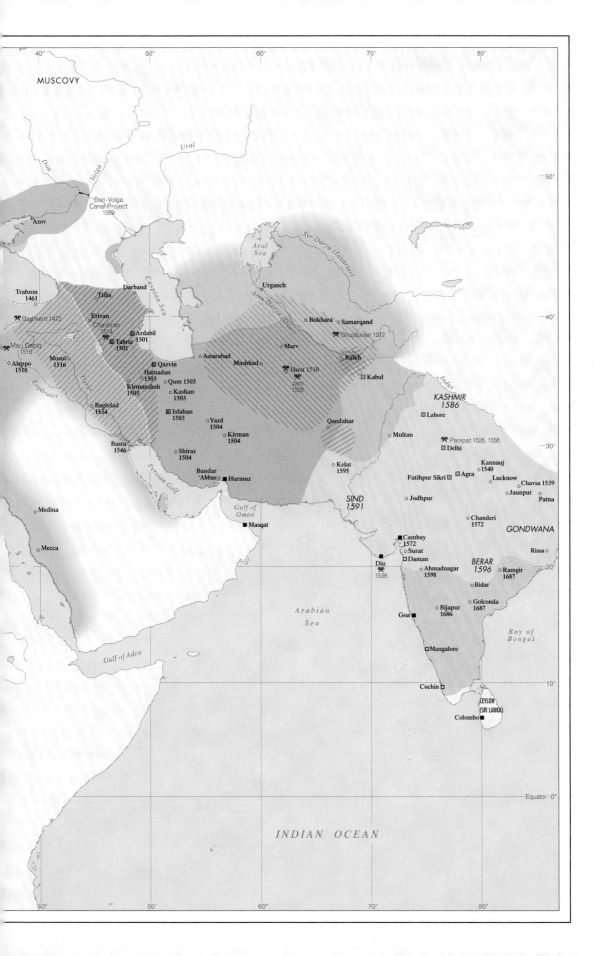

MUSCOVY

Don

Volga

Ural

Don-Volga
Canal Project
1569

Azov

Aral
Sea

Syr Darya (Jaxartes)

Caspian Sea

Trabzon
1461

Darband

Tiflis

⚔ Bashkent 1473

Erivan
Chaldiran
1514

Bukhara   Samarqand

⚔ Ghujduvan 1512

Ardabil
1501

Tabriz
1501

Marv

Astarabad

Balkh

⚔ Marj Dabiq
1516

Mosul
1516

Amu Darya (Oxus)

Aleppo
1516

Euphrates

Tigris

Qazvin

Hamadan
1503

Mashhad

⚔ Harat 1510
Jam
1528

Kabul

Kirmanshah
1503

Qum 1503

Kashan
1503

Qandahar

KASHMIR
1586

Baghdad
1534

Isfahan
1503

Yazd
1504

Lahore

Kirman
1504

Multan

Panipat 1526, 1556

Basra
1546

Shiraz
1504

Kelat
1595

Delhi

Kannauj
1540

Bandar
'Abbas

Hurmuz

Fatihpur Sikri   Agra

Lucknow
Chavsa 1539

Persian Gulf

Jaunpur

Patna

Jodhpur

SIND
1591

Gulf of
Oman

Chanderi
1572

GONDWANA

Medina

Masqat

Cambay
1572

Rissa

Red Sea

Mecca

Surat

Daman

BERAR
1596

Diu
1538

Ahmadnagar
1598

Ramgir
1687

Bidar

Arabian
Sea

Goa

Bijapur
1686

Golconda
1687

Gulf of Aden

Bay of
Bengal

Mangalore

Cochin

CEYLON
(SRI LANKA)

Colombo

INDIAN OCEAN

Equator 0°

50°

60°

70°

80°

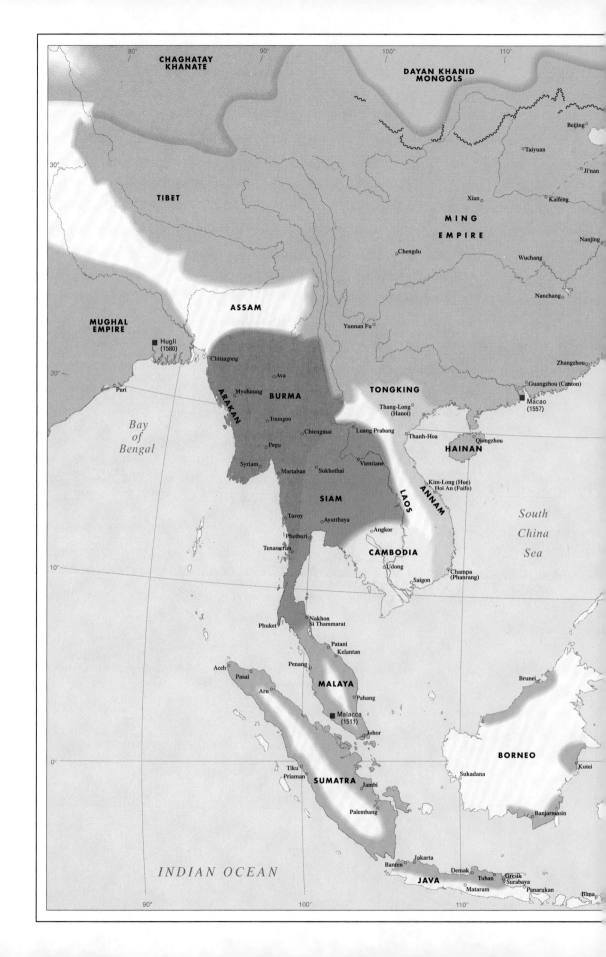

CHAGHATAY
KHANATE

DAYAN KHANID
MONGOLS

Beijing

Taiyuan

TIBET

Ji'nan

Kaifeng

MING

Xian

EMPIRE

Nanjing

Chengdu

Wuchang

ASSAM

Nanchang

MUGHAL
EMPIRE

Yunnan Fu

Hugli
(1580)

Chittagong

Zhangzhou

Ava

Guangzhou (Canton)

TONGKING

Myohaung

Macao
(1557)

BURMA

Thang-Long
(Hanoi)

ARAKAN

Puri

Chiengmai

Luang Prabang

Qiongzhou

Bay
of
Bengal

Toungoo

Thanh-Hoa

HAINAN

Pegu

Vientiane

Kim-Long (Hue)
Hoi An (Faifo)

Syriam

Martaban

Sukhothai

ANNAM

LAOS

South

SIAM

China

Tavoy

Ayutthaya

Sea

Phetburi

Angkor

Tenasserim

CAMBODIA

Udong

Champa
(Phanrang)

Saigon

Nakhon
Si Thammarat

Phuket

Patani

Kelantan

Penang

Brunei

Aceh

Pasai

MALAYA

Aru

Pahang

Malacca
(1511)

BORNEO

Kutei

Johor

Tiku
Priaman

Sukadana

SUMATRA

Jambi

Banjarmasin

Palembang

INDIAN OCEAN

Banten

Jakarta

Demak

Gresik

Tuban

Surabaya

JAVA

Mataram

Panarukan

Bima

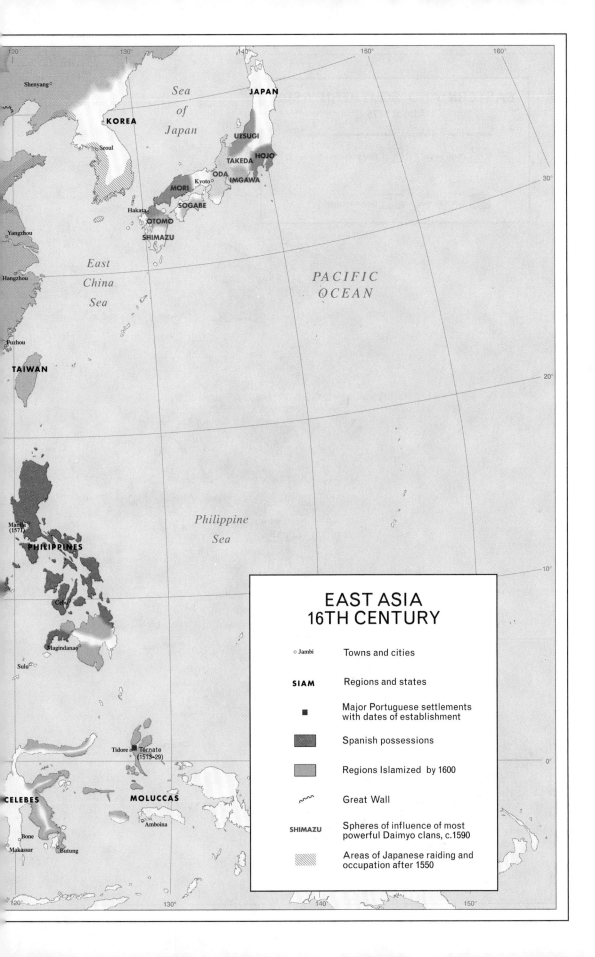

Shenyang

Sea
of
Japan

KOREA

Seoul

JAPAN

UESUGI

TAKEDA HOJO

ODA
MORI Kyoto IMGAWA

Hakata SOGABE

OTOMO

SHIMAZU

Yangzhou

Hangzhou

East
China
Sea

PACIFIC
OCEAN

Fuzhou

TAIWAN

30°

20°

PHILIPPINES

Manila
(1571)

Cebu

Magindanao

Sulu

Philippine
Sea

10°

EAST ASIA
16TH CENTURY

○ Jambi   Towns and cities

SIAM   Regions and states

■   Major Portuguese settlements
with dates of establishment

Spanish possessions

Regions Islamized by 1600

Great Wall

SHIMAZU   Spheres of influence of most
powerful Daimyo clans, c.1590

Areas of Japanese raiding and
occupation after 1550

Tidore Ternate
(1513–29)

CELEBES MOLUCCAS

Amboina

Bone

Makassar Butung

0°

120° 130° 140° 150°

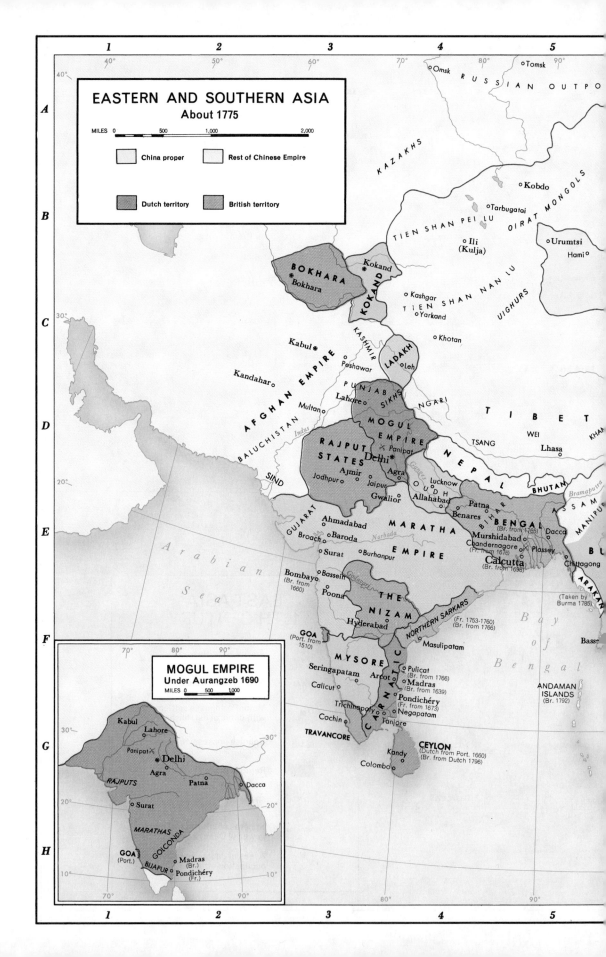

EASTERN AND SOUTHERN ASIA
About 1775

MILES 0   500   1,000   2,000

- China proper
- Rest of Chinese Empire
- Dutch territory
- British territory

RUSSIAN OUTPO

○ Omsk
○ Tomsk

KAZAKHS

○ Kobdo

○ Tarbugatai
OIRAT MONGOLS

TIEN SHAN PEI LU
○ Ili
(Kulja)
○ Urumtsi
○ Hami

○ Kashgar
TIEN SHAN NAN LU
○ Yarkand
UIGHURS

BOKHARA
* Bokhara
* Kokand
KOKAND

○ Khotan

* Kabul
AFGHAN EMPIRE
KASHMIR
LADAKH
○ Leh

○ Peshawar
○ Kandahar

PUNJAB
○ Lahore
SIKHS
NGARI

TIBET

BALUCHISTAN
○ Multan
Indus

MOGUL
EMPIRE
TSANG
WEI
KHAM
Lhasa

RAJPUT
STATES
Delhi ×Panipat
NEPAL
BHUTAN

SIND
○ Ajmir
○ Agra
Ganges
Lucknow
O U D H
Allahabad
Bramaputra
ASSAM
MANIPU

○ Jodhpur
○ Jaipur
○ Gwalior

GUJARAT
○ Ahmadabad
MARATHA
Patna
Benares
BIHAR
BENGAL
(Br. from 1765)
Dacca

Arabian
Sea

○ Broach
○ Baroda
Narbada
EMPIRE
Murshidabad
Chandernagore
(Fr. from 1676)
Plossey

○ Surat
○ Burhanpur
Calcutta
(Br. from 1698)
Chittagong
ARAKAN

Bombay○
(Br. from 1660)
○ Bassein
THE
NIZAM
Poona
Godavari
(Taken by
Burma 1785)

GOA
(Port. from 1510)
Hyderabad
NORTHERN SARKARS
(Fr. 1753-1760)
(Br. from 1766)
Bay
of
Bengal
Basse

MYSORE
Masulipatam

○ Calicut
Seringapatam
CARNATIC
Arcot
Pulicat
(Br. from 1766)
Madras
(Br. from 1639)
Pondichéry
(Fr. from 1673)

ANDAMAN
ISLANDS
(Br. 1792)

Trichinopoly
Negapatam
Tanjore

○ Cochin
TRAVANCORE
CEYLON
(Dutch from Port. 1660)
(Br. from Dutch 1796)
Kandy

Colombo○

MOGUL EMPIRE
Under Aurangzeb 1690

MILES 0   500   1,000

Kabul
○ Lahore
Panipat×
* Delhi
Agra
RAJPUTS
Patna
Dacca

○ Surat

MARATHAS
GOLCONDA
GOA
(Port.)
BIJAPUR
Madras
(Br.)
Pondichéry
(Fr.)

48

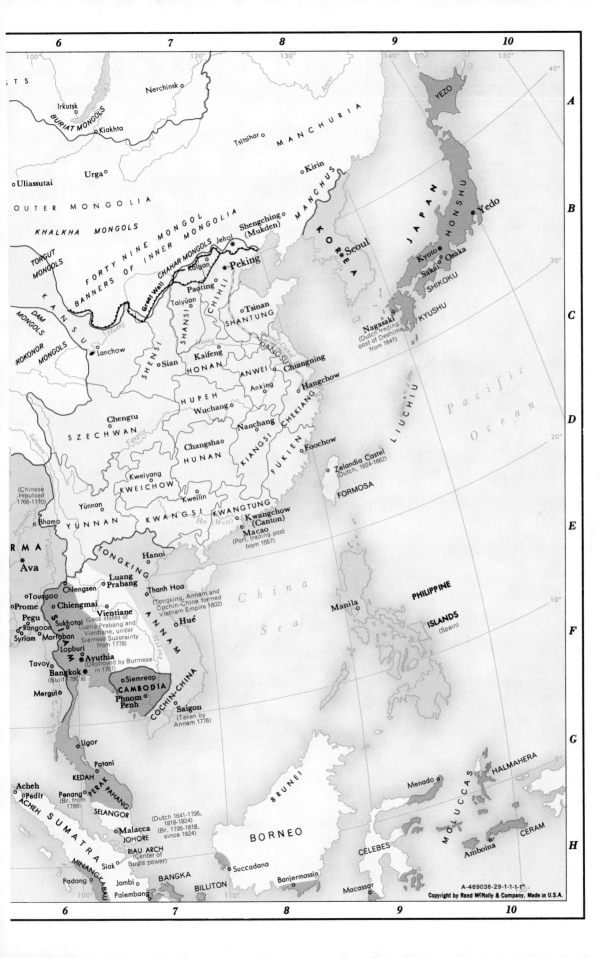

A · 6

6 · 100° · **7** · 120° · **8** · 130° · **9** · 140° · **10** · 150° · 40°

Nerchinsk

Irkutsk
BURIAT MONGOLS
Kiakhta
YEZO

Tsitsihar
MANCHURIA

A

Uliassutai
Urga
OUTER MONGOLIA
Kirin
MANCHUS
HONSHU
JAPAN

B

KHALKHA MONGOLS
Shengching
(Mukden)
KOREA
Seoul
Kyoto
Sakai
Yedo
30°

TORGUT MONGOLS
FORTY NINE MONGOL
BANNERS OF INNER MONGOLIA
CHAHAR MONGOLS
Jehol
Kalgan
Great Wall
Peking
CHIHLI
Osaka
SHIKOKU

KANSU
DAM MONGOLS
Paoting
Taiyüan
SHANSI
Tsinan
SHANTUNG
KYUSHU

C

KOKONOR MONGOLS
Lanchow
Huang
Sian
SHENSI
Kaifeng
HONAN
ANWEI
Chiangning
Nagasaki
(Dutch trading post of Deshima from 1641)
LIUCHIU

Anking
HUPEH
Wuchang
Hangchow
CHEKIANG

Chengtu
SZECHWAN
Yangtze
Nanchang
KIANGSI
Foochow
FUKIEN
Pacific Ocean

D

Changshao
HUNAN
20°

(Chinese repulsed 1766-1770)
Salween
Kweiyang
KWEICHOW
Kweilin
Zelandia Castel
(Dutch, 1624-1662)

Yünnan
KWANGSI
KWANGTUNG
Hsi (West)
Kwangchow
(Canton)
FORMOSA

E

Bhamo
Irrawaddy
YUNNAN
Macao
(Port. trading post from 1557)

BURMA
Ava
TONGKING
Hanoi
Hué

PHILIPPINE

F

Toungoo
Chiengsen
Luang Prabang
Thanh Hoa
(Tongking, Annam and Cochin-China formed Vietnam Empire 1802)
China Sea
Manila
ISLANDS
(Spain)
10°

Prome
Pegu
Chiengmai
Vientiane
(Laos states of Luang Prabang and Vientiane, under Siamese Suzerainty from 1778)

Rangoon
Sukhotai
Hué
ANNAM
Syriam
Martaban
Lopburi
Ayuthia
(Destroyed by Burmese in 1767)

Tavoy
Bangkok
(Built 1780's)
Mekong

Mergui
Siemreap
CAMBODIA
Phnom Penh
COCHIN-CHINA
Saigon
(Taken by Annam 1776)

G

Ligor

Patani

KEDAH
BRUNEI
Menado
HALMAHERA

Acheh
Pedir
Penang
(Br. from 1786)
PERAK
PAHANG
SELANGOR
MOLUCCAS
CERAM

ACHEH
SUMATRA
Malacca
JOHORE
(Dutch 1641-1795, 1818-1824) (Br. 1795-1818, since 1824)
BORNEO
CELEBES
Amboina

H

MINANGKABAU
Padang
RIAU ARCH
(Center of Bugis power)
Siak
BANGKA
BILLITON
Succadana
Banjermassin
Macassar
A-469036-29-1-1-1-1*
Copyright by Rand McNally & Company, Made in U.S.A.

Jambi
Palembang · 100° · **7** · 110° · **8** · **9** · Macassar · **10**

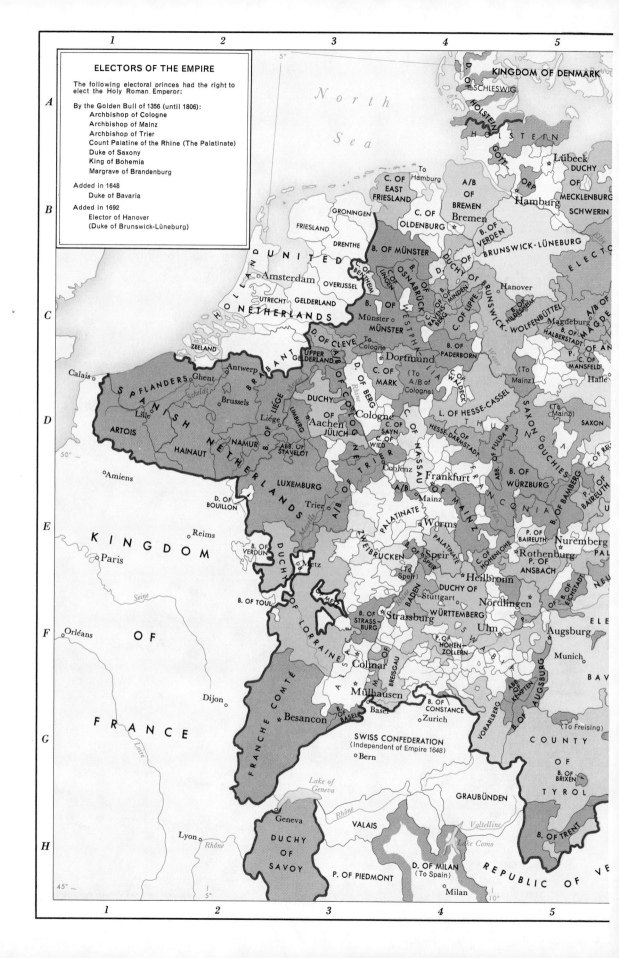

ELECTORS OF THE EMPIRE

The following electoral princes had the right to
elect the Holy Roman Emperor:

By the Golden Bull of 1356 (until 1806):
Archbishop of Cologne
Archbishop of Mainz
Archbishop of Trier
Count Palatine of the Rhine (The Palatinate)
Duke of Saxony
King of Bohemia
Margrave of Brandenburg

Added in 1648
Duke of Bavaria

Added in 1692
Elector of Hanover
(Duke of Brunswick-Lüneburg)

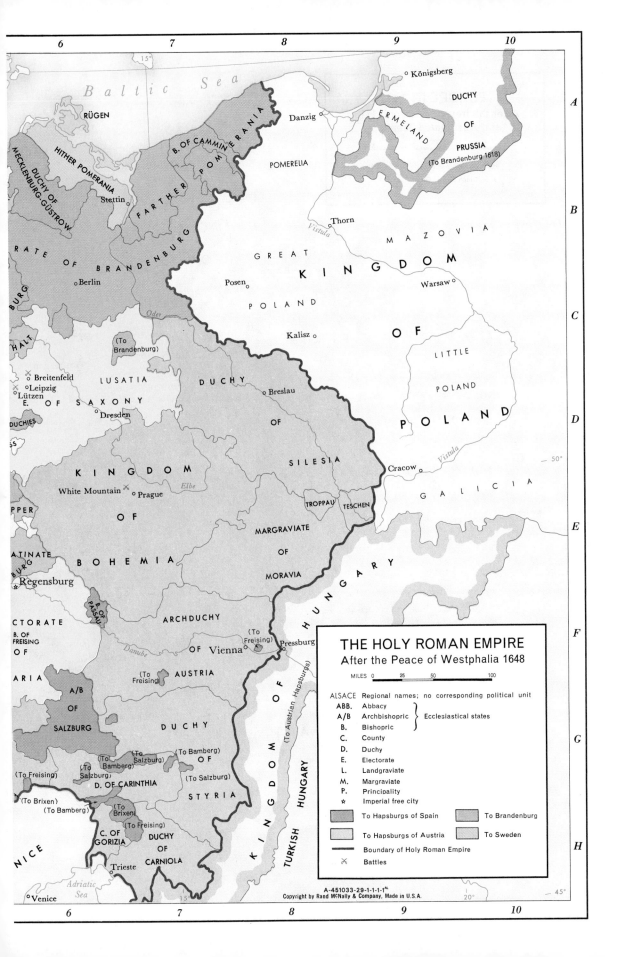

THE HOLY ROMAN EMPIRE
After the Peace of Westphalia 1648

MILES 0   25   50   100

ALSACE Regional names; no corresponding political unit
ABB.   Abbacy
A/B   Archbishopric } Ecclesiastical states
B.   Bishopric
C.   County
D.   Duchy
E.   Electorate
L.   Landgraviate
M.   Margraviate
P.   Principality
☆   Imperial free city

To Hapsburgs of Spain   To Brandenburg
To Hapsburgs of Austria   To Sweden
—— Boundary of Holy Roman Empire
✕   Battles

A-451033-29-1-1-1-1ᴬᴸ
Copyright by Rand McNally & Company, Made in U.S.A.

Map labels, reading generally top to bottom:

Baltic Sea
Königsberg
RÜGEN
DUCHY OF PRUSSIA
(To Brandenburg 1618)
HITHER POMERANIA
DUCHY OF MECKLENBURG-GÜSTROW
B. OF CAMMIN
FARTHER POMERANIA
Danzig
ERMELAND
Stettin
POMERELIA
RATE OF BRANDENBURG
BURG
Thorn
Vistula
MAZOVIA
GREAT
Berlin
Oder
Warsaw
KINGDOM
POLAND
ALT
HALT
Posen
OF
(To Brandenburg)
LITTLE
Breitenfeld
LUSATIA
Kalisz
POLAND
Leipzig
Lützen
E. OF SAXONY
DUCHY
Breslau
DUCHIES
Dresden
OF
50°
SS
KINGDOM
SILESIA
Cracow
GALICIA
PPER
White Mountain
Prague
Elbe
Vistula
TROPPAU
TESCHEN
ATINATE
OF
MARGRAVIATE
URG
BOHEMIA
OF
Regensburg
MORAVIA
B. OF PASSAU
HUNGARY
CTORATE
ARCHDUCHY
B. OF FREISING
Danube
(To Freising)
Pressburg
OF
(To Freising)
OF Vienna
ARIA
A/B OF SALZBURG
(To Freising)
AUSTRIA
(To Austrian Hapsburgs)
(To Bamberg)
(To Salzburg)
(To Bamberg)
DUCHY
(To Freising)
(To Salzburg)
OF
KINGDOM OF HUNGARY
(To Salzburg)
(To Bamberg)
D. OF CARINTHIA
(To Brixen)
(To Bamberg)
STYRIA
TURKISH HUNGARY
(To Brixen)
Brixen
(To Freising)
C. OF GORIZIA
DUCHY OF CARNIOLA
NICE
Trieste
Adriatic Sea
Venice
45°

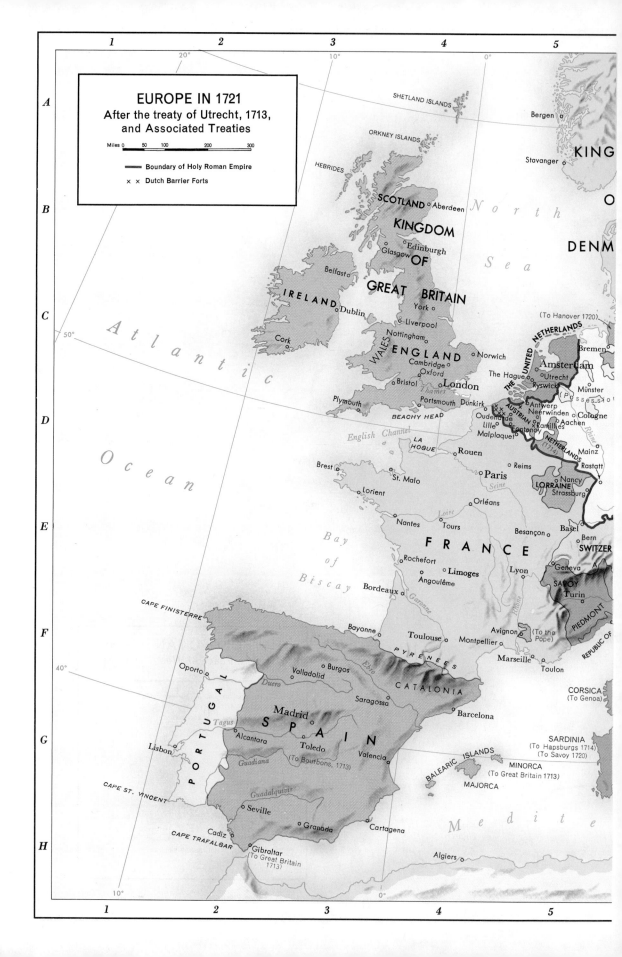

EUROPE IN 1721
After the treaty of Utrecht, 1713, and Associated Treaties

Miles 0   50   100   200   300

——— Boundary of Holy Roman Empire
x x Dutch Barrier Forts

20°   10°   0°

SHETLAND ISLANDS

Bergen

ORKNEY ISLANDS

KING

Stavanger

O

HEBRIDES

North

DENM

Sea

SCOTLAND   o Aberdeen

KINGDOM

o Edinburgh
Glasgow o

Belfast o   OF

IRELAND   GREAT   BRITAIN

o Dublin   York o

Cork o   o Liverpool   (To Hanover 1720)

Nottingham o   NETHERLANDS   o Bremen

ENGLAND   o Norwich   The Hague o   THE UNITED   o Utrecht
WALES   Cambridge o   Amsterdam   Ryswick o   o Münster

o Bristol   Oxford o   Antwerp   Possession
Plymouth o   London   THE   x x   o Cologne
Portsmouth o   Dunkirk o   AUSTRIAN   Neerwinden o   o Aachen
BEACHY HEAD   Oudenarde o   Ramillies   NETHERLANDS   o Mainz
LA   Lille o   o Fontenoy   (1714)
HOGUE   Malplaquet o   o Rastatt

English Channel   Rouen o   o Reims   Rhine

Atlantic   Brest o   St. Malo o   Paris   Nancy o
Seine   o   LORRAINE   Strassburg o
Lorient o   Orléans o

Ocean   Nantes o   Tours o   Loire   Besançon o   Basel o   Bern o
o   SWITZER

FRANCE   Geneva o
Rochefort o   Lyon o   SAVOY
Bay   o Limoges   Turin o
of   Angoulême o   PIEDMONT
Biscay   Bordeaux o   Garonne   Avignon o   (To the   REPUBLIC OF
Pope)

CAPE FINISTERRE   Bayonne o   Toulouse o   Montpellier o   CORSICA
Toulon o   (To Genoa)

40°   Oporto o   Valladolid o   Burgos o   Marseille o
Duero   PYRENEES   SARDINIA
Saragossa o   CATALONIA   (To Hapsburgs 1714)
Tagus   Madrid   o Barcelona   (To Savoy 1720)
PORTUGAL   o   MINORCA
Alcantara o   SPAIN   Valencia o   BALEARIC ISLANDS   (To Great Britain 1713)
Lisbon o   Toledo o   MAJORCA
Guadiana   (To Bourbons, 1713)
CAPE ST. VINCENT   Guadalquivir   Cartagena o   Medite

Seville o   Mediter

Cadiz o   Granada o
CAPE TRAFALGAR   Gibraltar   Algiers o
(To Great Britain
1713)

10°   0°

52

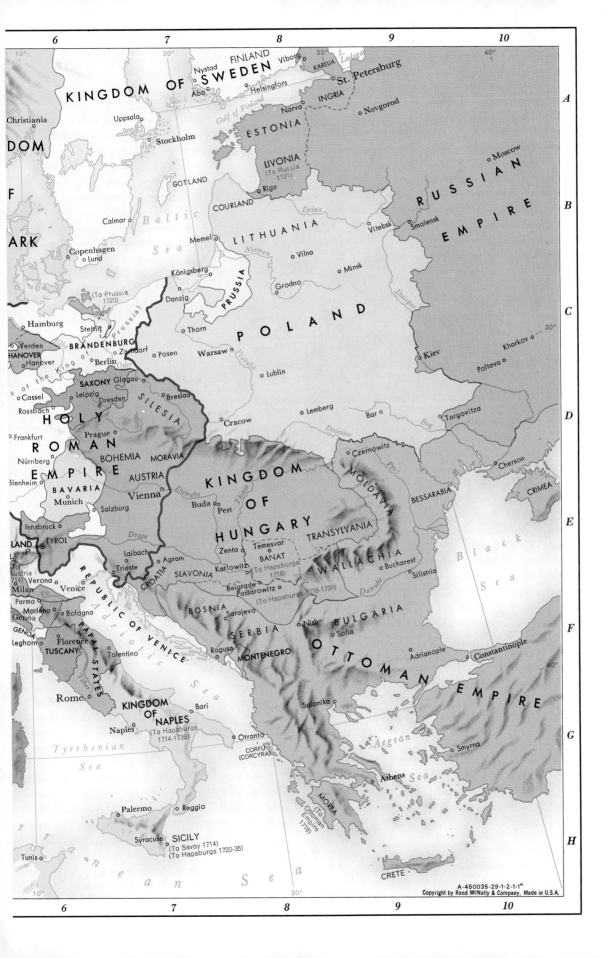

KINGDOM OF SWEDEN

FINLAND

Nystad
Åbo
Helsingfors
Viborg
KARELIA
L. Ladoga
St. Petersburg
INGRIA
Narva
Novgorod

Christiania

Uppsala

Stockholm

DOM
F
ARK

Calmar

Copenhagen
Lund

GOTLAND

ESTONIA

LIVONIA
(To Russia 1721)
Riga

COURLAND

Moscow

RUSSIAN EMPIRE

Baltic Sea

Memel

LITHUANIA

Dvina

Vitebsk
Smolensk

Königsberg
(To Prussia 1720)
Danzig

PRUSSIA

Vilna

Minsk

Grodno

Hamburg
Stettin
HANOVER
Verden
Hanover

BRANDENBURG
Zandorf
Berlin

Thorn

POLAND

Posen

Warsaw

Vistula

Kiev

Kharkov

Poltava

Dnieper

50°

s of the King of Prussia

Cassel
Rossbach

SAXONY
Leipzig
Dresden
Glogau
Breslau
SILESIA

Cracow

Lublin

Lemberg

Bug

Bar

Targovitza

Dniester

HOLY ROMAN EMPIRE

Frankfurt
Nürnberg
Blenheim

Prague
BOHEMIA
AUSTRIA
BAVARIA
Munich

MORAVIA

Czernowitz

Pruth

KINGDOM OF HUNGARY

MOLDAVIA

BESSARABIA

Cherson

CRIMEA

Salzburg

Vienna

Buda
Pest

Danube

Theiss

LAND
P
To Austria 1714)
Verona
Milan
Parma
Modena
Bologna
GENOA
Leghorn

Innsbruck
TYROL

Laibach
Trieste

Agram

CROATIA

Zenta

Temesvar
BANAT
(To Hapsburgs 1718)

Karlowitz

SLAVONIA

TRANSYLVANIA

WALLACHIA

Bucharest

Drave

REPUBLIC OF VENICE

Venice

Po

Belgrade
Passarowitz
(To Hapsburgs 1718-1739)

Silistria

Danube

Black Sea

40°

BOSNIA

Sarajevo

SERBIA

Nish

Sofia

BULGARIA

OTTOMAN EMPIRE

TUSCANY
Florence
PAPAL STATES
Tolentino

Adriatic Sea

Ragusa

MONTENEGRO

Adrianople

Constantinople

Rome

Tiber

KINGDOM OF NAPLES
(To Hapsburgs 1714-1735)

Bari

Salonika

Tyrrhenian Sea

Naples

Otranto

CORFU (CORCYRA)

Aegean Sea

Smyrna

Athens

Palermo
Reggio

MOREA
(To Ottoman Empire 1718)

Syracuse
SICILY
(To Savoy 1714)
(To Hapsburgs 1720-35)

Tunis

CRETE

Mediterranean Sea

A-450035-29-1-2-1-1
Copyright by Rand McNally & Company, Made in U.S.A.

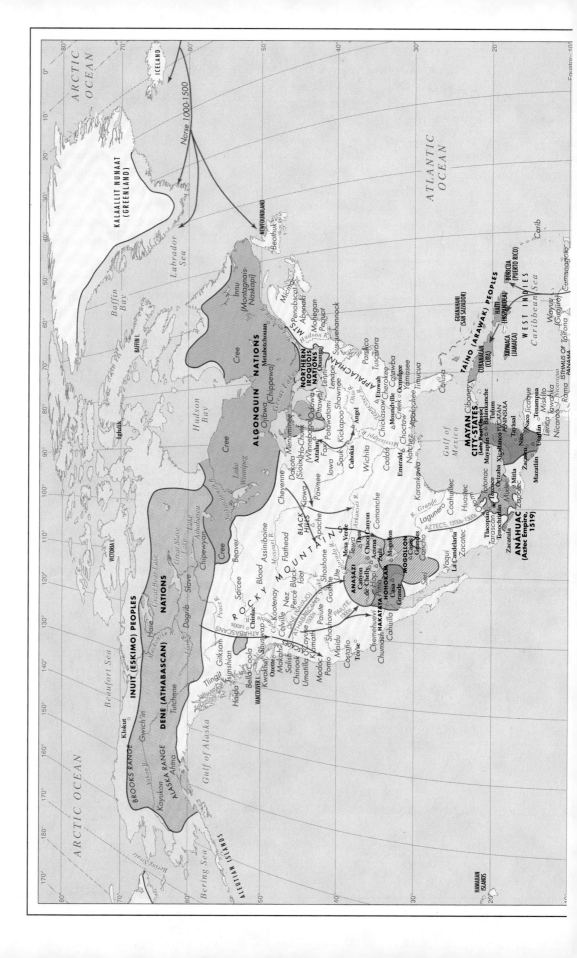

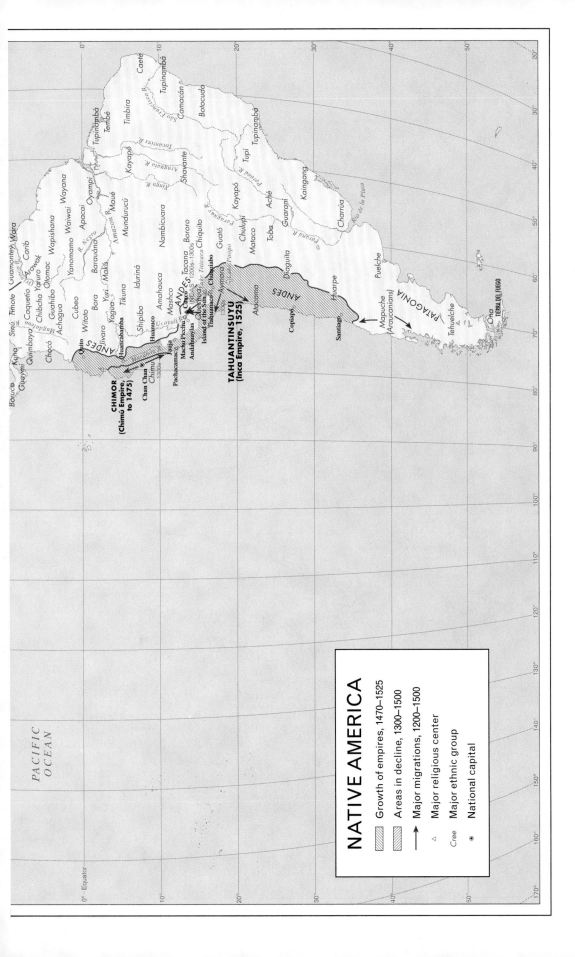

PACIFIC
OCEAN

0° Equator

NATIVE AMERICA

Growth of empires, 1470–1525

Areas in decline, 1300–1500

Major migrations, 1200–1500

△ Major religious center

Cree Major ethnic group

⊛ National capital

Borucá
Kuna
Guaymí
Timote
Guamonte
Wara
Sinú
Quimbaya
Caquetío
Yaruro
Carib
Chibcha
Yavavak
Chocó
Otomac
Guahibo
Achagua
Witoto
Cubeo
Bora
Yuri
Tikuna
Yagua
Makú
Jívaro
Huancabamba
Shipibo
Huánuco
Mascho
Amahauca
Nambicuara
Tacana
Bororo
Chiquito
Chiquiabo
Guató
Guaraní
Chulupí
Mataco
Toba
Aché
Kaingang
Charrúa

Wayana
Waiwai
Wapishana
Barauána
Yanomamo
Munduracú
Apacai
Oyampi
Kayapó
Shavante
Tupinambá
Tupi
Kayapó

Quito
ANDES
CHIMOR
(Chimú Empire,
to 1475)
Chan Chan
Chimú
1300s
Pachacamac
Andahuaylas
Machu Picchu
Cuzco
INCAS 1200s–1300s
Jauja
Quechua
Tiahuanaco
Island of the Sun
Lake Titicaca 1300s
Aymara
TAHUANTINSUYU
(Inca Empire, 1525)
ANDES
Atacama
Copiapó
Diaguita
Santiago
Huarpe
Mapuche
(Araucanians)
PATAGONIA
Puelche
Tehuelche
Ona
TIERRA DEL FUEGO

Caeté
Tupinambá
Tembé
Timbira
São Francisco R.
Camacán
Botocudo

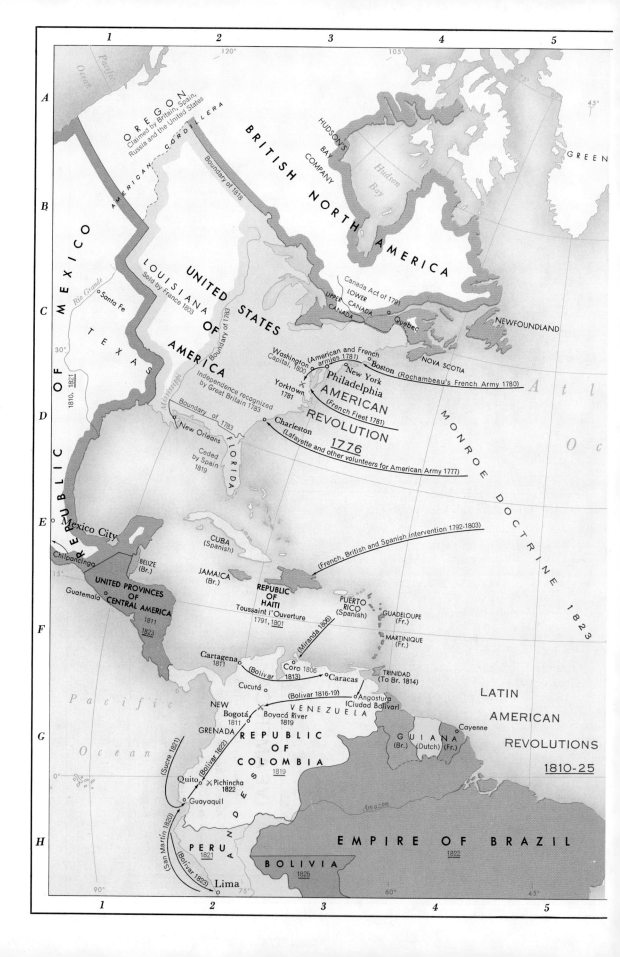

A B C D E F G H

1   2   3   4   5

Pacific Ocean

OREGON
Claimed by Britain, Spain,
Russia and the United States

BRITISH NORTH AMERICA

HUDSON'S BAY COMPANY

Hudson Bay

GREEN

AMERICAN CORDILLERA

Boundary of 1818

UNITED STATES OF AMERICA

LOUISIANA
Sold by France 1803

Rio Grande

Santa Fe

REPUBLIC OF MEXICO

TEXAS

1810, 1821

Boundary of 1783

Independence recognized
by Great Britain 1783

Mississippi

Boundary of 1783

New Orleans

FLORIDA
Ceded by Spain 1819

Canada Act of 1791
UPPER CANADA   LOWER CANADA

Quebec

NEWFOUNDLAND

NOVA SCOTIA

Washington Capital, 1800
(American and French armies 1781)
New York
Boston (Rochambeau's French Army 1780)

Philadelphia
AMERICAN
(French Fleet 1781)
Yorktown 1781
REVOLUTION
1776

Charleston
(Lafayette and other volunteers for American Army 1777)

Atl

MONROE DOCTRINE 1823

Oc

Mexico City

Chilpancingo

BELIZE (Br.)

UNITED PROVINCES OF CENTRAL AMERICA
Guatemala
1811
1823

CUBA (Spanish)

JAMAICA (Br.)

REPUBLIC OF HAITI
Toussaint l'Ouverture
1791, 1801

PUERTO RICO (Spanish)

GUADELOUPE (Fr.)

MARTINIQUE (Fr.)

(French, British and Spanish intervention 1792-1803)

Cartagena 1811

(Bolivar 1813)

Coro 1806

(Miranda 1806)

Caracas

TRINIDAD (To Br. 1814)

Cucutá

NEW

Bogotá 1811

GRENADA

(Bolivar 1816-19)
VENEZUELA
Boyacá River 1819
Angostura (Ciudad Bolivar)

REPUBLIC OF COLOMBIA
1819

(Sucre 1821)

Quito

(Bolivar 1822)

Pichincha 1822

Guayaquil

GUIANA
(Br.) (Dutch) (Fr.)

Cayenne

LATIN AMERICAN REVOLUTIONS
1810-25

Pacific Ocean

Amazon

EMPIRE OF BRAZIL
1822

(San Martín 1820)

PERU
1821

(Bolivar 1823)

BOLIVIA
1825

Lima

1   2   3   4   5

56

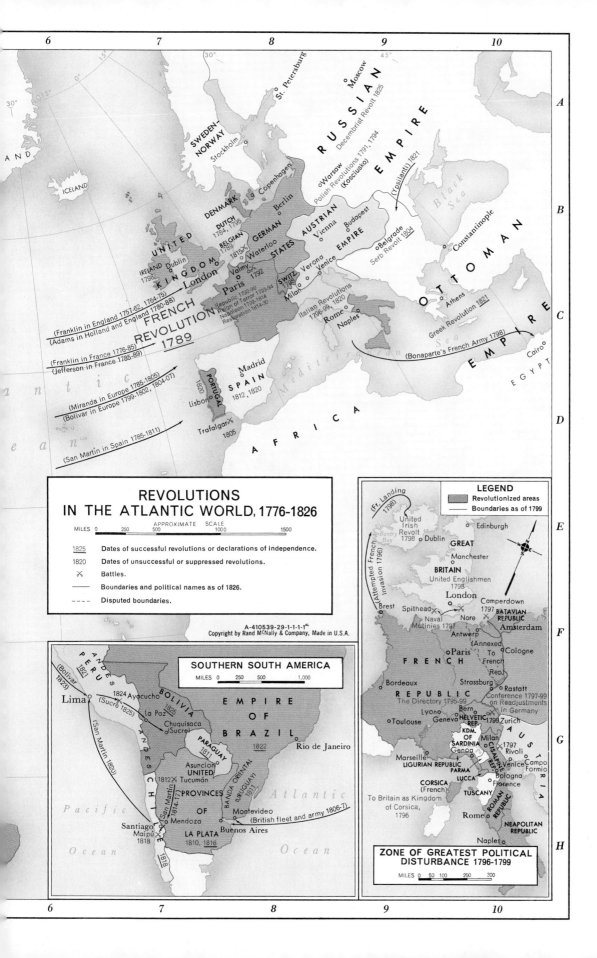

REVOLUTIONS IN THE ATLANTIC WORLD, 1776-1826

6   7   8   9   10

ICELAND

RUSSIAN EMPIRE

Moscow

Decembrist Revolt 1825

St. Petersburg

SWEDEN-NORWAY

Stockholm

DENMARK

Copenhagen

Warsaw

Polish Revolutions 1791, 1794
(Kosciusko)

(Ypsilanti) 1821

Black Sea

OTTOMAN EMPIRE

Constantinople

UNITED KINGDOM

IRELAND Dublin
1798

London

Berlin

DUTCH
1784, 1795

BELGIUM
1789

1815 × Waterloo

GERMAN STATES

AUSTRIAN EMPIRE

Vienna

Budapest

Belgrade 1804

Serb Revolt 1804

SWITZ. 1847

Verona

Venice

Milan

Valmy
1792

Paris

FRENCH REVOLUTION 1789

Republic 1792-99
Reign of Terror 1793-94
Napoleon 1799-1814
Restoration 1814-30

Italian Revolutions
1796-99, 1820

Rome

Naples

Athens

Greek Revolution 1821

(Bonaparte's French Army 1798)

Cairo

EGYPT

(Franklin in England 1757-62, 1764-75)

(Adams in Holland and England 1780-88)

(Franklin in France 1776-85)

(Jefferson in France 1785-89)

(Miranda in Europe 1785-1805)

(Bolivar in Europe 1799-1802, 1804-07)

(San Martin in Spain 1785-1811)

Madrid

SPAIN
1812, 1820

PORTUGAL
1820

Lisbon

Trafalgar ×
1805

AFRICA

Mediterranean Sea

Atlantic Ocean

A
B
C
D
E
F
G
H

**REVOLUTIONS
IN THE ATLANTIC WORLD, 1776-1826**

MILES 0   250   500   1000   1500

APPROXIMATE SCALE

<u>1825</u> Dates of successful revolutions or declarations of independence.

1820 Dates of unsuccessful or suppressed revolutions.

× Battles.

—— Boundaries and political names as of 1826.

---- Disputed boundaries.

A-410539-29-1-1-1-1^AL
Copyright by Rand McNally & Company, Made in U.S.A.

LEGEND

▨ Revolutionized areas

—— Boundaries as of 1799

**ZONE OF GREATEST POLITICAL
DISTURBANCE 1796-1799**

MILES 0   50   100   200   300

(Fr. Landing 1798)

United Irish Revolt 1798

Edinburgh

Dublin

GREAT BRITAIN

Manchester

United Englishmen 1798

(Attempted French Invasion 1796)

Bantry Bay

London

Brest

Spithead

Naval Mutinies 1797

Nore

Camperdown 1797

BATAVIAN REPUBLIC

Amsterdam

Antwerp

(Annexed To French Rep.)

Cologne

FRENCH REPUBLIC
The Directory 1795-99

Paris

Bordeaux

Strassburg

Rastatt Conference 1797-99 on Readjustments in Germany

Lyons

Bern

Geneva

HELVETIC REP.

1799 Zurich

Toulouse

KDM. OF SARDINIA

Milan

1797 Rivoli

AUSTRIA

Marseille

LIGURIAN REPUBLIC

Genoa

CISALPINE REP.

Venice

Campo Formio

PARMA

LUCCA

Bologna

Florence

CORSICA (French)

To Britain as Kingdom of Corsica, 1796

TUSCANY

ROMAN REP.

Rome

NEAPOLITAN REPUBLIC

Naples

SOUTHERN SOUTH AMERICA

MILES 0   250   500   1,000

PERU

(Bolivar 1823)
1821

Lima

1824 Ayacucho
1825 (Sucre 1825)

La Paz

BOLIVIA

Chuquisaca
Sucre

EMPIRE OF BRAZIL
1822

Rio de Janeiro

(San Martin 1820)

ANDES

CHILE

PARAGUAY
1811

Asuncion

1812 × Tucumán

UNITED PROVINCES OF LA PLATA
1810, 1816

BANDA ORIENTAL (URUGUAY) 1811

Montevideo

(British fleet and army 1806-7)

Buenos Aires

Santiago

Maipú ×
1818

Mendoza

San Martin 1814-17

1818

Pacific Ocean

Atlantic Ocean

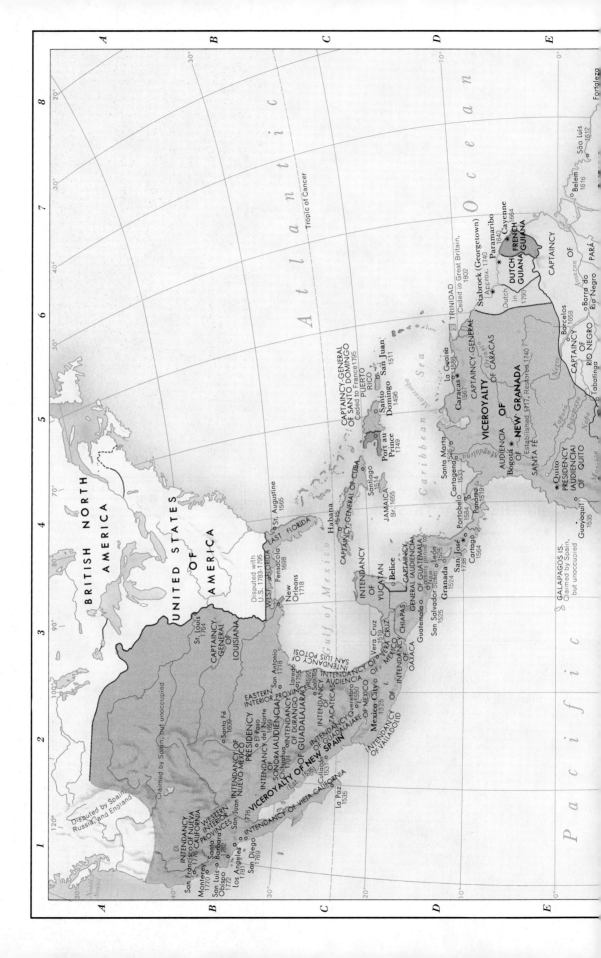

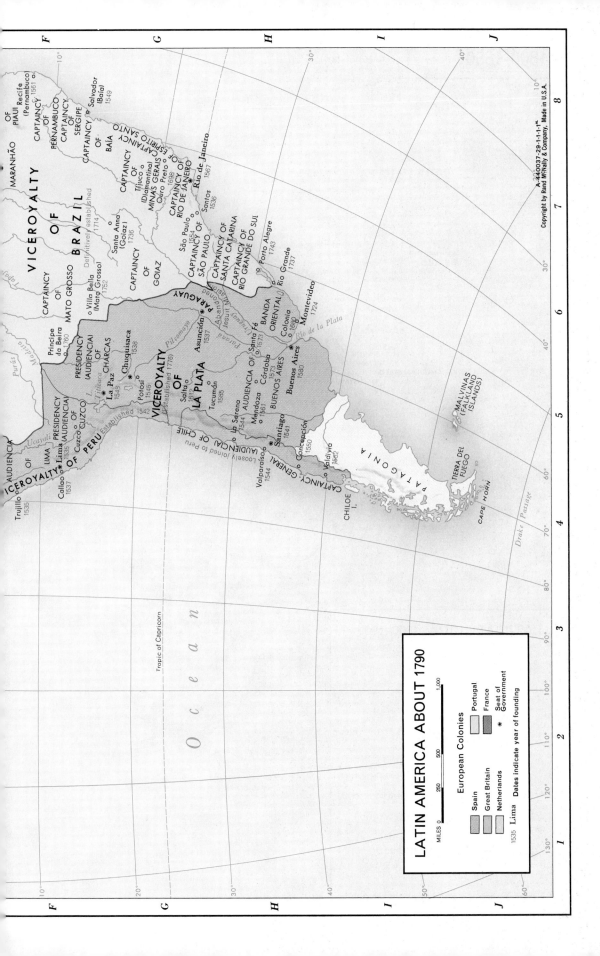

LATIN AMERICA ABOUT 1790

European Colonies

- Spain
- Great Britain
- Netherlands
- Portugal
- France
- * Seat of Government

1535 Lima Dates indicate year of founding

MILES 0   250   500   1,000

VICEROYALTY OF BRAZIL

MARANHÃO

CAPTAINCY OF PIAUI Recife (Pernambuco) 1561 o

CAPTAINCY OF PERNAMBUCO

CAPTAINCY OF SERGIPE

CAPTAINCY OF BAÍA Salvador (Baía) 1549

CAPTAINCY OF ESPÍRITO SANTO

CAPTAINCY OF MINAS GERAIS Tijuco (Diamantina) o Ouro Preto 1698

CAPTAINCY OF MATO GROSSO Definitively established 1714

Santa Anna (Goiaz) 1736

o Villa Bella (Mato Grosso) 1752

CAPTAINCY OF GOIAZ

Príncipe da Beira 1760

CAPTAINCY OF RIO DE JANEIRO Rio de Janeiro 1567

São Paulo 1554 CAPTAINCY OF SÃO PAULO Santos 1536

CAPTAINCY OF SANTA CATARINA

CAPTAINCY OF RIO GRANDE DO SUL Porto Alegre 1743 o Rio Grande 1737

PARAGUAY Asunción 1537

PRESIDENCY (AUDIENCIA) OF CHARCAS Chuquisaca 1538

La Paz 1548 Potosí 1546

VICEROYALTY OF LA PLATA (Established 1776)

Salta 1582 Tucumán 1585 Córdoba 1573 Santa Fé 1573

BANDA ORIENTAL Colonia 1680 Montevideo 1724

Mendoza 1561 AUDIENCIA OF BUENOS AIRES Buenos Aires 1580

PRESIDENCY (AUDIENCIA) OF CUZCO Cuzco 1535

VICEROYALTY OF PERU Established 1542

AUDIENCIA OF LIMA Lima 1535 Callao 1537

Trujillo 1535

VICEROYALTY OF PERU

La Serena 1544

Santiago 1541 CAPTAINCY GENERAL (AUDIENCIA) OF CHILE Loosely joined to Peru

Valparaíso 1544 Concepción 1550

Valdivia 1552

CHILOE I.

PATAGONIA

TIERRA DEL FUEGO

CAPE HORN

Drake Passage

MALVINAS (FALKLAND ISLANDS)

Río de la Plata

Tropic of Capricorn

O c e a n

A-440037-29-1-1-1-1™
Copyright by Rand McNally & Company. Made in U.S.A.

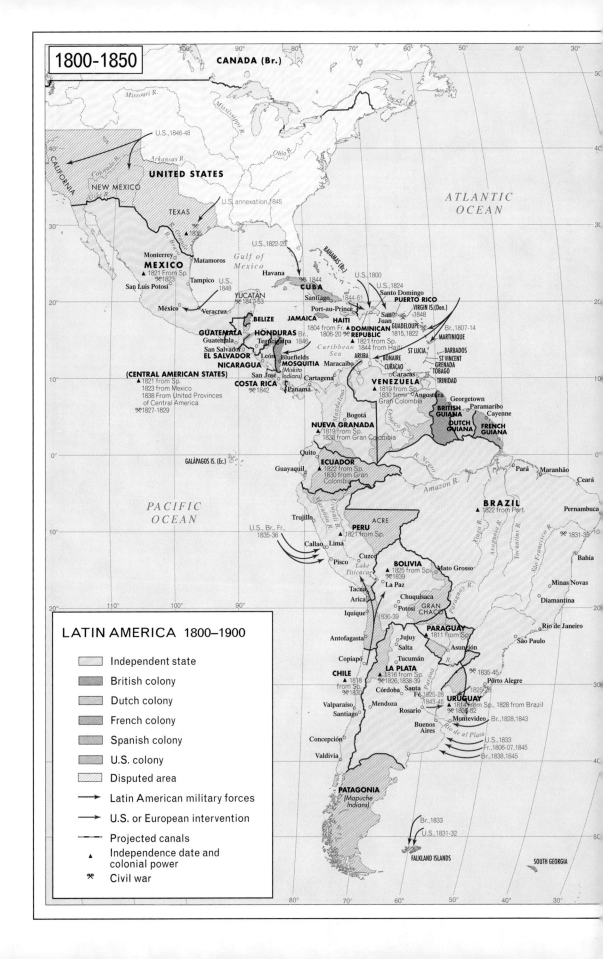

1800-1850

CANADA (Br.)

Missouri R.

Mississippi R.

UNITED STATES

U.S.,1846-48

CALIFORNIA

Arkansas R.

Colorado R.

NEW MEXICO

Red R.

TEXAS

▲1836

U.S. annexation,1845

R. Grande

U.S.,1822-25

ATLANTIC OCEAN

Monterrey

Matamoros

MEXICO
▲1821 From Sp.
✖1823

Gulf of Mexico

Havana

U.S.,1800

BAHAMAS (Br.)

Santo Domingo

U.S.,1824

PUERTO RICO

VIRGIN IS.(Den.)
✖1848

San Luis Potosí

Tampico

U.S.,
1848

YUCATÁN
✖1847-53

CUBA ✖1844

Santiago

JAMAICA

Port-au-Prince

San
Juan

GUADELOUPE
1815,1822

Br.,1807-14

México

Veracruz

BELIZE

HAITI
▲1804 from Fr.

**DOMINICAN
REPUBLIC**
▲1821 from Sp.
1844 from Haiti

MARTINIQUE

GUATEMALA
Guatemala

HONDURAS
Tegucigalpa

Br.,
1806-20

Caribbean Sea

ST LUCIA

BARBADOS
ST VINCENT
GRENADA
TOBAGO

San Salvador
EL SALVADOR

León

Br.,
1846

BONAIRE

ARUBA

NICARAGUA

Bluefields
MOSQUITIA
(Miskito Indians)

CURAÇAO

Maracaibo

Caracas

TRINIDAD

(CENTRAL AMERICAN STATES)
▲1821 from Sp.
1823 from Mexico
1838 From United Provinces
of Central America
✖1827-1829

San José

COSTA RICA
✖1842

Cartagena

Panamá

VENEZUELA
▲1819 from Sp.
1830 from
Gran Colombia

Angostura

Georgetown

Paramaribo

Cayenne

**BRITISH
GUIANA**

**DUTCH
GUIANA**

**FRENCH
GUIANA**

Bogotá

NUEVA GRANADA
▲1819 from Sp.
1830 from Gran Colombia

R. Negro

Orinoco R.

Magdalena R.

Quito

GALÁPAGOS IS. (Ec.)

ECUADOR
▲1822 from Sp.
1830 from Gran
Colombia

Guayaquil

Amazon R.

Pará

Maranhão

Ceará

*PACIFIC
OCEAN*

Marañon R.

Ucayali R.

ACRE

BRAZIL
▲1822 from Port.

Pernambuca

Trujillo

U.S., Br., Fr.,
1835-36

PERU
▲1821 from Sp.

✖1831-35

Bahia

Callao

Lima

Cuzco

*Lake
Titicaca*

BOLIVIA
▲1825 from Sp.
✖1839

Mato Grosso

Minas Novas

Pisco

La Paz

Diamantina

Tacna

Chuquisaca

Xingu R.

Tocantins R.

São Francisco R.

Arica

Potosí

GRAN
CHACO

Araguaia R.

Paraguay R.

Iquique

✖1836-39

Rio de Janeiro

Antofagasta

Jujuy

Salta

PARAGUAY
▲1811 from Sp.

São Paulo

Asunción

LATIN AMERICA 1800–1900

Independent state

British colony

Dutch colony

French colony

Spanish colony

U.S. colony

Disputed area

→ Latin American military forces

→ U.S. or European intervention

⊶ Projected canals

▲ Independence date and
colonial power

✖ Civil war

Copiapó

Tucumán

LA PLATA
▲1816 from Sp.
✖1826,1838-39

CHILE
▲1818
from Sp.
✖1830

Córdoba

Santa
Fé

✖1835-45

✖1825-28

Pôrto Alegre

1825-26

Valparaíso

Mendoza

Rosario

1843-45

URUGUAY
▲1814 from Sp., 1828 from Brazil
✖1836-52

Paraná R.

Santiago

Buenos
Aires

Montevideo

Br.,1828,1843

Concepción

Rio de al Plata

U.S.,1833
Fr.,1806-07,1845
Br.,1838,1845

Valdivia

PATAGONIA
(Mapuche Indians)

Br.,1833

U.S.,1831-32

FALKLAND ISLANDS

SOUTH GEORGIA

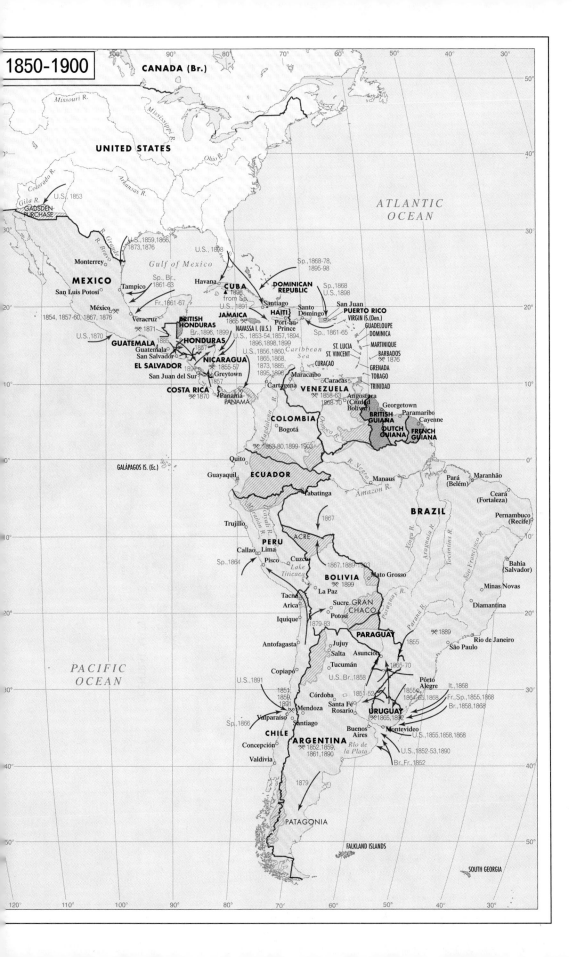

1850-1900

CANADA (Br.)

Missouri R.

Mississippi R.

UNITED STATES

Ohio R.

ATLANTIC
OCEAN

Colorado R.

Arkansas R.

Gila R. U.S., 1853
GADSDEN
PURCHASE

U.S.,1859,1866,
1873,1876

U.S., 1858

Sp.,1868-78,
1895-98

Monterrey
R. Grande
R. Bravo
Gulf of Mexico

Sp., Br.,
1861-63

Havana

CUBA
▲1898
from Sp.

DOMINICAN
REPUBLIC

Sp.,1868
U.S.,1898

MEXICO

San Luis Potosí

Tampico

Fr.,1861-67

U.S., 1891

Santiago

Santo
Domingo

San Juan

PUERTO RICO

México
1854, 1857-60, 1867, 1876

Veracruz

✠1871

JAMAICA
1865

HAITI
Port-au-
Prince

VIRGIN IS.(Den.)
GUADELOUPE
DOMINICA

U.S.,1870

BRITISH
HONDURAS

1885

NAVASSA I. (U.S.)
Br.,1896, 1899
U.S., 1853-54,1857,1894,
1896,1898,1899

Sp., 1861-65

ST. LUCIA
ST. VINCENT

MARTINIQUE
BARBADOS
✠1876

GUATEMALA

HONDURAS
1857

Guatemala
San Salvador

NICARAGUA
1855-57

U.S.,1856,1860,
1865,1868,
1873,1885,
1895,1898

GRENADA

TOBAGO

*Caribbean
Sea*

CURAÇAO

EL SALVADOR

✠1855

Greytown
1857

Maracaibo

Caracas

TRINIDAD

San Juan del Sur

COSTA RICA
✠1870

Panamá
PANAMA

Cartagena

VENEZUELA
✠1858-63
1868-70

Angostura
(Ciudad
Bolívar)

Georgetown

Paramaribo

Cayenne

Magdalena R.

COLOMBIA
Bogotá

Orinoco R.

BRITISH
GUIANA

DUTCH
GUIANA

FRENCH
GUIANA

1863-80,1899-1903

GALÁPAGOS IS. (Ec.)

Quito

R. Negro

Manaus

Pará
(Belém)

Maranhão

Guayaquil

ECUADOR

Tabatinga

Amazon R.

Ceará
(Fortaleza)

Marañón R.

1867

BRAZIL

Pernambuco
(Recife)

Trujillo

Ucayali R.

ACRE

PERU

Callao

Lima

Pisco

Cuzco

*Lake
Titicaca*

Sp.,1864

1867, 1889,1903

BOLIVIA
✠1899

Mato Grosso

Xingú R.

Araguaia R.

Tocantins R.

São Francisco R.

Bahia
(Salvador)

Minas Novas

La Paz

Tacna

Arica

Sucre

GRAN
CHACO

Diamantina

Iquique

1879-83

Paraguay R.

✠1889

Antofagasta

Copiapó

U.S.,1891

Jujuy

Salta

Asunción

Tucumán

1855

PARAGUAY

1865-70

Paraná R.

Rio de Janeiro

São Paulo

U.S.,Br.,1858

Pôrto
Alegre

It.,1868

PACIFIC
OCEAN

1851-52

1851,
1859,
1891

Córdoba

Mendoza

Santa Fé
Rosario

Fr.,Sp.,1855,1868

1855,
1864,65, 1868

Br.,1858,1868

Valparaíso

Sp.,1866

Santiago

CHILE

Concepción

ARGENTINA
✠1852,1859,
1861,1890

URUGUAY
✠1865,1892

Buenos
Aires

*Río de
la Plata*

Montevideo

U.S.,1855,1858,1868

U.S.,1852-53,1890

Valdivia

Br.,Fr.,1852

1879

PATAGONIA

FALKLAND ISLANDS

SOUTH GEORGIA

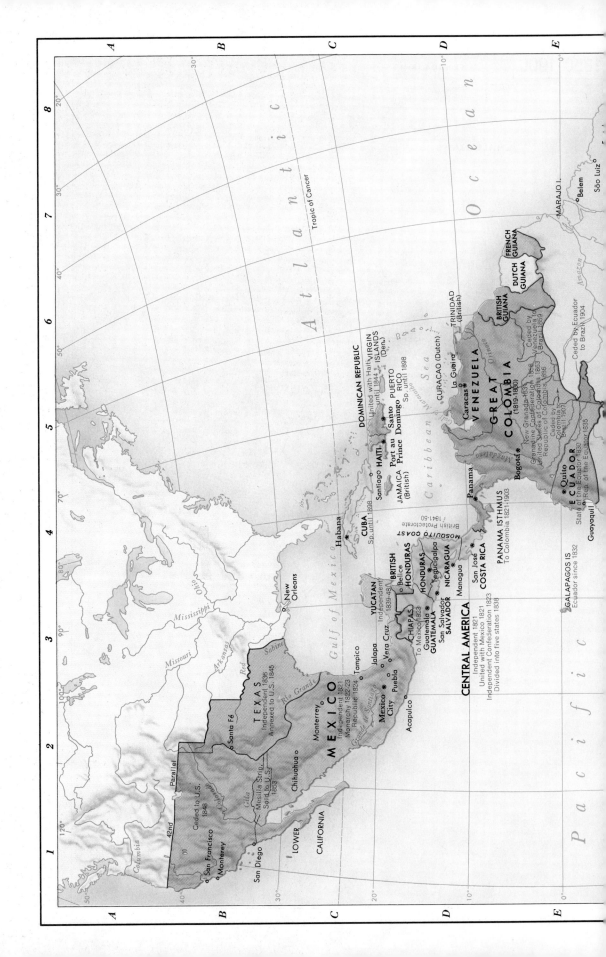

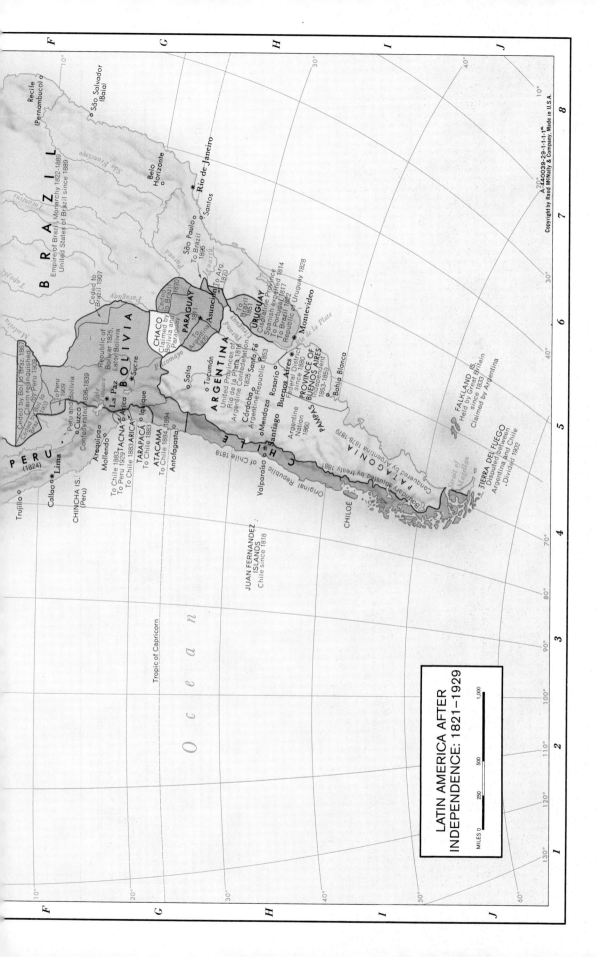

LATIN AMERICA AFTER
INDEPENDENCE: 1821–1929

MILES 0   250   500   1,000

BRAZIL
Empire of Brazil Monarchy 1822–1889
United States of Brazil since 1889

Recife
(Pernambuco)

São Salvador
(Baia)

Belo
Horizonte

Rio de Janeiro

Santos

São Paulo
To Brazil
1895

To Arg.
1870

Ceded to
Brazil 1907

Ceded by Bol. to Braz. 1867
Claim relinquished
by Peru 1909

Ceded by Bol. to
Braz. 1903

PERU
(1824)

Trujillo

Callao

Lima

CHINCHA IS.
(Peru)

Arequipa
Mollendo

To Peru 1929
Cuzco

Peru and Bolivia
Confederated 1836–1839

To Peru
1909

Republic of
Bolívar 1825,
Later Bolivia

BOLIVIA

La Paz

Lake
Titicaca

Sucre

TACNA
ARICA
To Chile 1883

TARAPACÁ
To Chile 1883

ATACAMA
To Chile 1884, 1894

Antofagasta

Iquique

Salta

Tucumán

Córdoba

Mendoza

Santiago

Valparaíso

Original Republic of Chile 1818

C H I L E

Boundary adjusted by treaty 1881

P A T A G O N I A
Conquered by Argentina 1878–1879

CHILOÉ

JUAN FERNANDEZ
ISLANDS
Chile since 1818

Tropic of Capricorn

O c e a n

PARAGUAY
1811

Ceded by Braz. 1927

CHACO
Claimed by
Bolivia and
Paraguay

Asunción

ARGENTINA
United Provinces of
Río de la Plata or
Argentine Confederation 1816
1825

Santa Fe
1853

Rosario

Buenos Aires

PROVINCE OF
BUENOS AIRES
Independent
1853–1859

Federal District
since 1880

Argentine
Nation
1860

Argentine Republic

P A M P A S

Bahía Blanca

URUGUAY
Cisplatine Province
Spanish Province
Expelled 1814
To Portugal 1817
To Brazil 1822
Republic of Uruguay 1828

Montevideo

To
Brazil
1851

Río de la Plata

FALKLAND IS.
Held by Great Britain
since 1833
Claimed by Argentina

TIERRA DEL FUEGO
Disputed between
Argentina and Chile
Divided 1902

Strait of Magellan

São Francisco

Tocantins

Tapajós

Madeira

Paraguay

Pilcomayo

Paraná

Uruguay

Iguassú

A-140039-29-1-1-1-1"
Copyright by Rand McNally & Company. Made in U.S.A.

63

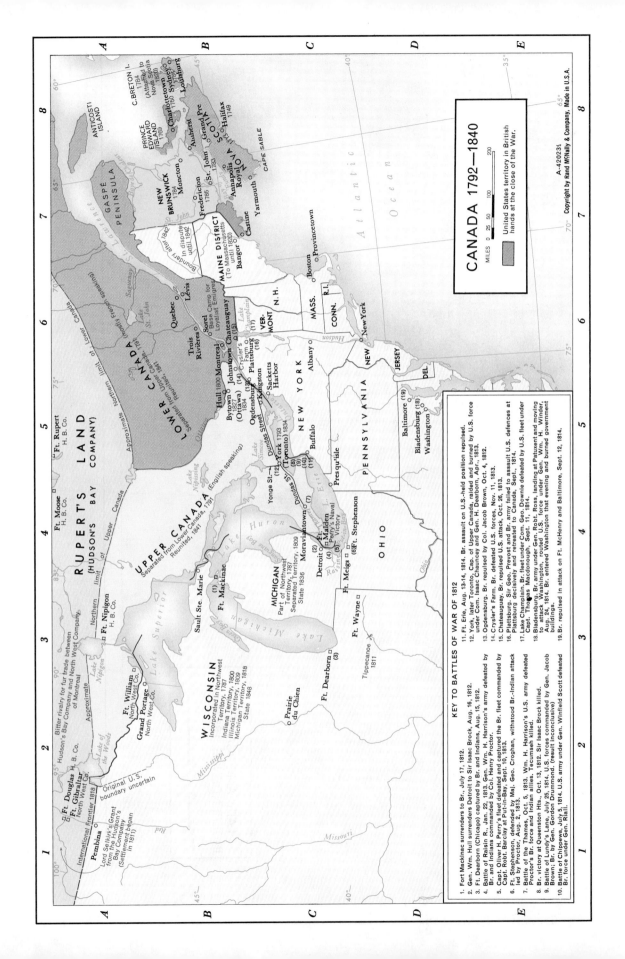

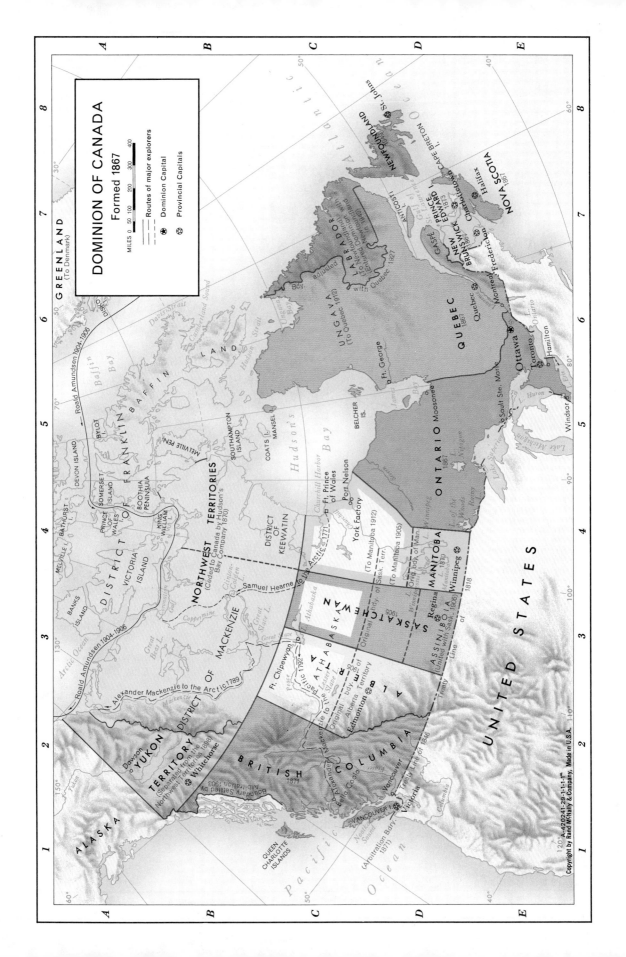

DOMINION OF CANADA
Formed 1867

MILES 0 50 100 200 300 400

---- Routes of major explorers
⊛ Dominion Capital
⊛ Provincial Capitals

GREENLAND
(To Denmark)

Roald Amundsen 1904-1906

DISTRICT OF FRANKLIN

BANKS ISLAND
VICTORIA ISLAND
MELVILLE I.
BATHURST
PRINCE OF WALES
SOMERSET ISLAND
DEVON ISLAND
BYLOT
BOOTHIA PENINSULA
KING WILLIAM
MELVILLE PEN.
SOUTHAMPTON ISLAND
MANSEL
COATS I.

BAFFIN LAND

Baffin Bay
Davis Strait
Cumberland Sound
Hudson Strait
Ungava Bay

Arctic Ocean
Roald Amundsen 1904-1906
Alexander Mackenzie to the Arctic 1789

DISTRICT OF MACKENZIE

Coppermine
Great Bear L.
Great Slave L.
Mackenzie
Athabasca L.
Caribou L.
Colen L.

Samuel Hearne to the Arctic 1771

NORTHWEST TERRITORIES
(Ceded to Canada by Hudson's Bay Company 1870)

DISTRICT OF KEEWATIN

Churchill Harbor
Ft. Prince of Wales
Port Nelson
York Factory

Hudson's Bay

BELCHER IS.

UNGAVA
(To Quebec 1912)

LABRADOR
(To Newfoundland 1927)
Bdy. adjusted with Quebec 1927

LABRADOR (To Newfoundland with Newfoundland 1949)

Gulf of St. Lawrence

ANTICOSTI I.
NEWFOUNDLAND
St. John's
CAPE BRETON I.
PRINCE EDWARD I. 1873
Charlottetown
GASPÉ
NOVA SCOTIA 1867
Halifax
NEW BRUNSWICK
Fredericton
Montreal
QUEBEC 1867
Quebec
Ottawa
Ft. George
James Bay

Moosonee
ONTARIO 1867
L. Nipigon
L. of the Woods
L. Superior
Sault Ste. Marie
L. Huron
Georgian Bay
L. Ontario
Toronto
Hamilton
Windsor
L. Erie
Lake Michigan

(To Manitoba 1912)
(To Sask. Terr.)
(Old body. of Sask. Terr.)
(To Manitoba 1905)
MANITOBA 1870
Winnipeg

SASKATCHEWAN 1905
Regina

ASSINIBOIA
(United with Sask. 1905)
Original Line of 1818

ATHABASKA

ALBERTA 1905
Edmonton
Alberta Territory
Original bdy. of 1905

Ft. Chipewyan 1792
Peace
Lesser Slave L.

Sir Alexander Mackenzie to the Pacific 1793

YUKON TERRITORY
(Separated from the Northwest Territories 1898)
Dawson
Whitehorse
Boundary settled by Arbitration 1903

ALASKA

BRITISH COLUMBIA 1871

Bella Coola
Vancouver
VANCOUVER I.
Victoria
Nootka Sound
(Arbitration Bdry. 1871)

Treaty Line of 1846
Columbia

UNITED STATES

QUEEN CHARLOTTE ISLANDS

Pacific Ocean

Atlantic Ocean

120° 130° 150° 60° 50° 50° 40° 40° 30° 50° 70° 80° 90° 100° 110°

A B C D E

1 2 3 4 5 6 7 8

A-420241-29-1-1-1-1"
Copyright by Rand McNally & Company, Made in U.S.A.

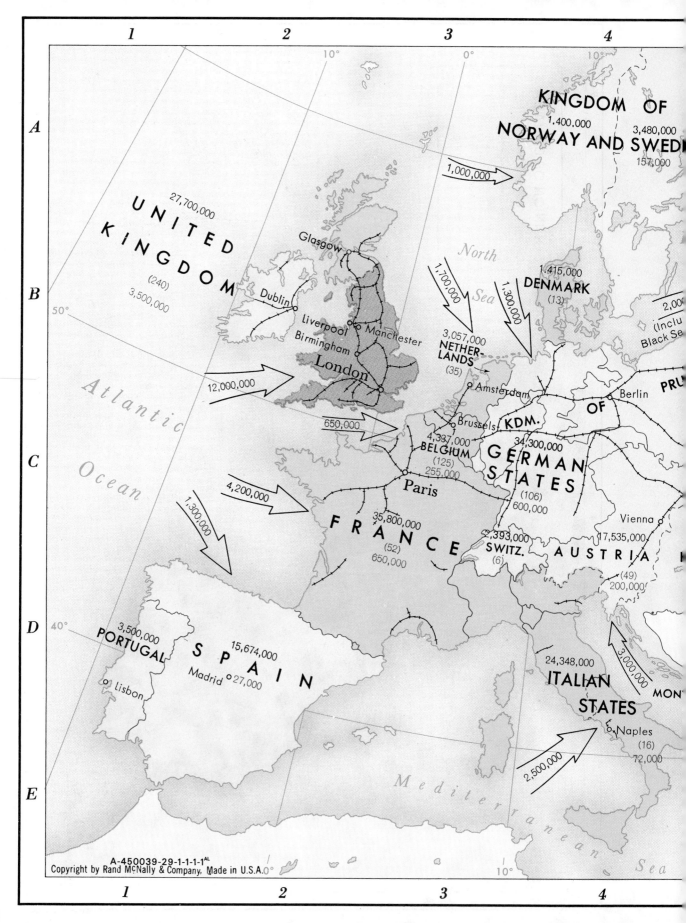

KINGDOM OF
NORWAY AND SWEDE
1,400,000   3,480,000
157,000

1,000,000

UNITED
27,700,000

KINGDOM

(240)
3,500,000

1,700,000   1,300,000   DENMARK   1,415,000
                                          (13)

2,00
(Inclu
Black Se

Glasgow

Dublin

Liverpool
Birmingham   Manchester

London

3,057,000
NETHER-
LANDS
(35)

Amsterdam

Brussels   KDM.   OF   Berlin   PRU
12,000,000

650,000
4,337,000
BELGIUM
(125)
255,000

GERMAN
STATES
34,300,000

4,200,000

Paris

(106)
600,000

Vienna

Atlantic

1,300,000

F R A N C E
35,800,000
(52)
650,000

2,393,000
SWITZ.
(6)

AUSTRIA
17,535,000

Ocean

(49)
200,000

3,500,000
PORTUGAL

15,674,000
S P A I N

3,000,000

ITALIAN

Lisbon

Madrid ○ 27,000

STATES
24,348,000

MON

Naples
(16)
72,000

2,500,000

North   Sea

Mediterranean   Sea

A-450039-29-1-1-1-1^{AL}
Copyright by Rand McNally & Company, Made in U.S.A.

66

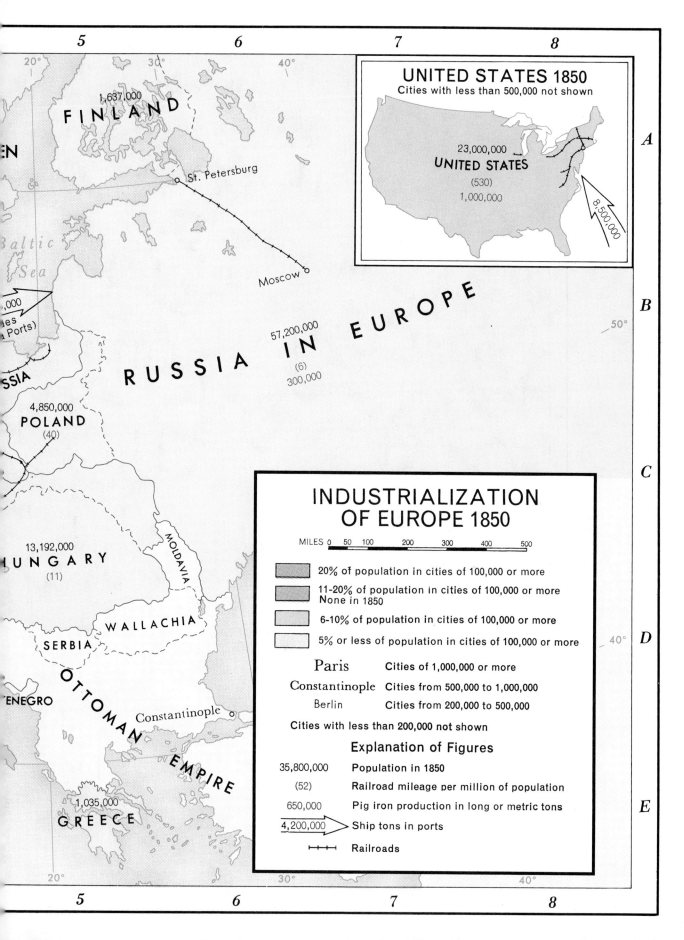

FINLAND

1,637,000

St. Petersburg

Moscow

Baltic Sea

RUSSIA IN EUROPE

57,200,000
(6)
300,000

SSIA

POLAND
4,850,000
(40)

HUNGARY
13,192,000
(11)

MOLDAVIA

WALLACHIA

SERBIA

TENEGRO

OTTOMAN EMPIRE

Constantinople

GREECE
1,035,000

UNITED STATES 1850
Cities with less than 500,000 not shown

23,000,000
UNITED STATES
(530)
1,000,000

8,500,000

INDUSTRIALIZATION
OF EUROPE 1850

MILES 0   50 100   200   300   400   500

20% of population in cities of 100,000 or more

11-20% of population in cities of 100,000 or more
None in 1850

6-10% of population in cities of 100,000 or more

5% or less of population in cities of 100,000 or more

Paris   Cities of 1,000,000 or more

Constantinople   Cities from 500,000 to 1,000,000

Berlin   Cities from 200,000 to 500,000

Cities with less than 200,000 not shown

Explanation of Figures

35,800,000   Population in 1850

(52)   Railroad mileage per million of population

650,000   Pig iron production in long or metric tons

4,200,000   Ship tons in ports

⊢⊢⊢⊢⊢   Railroads

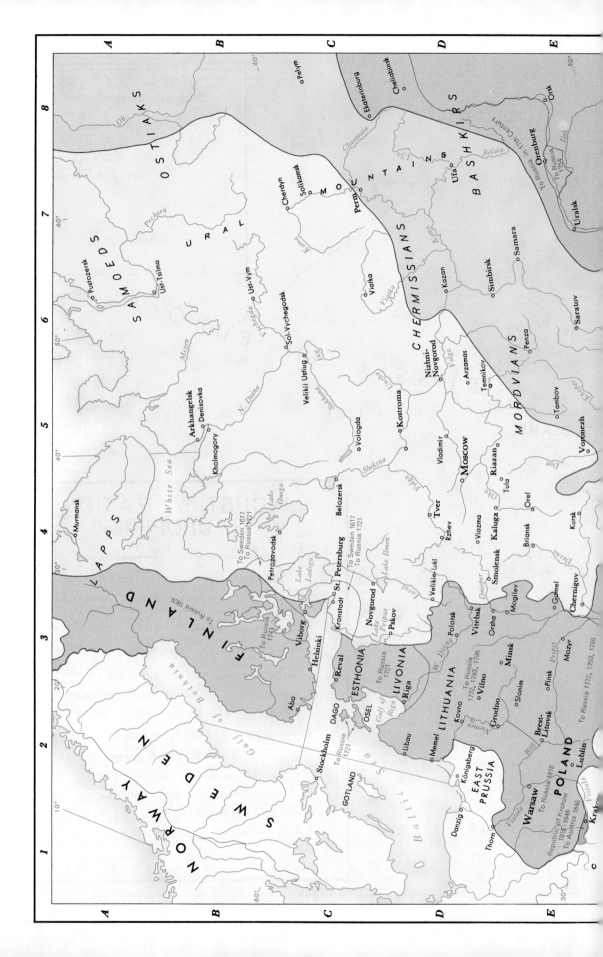

68

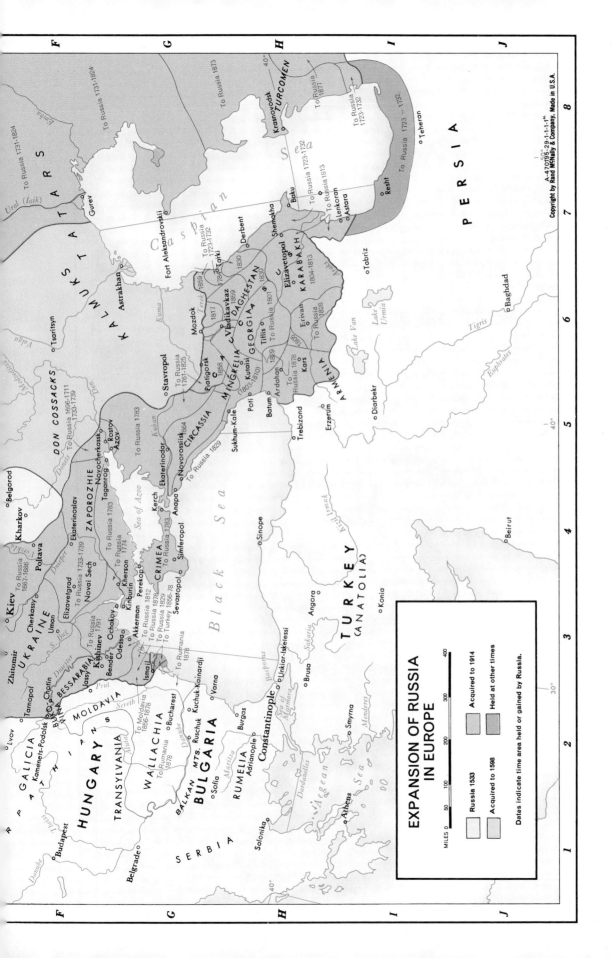

EXPANSION OF RUSSIA IN EUROPE

MILES 0   50   100   200   300   400

Russia 1533 | Acquired to 1914
Acquired to 1598 | Held at other times

Dates indicate time area held or gained by Russia.

A-47016-29-1-1-1-1

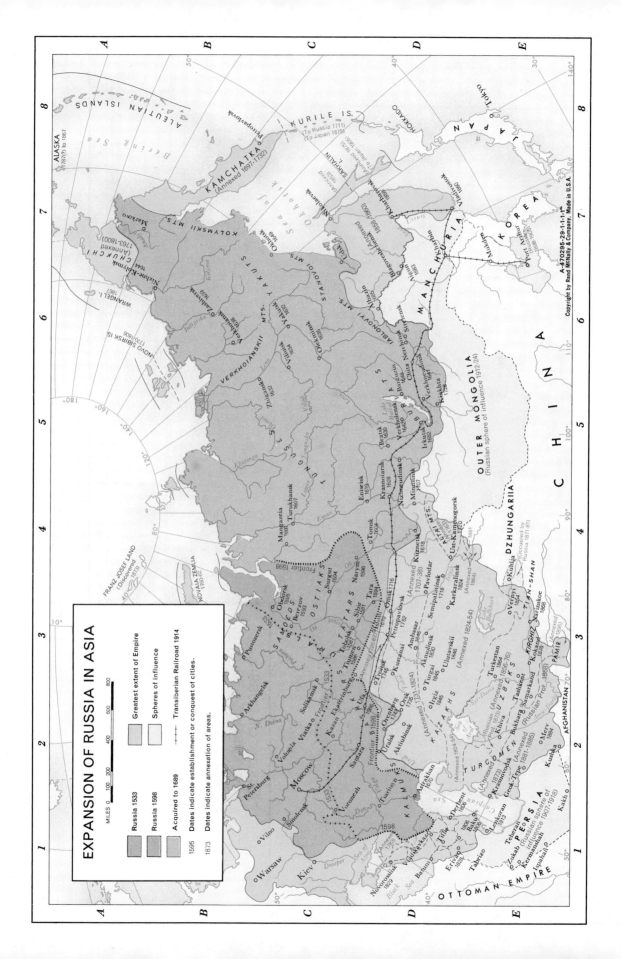

EXPANSION OF RUSSIA IN ASIA

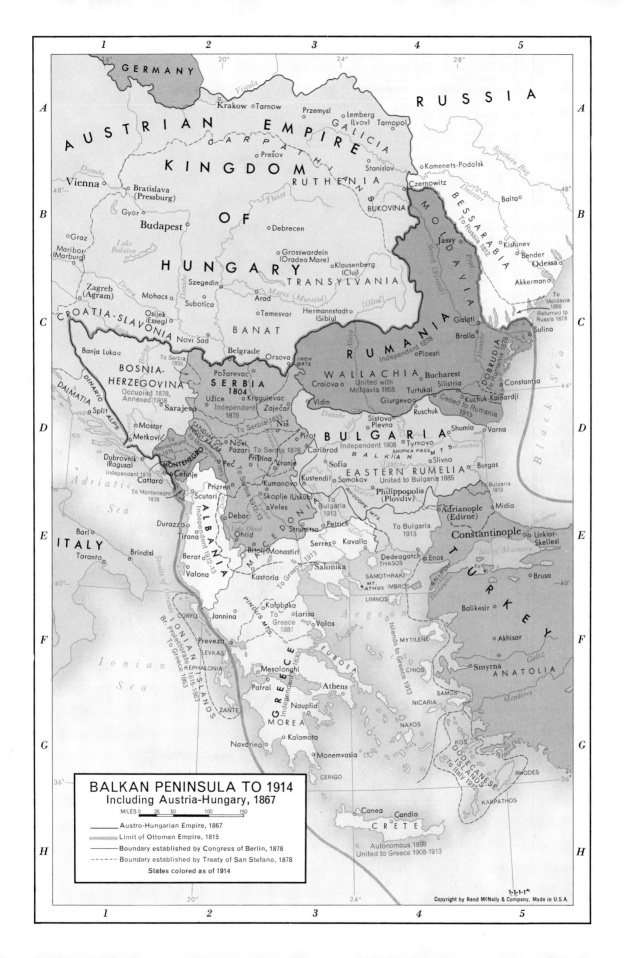

BALKAN PENINSULA TO 1914
Including Austria-Hungary, 1867

MILES 0   25   50   100   150

———— Austro-Hungarian Empire, 1867
▒▒▒▒ Limit of Ottoman Empire, 1815
———— Boundary established by Congress of Berlin, 1878
- - - - Boundary established by Treaty of San Stefano, 1878
States colored as of 1914

Copyright by Rand McNally & Company, Made in U.S.A.

71

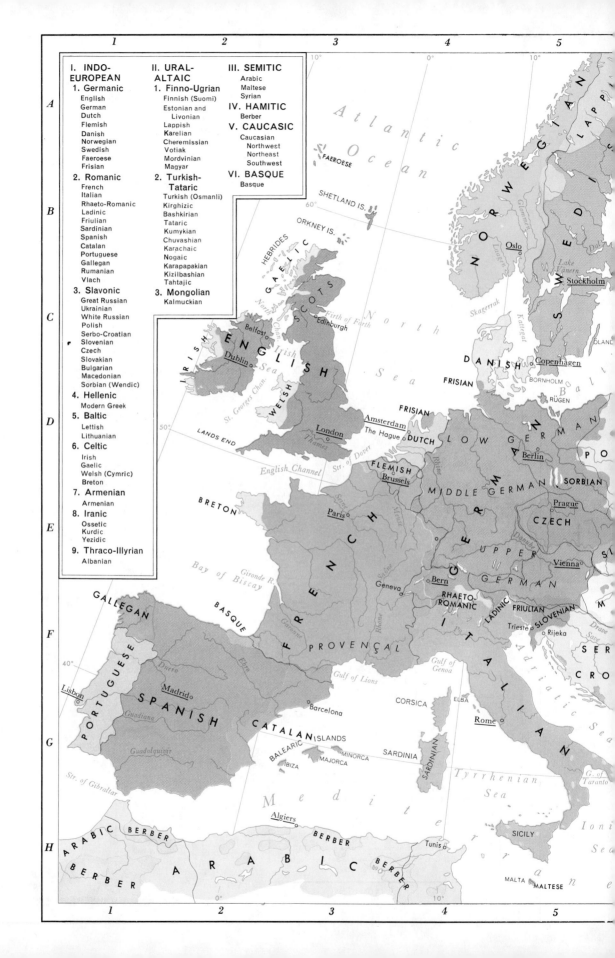

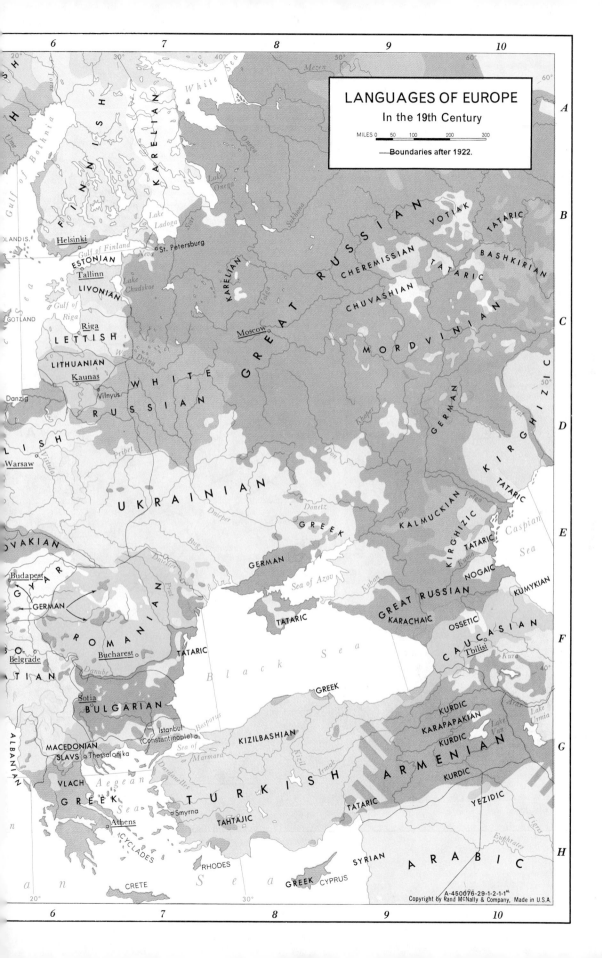

LANGUAGES OF EUROPE
In the 19th Century

MILES 0   50   100   200   300

—— Boundaries after 1922.

FINNISH
KARELIAN
Umeå
Gulf of Bothnia
White Sea
Mezen
Onega
60°

Helsinki
ÅLAND IS.
ESTONIAN
Tallinn
LIVONIAN
St. Petersburg
Neva
Lake Ladoga
Svir
Lake Onega
Sukhona

GOTLAND
Gulf of Finland
Lake Chudskoe
Gulf of Riga
Riga
LETTISH
KARELIAN
GREAT RUSSIAN
CHEREMISSIAN
VOTIAK
TATARIC
TATARIC
BASHKIRIAN

LITHUANIAN
Kaunas
WHITE
Vilnyus
West Dvina
Volga
CHUVASHIAN
MORDVINIAN
Moscow
Danzig
RUSSIAN
GERMAN
KIRGHIZIC
50°

POLISH
Warsaw
Vistula
Pripet
Bug
UKRAINIAN
Dnieper
Donetz
Don
GREEK
Khoper
KALMUCKIAN
Volga
TATARIC
Ural

SLOVAKIAN
MAGYAR
Budapest
GERMAN
Danube
Dniester
Prut
GERMAN
Sea of Azov
Kuban
GREAT RUSSIAN
KARACHAIC
KIRGHIZIC
TATARIC
NOGAIC
Caspian Sea
KUMYKIAN

ROMANIAN
Bucharest
TATARIC
TATARIC
Black Sea
OSSETIC
CAUCASIAN
Tbilisi
Kura
40°

BO-
Belgrade
CROATIAN
Danube
Sofia
BULGARIAN
GREEK
Kizil Irmak

ALBANIAN
MACEDONIAN
SLAVS
Thessaloníka
Istanbul (Constantinople)
Bosporus
Sea of Marmara
Dardanelles
KIZILBASHIAN
KURDIC
KARAPAPAKIAN
KURDIC
ARMENIAN
Lake Van
Arax
Lake Urmia

VLACH
GREEK
Aegean Sea
TURKISH
KURDIC
YEZIDIC
Tigris

Athens
Smyrna
TAHTAJIC
TATARIC
Euphrates

CYCLADES
RHODES
CRETE
Sea
GREEK
CYPRUS
SYRIAN
ARABIC

A-450076-29-1-2-1-1^{AL}
Copyright by Rand McNally & Company, Made in U.S.A.

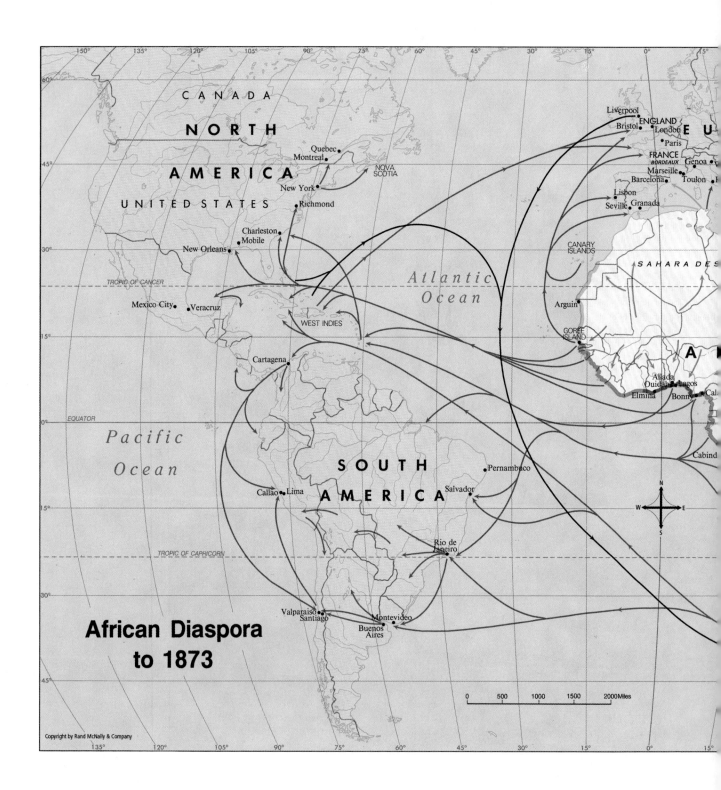

CANADA

NORTH

AMERICA

UNITED STATES

Quebec
Montreal
New York
Richmond
Charleston
Mobile
New Orleans

Mexico City • Veracruz

TROPIC OF CANCER

WEST INDIES

Cartagena

EQUATOR

Pacific

Ocean

SOUTH

Callao • Lima

AMERICA

Pernambuco

Salvador

TROPIC OF CAPRICORN

Rio de Janeiro

African Diaspora

to 1873

Valparaíso
Santiago
Montevideo
Buenos
Aires

NOVA
SCOTIA

Atlantic

Ocean

Liverpool
Bristol ENGLAND London
Paris
FRANCE
BORDEAUX Genoa
Marseille
Barcelona Toulon
Lisbon
Seville • Granada

CANARY
ISLANDS

SAHARA DES

Arguin

GOREE
ISLAND

A

Allada
Ouidah • Lagos
Elmina Bonn Cal

Cabind

E U

N
W — E
S

Copyright by Rand McNally & Company

0   500   1000   1500   2000 Miles

74

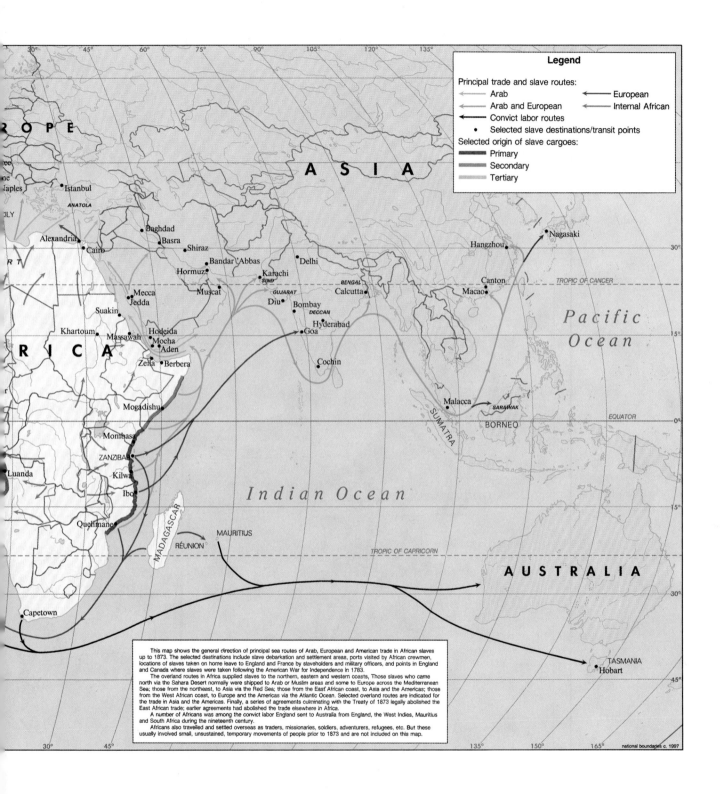

Legend

Principal trade and slave routes:

→ Arab   → European
→ Arab and European   → Internal African
→ Convict labor routes
• Selected slave destinations/transit points

Selected origin of slave cargoes:
▬ Primary
▬ Secondary
▬ Tertiary

EUROPE
ASIA
AFRICA
Pacific Ocean
Indian Ocean
AUSTRALIA

ANATOLA
SICILY
Naples
Istanbul
Alexandria
Cairo
Baghdad
Basra
Shiraz
Bandar 'Abbas
Delhi
Hormuz
Karachi
SIND
Mecca
Jedda
Muscat
GUJARAT
Diu
Bombay
DECCAN
Calcutta
BENGAL
Hyderabad
Goa
Hangzhou
Canton
Macao
Nagasaki
TROPIC OF CANCER
Suakin
Khartoum
Massawah
Hodeida
Mocha
Aden
Zeila
Berbera
Cochin
Mogadishu
Mombasa
ZANZIBAR
Kilwa
Ibo
Luanda
Quelimane
MADAGASCAR
RÉUNION
MAURITIUS
Capetown
SUMATRA
Malacca
SARAWAK
BORNEO
EQUATOR
TROPIC OF CAPRICORN
TASMANIA
Hobart

Pacific Ocean

Indian Ocean

This map shows the general direction of principal sea routes of Arab, European and American trade in African slaves up to 1873. The selected destinations include slave debarkation and settlement areas, ports visited by African crewmen, locations of slaves taken on home leave to England and France by slaveholders and military officers, and points in England and Canada where slaves were taken following the American War for Independence in 1783.

The overland routes in Africa supplied slaves to the northern, eastern and western coasts, Those slaves who came north via the Sahara Desert normally were shipped to Arab or Muslim areas and some to Europe across the Mediterranean Sea; those from the northeast, to Asia via the Red Sea; those from the East African coast, to Asia and the Americas; those from the West African coast, to Europe and the Americas via the Atlantic Ocean. Selected overland routes are indicated for the trade in Asia and the Americas. Finally, a series of agreements culminating with the Treaty of 1873 legally abolished the East African trade; earlier agreements had abolished the trade elsewhere in Africa.

A number of Africans was among the convict labor England sent to Australia from England, the West Indies, Mauritius and South Africa during the nineteenth century.

Africans also travelled and settled overseas as traders, missionaries, soldiers, adventurers, refugees, etc. But these usually involved small, unsustained, temporary movements of people prior to 1873 and are not included on this map.

national boundaries c. 1997

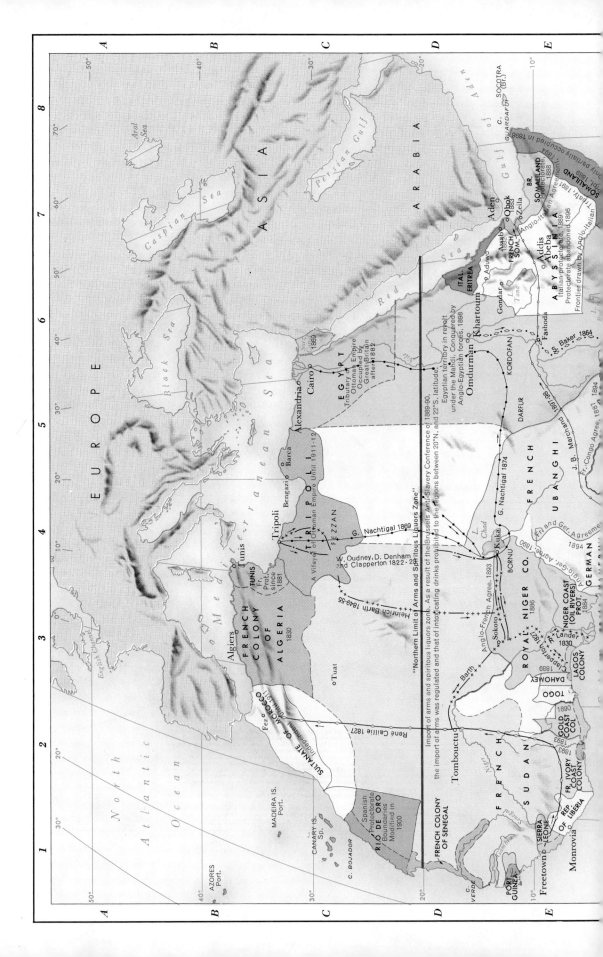

A *Vilayet* of Ottoman Empire Until 1911-12

E G Y P T
Tributary of Ottoman Empire
Occupied by Great Britain after 1882

W. Oudney, D. Denham and Clapperton 1822-25

G. Nachtigal 1869

"Northern Limit of Arms and Spirituous Liquors Zone"

Import of arms and spirituous liquors zone. As a result of the Brussels Anti-Slavery Conference of 1889-90, the import of arms was regulated and that of intoxicating drinks prohibited to the regions between 20°N, and 22°S, latitude

Egyptian territory in revolt under the Mahdi. Conquered by Anglo-Egyptian forces, 1898

Heinrich Barth 1849-55

René Caillié 1827

F R E N C H   C O L O N Y   O F   A L G E R I A
1830

FRENCH COLONY OF SENEGAL

TUNIS Fr. Prot. since 1881

SULTANATE OF MOROCCO Independent until 1912

Spanish Protectorate RIO DE ORO Boundaries Modified in 1900

Fez

Tuat

Algiers

Tunis

Tripoli

Bengazi

Barca

Alexandria

Cairo
1869

Khartoum

Omdurman

Tombouctou

Kuka

L. Chad

BORNU

KORDOFAN

DARFUR

F R E N C H   U B A N G H I

N. S. Baker 1864

Fashoda

G E R M A N

Anglo-French Agree, 1893

Fr. and Ger. Agreement 1894

Anglo-Ger. Agree. 1890

J. B. Marchand, 1896-98

Fr.-Congo Agree, 1894

G. Nachtigal 1874

Barth

Sokoto

Lander 1830

Clapperton 1827

ROYAL NIGER CO. 1886

NIGER COAST (OIL RIVERS) PROT. 1884

DAHOMEY 1889

TOGO 1890

LAGOS COLONY

GOLD COAST COL. 1893

IVORY COAST COLONY 1893

FR.

REP. OF LIBERIA

SIERRA LEONE

PORT. GUINEA

F R E N C H   S U D A N

Senegal

Monrovia

Freetown

Gambia

C. VERDE

ITAL. ERITREA

BR. SOMALILAND 1884

FRENCH SOM. 1888

Assab 1882

Obok 1883

Zeila

Aden

Gulf of Aden

SOCOTRA (Br.)

C. GUARDAFUI

SOMALILAND (Treaty, 1891) only partially occupied in 1898

Italian protectorate, 1889 Protectorate abandoned 1896 Frontier drawn by Anglo-Italian Agreement, 1894

A B Y S S I N I A

Addis Abeba

Aduwa

Gondar

L. Tana

Red Sea

A R A B I A

Persian Gulf

A S I A

Black Sea

Caspian Sea

Aral Sea

E U R O P E

M e d i t e r r a n e a n   S e a

N o r t h   A t l a n t i c   O c e a n

English Channel

AZORES Port.

MADEIRA IS. Port.

CANARY IS. Sp.

C. BOJADOR

FEZZAN

T R I P O L I

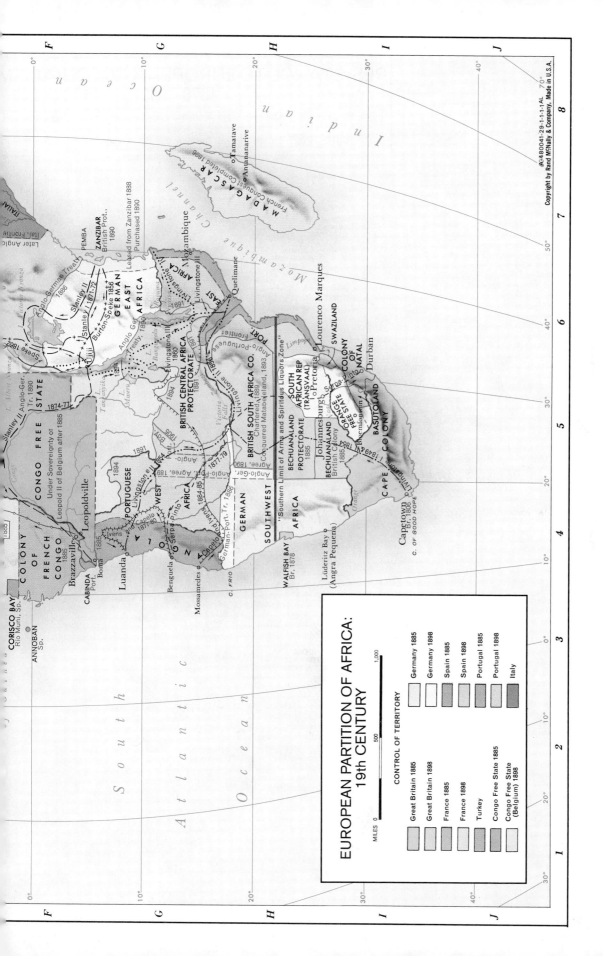

EUROPEAN PARTITION OF AFRICA: 19th CENTURY

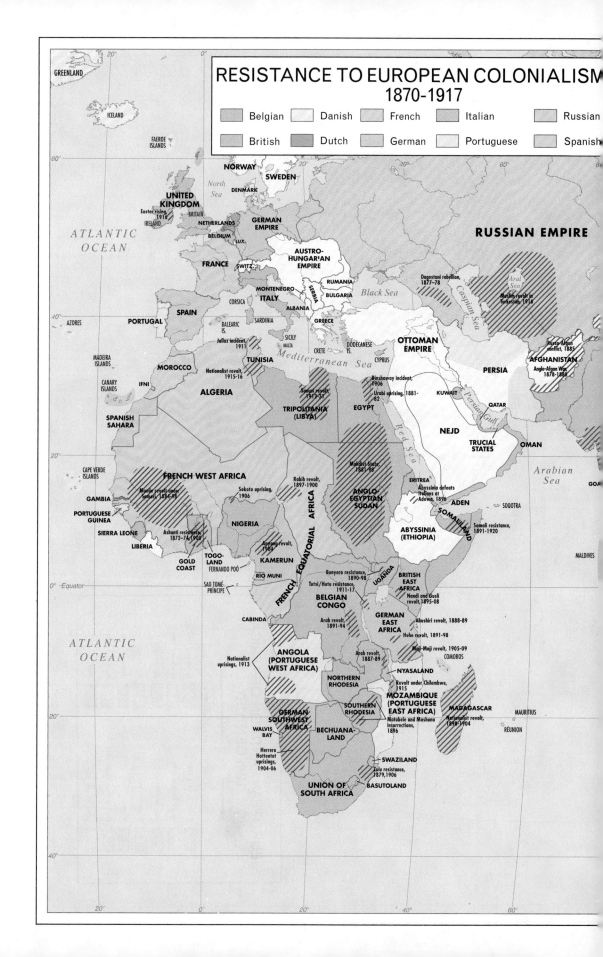

RESISTANCE TO EUROPEAN COLONIALISM
1870-1917

Belgian	Danish	French	Italian	Russian
British	Dutch	German	Portuguese	Spanish

GREENLAND

ICELAND

FAEROE ISLANDS

NORWAY

SWEDEN

DENMARK

UNITED KINGDOM

Easter rising, 1916

IRELAND

BRITAIN

NETHERLANDS

BELGIUM

LUX.

GERMAN EMPIRE

RUSSIAN EMPIRE

ATLANTIC OCEAN

FRANCE

SWITZ.

AUSTRO-HUNGARIAN EMPIRE

RUMANIA

MONTENEGRO

SERBIA

BULGARIA

North Sea

Black Sea

Dagestani rebellion, 1877–78

Aral Sea

Muslim revolt in Turkestan, 1916

Caspian Sea

CORSICA

ITALY

ALBANIA

GREECE

AZORES

PORTUGAL

SPAIN

BALEARIC IS.

SARDINIA

SICILY

MALTA

CRETE

DODECANESE IS.

CYPRUS

OTTOMAN EMPIRE

Russo-Afgan conflict, 1885

AFGHANISTAN

Anglo-Afgan War, 1878–1880

PERSIA

MADEIRA ISLANDS

MOROCCO

Jallaz incident, 1911

TUNISIA

Nationalist revolt, 1915-16

Mediterranean Sea

Denshaway incident, 1906

Urabi uprising, 1881–82

KUWAIT

Persian Gulf

QATAR

CANARY ISLANDS

IFNI

ALGERIA

Sanusi revolt, 1912-31

TRIPOLITANIA (LIBYA)

EGYPT

Red Sea

NEJD

TRUCIAL STATES

OMAN

SPANISH SAHARA

Arabian Sea

GOA

CAPE VERDE ISLANDS

FRENCH WEST AFRICA

Mandin revolt under Samori, 1894–98

Rabih revolt, 1897-1900

Sokoto uprising, 1906

Mahdist State, 1881-98

ANGLO-EGYPTIAN SUDAN

ERITREA

Abyssinia defeats Italians at Adowa, 1896

ADEN

SOQOTRA

SOMALILAND

Somali resistance, 1891-1920

GAMBIA

PORTUGUESE GUINEA

SIERRA LEONE

LIBERIA

Ashanti resistance, 1872-74, 1900

GOLD COAST

TOGO-LAND

FERNANDO POÓ

NIGERIA

KAMERUN

RÍO MUNI

Apranna revolt, 1904

SAO TOMÉ-PRÍNCIPE

FRENCH EQUATORIAL AFRICA

Bunyoro resistance, 1890-98

Tutsi/Hutu resistance, 1911-17

UGANDA

BRITISH EAST AFRICA

Nandi and Gusli revolt, 1895-08

ABYSSINIA (ETHIOPIA)

MALDIVES

Equator

CABINDA

BELGIAN CONGO

Arab revolt, 1891-94

GERMAN EAST AFRICA

Abushiri revolt, 1888-89

Hehe revolt, 1891-98

ATLANTIC OCEAN

Nationalist uprisings, 1913

Arab revolt, 1887-89

ANGOLA (PORTUGUESE WEST AFRICA)

Maji-Maji revolt, 1905-09

COMOROS

NORTHERN RHODESIA

NYASALAND

Revolt under Chilembwe, 1915

MOZAMBIQUE (PORTUGUESE EAST AFRICA)

MADAGASCAR

Nationalist revolt, 1898-1904

MAURITIUS

RÉUNION

SOUTHERN RHODESIA

GERMAN SOUTHWEST AFRICA

WALVIS BAY

BECHUANA-LAND

Matabele and Mashona insurrections, 1896

Herrero Hottentot uprisings, 1904-06

SWAZILAND

Zulu resistance, 1879, 1906

UNION OF SOUTH AFRICA

BASUTOLAND

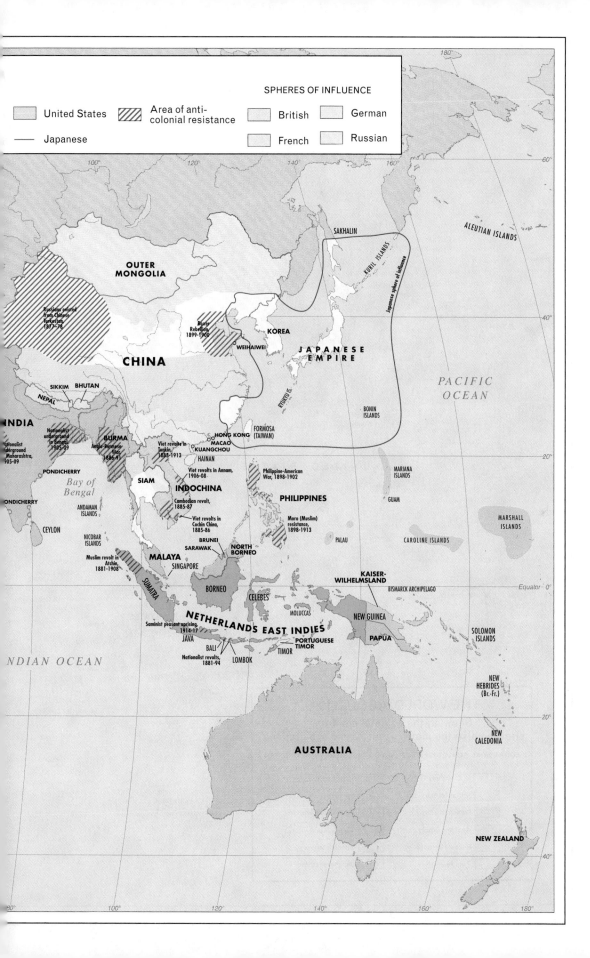

SPHERES OF INFLUENCE

United States

Japanese

Area of anti-colonial resistance

British

French

German

Russian

OUTER MONGOLIA

Russians evicted from Chinese Turkestan, 1877-78

Boxer Rebellion, 1899-1900

KOREA

WEIHAIWEI

CHINA

JAPANESE EMPIRE

SAKHALIN

KURIL ISLANDS

Japanese sphere of influence

ALEUTIAN ISLANDS

PACIFIC OCEAN

SIKKIM   BHUTAN

NEPAL

INDIA

Nationalist underground in Bengal, 1905-09

Nationalist underground in Maharashtra, 1905-09

BURMA

Anglo-Burmese War, 1886-91

Viet revolts in Tonkin, 1893-1913

HONG KONG
MACAO
KUANGCHOU
HAINAN

FORMOSA (TAIWAN)

RYUKYU IS.

BONIN ISLANDS

PONDICHERRY

Bay of Bengal

PONDICHERRY

SIAM

INDOCHINA

Viet revolts in Annam, 1906-08

Cambodian revolt, 1885-87

Viet revolts in Cochin China, 1885-86

Philippine-American War, 1898-1902

PHILIPPINES

MARIANA ISLANDS

GUAM

CEYLON

ANDAMAN ISLANDS

NICOBAR ISLANDS

Muslim revolt in Atchin, 1881-1908

MALAYA

SINGAPORE

SUMATRA

BRUNEI
SARAWAK

NORTH BORNEO

Moro (Muslim) resistance, 1898-1913

PALAU

MARSHALL ISLANDS

CAROLINE ISLANDS

BORNEO

CELEBES

MOLUCCAS

KAISER-WILHELMSLAND

NEW GUINEA

Equator   0°

BISMARCK ARCHIPELAGO

SOLOMON ISLANDS

NETHERLANDS EAST INDIES

Saminist peasant uprising, 1914-17

JAVA   BALI

Nationalist revolts, 1881-94   LOMBOK

TIMOR

PORTUGUESE TIMOR

PAPUA

INDIAN OCEAN

NEW HEBRIDES (Br.-Fr.)

NEW CALEDONIA

20°

AUSTRALIA

NEW ZEALAND

40°

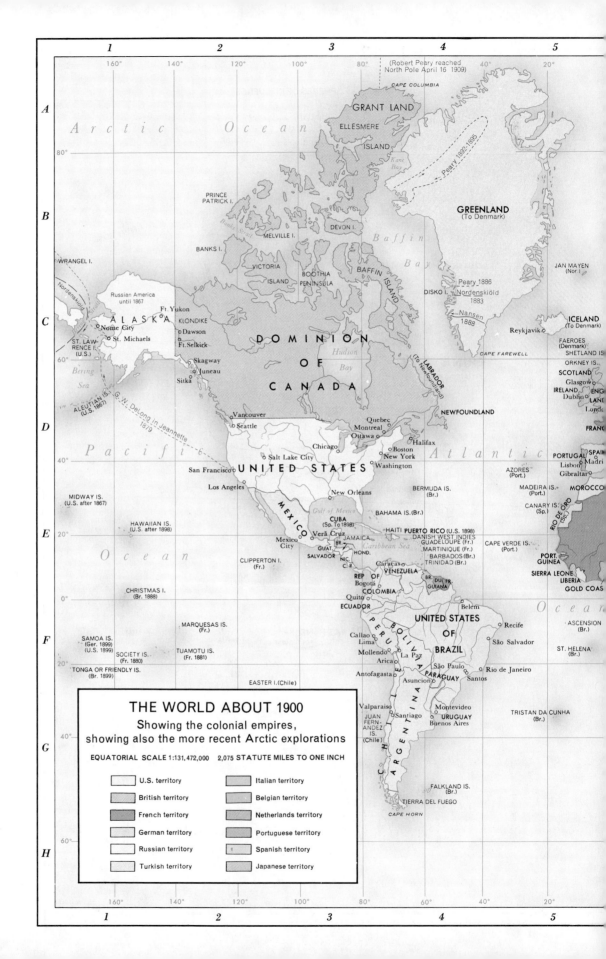

(Robert Peary reached
North Pole April 16 1909)

CAPE COLUMBIA

GRANT LAND

ELLESMERE

ISLAND

Peary 1892-1895

GREENLAND
(To Denmark)

Arctic Ocean

PRINCE
PATRICK I.

Banks Strait

MELVILLE I.

DEVON I.

Baffin

JAN MAYEN
(Nor.)

BANKS I.

Bay

VICTORIA

ISLAND

BOOTHIA
PENINSULA

BAFFIN ISLAND

Peary 1886

DISKO I. Nordenskiöld
1883

ICELAND
(To Denmark)

WRANGEL I.

Nansen
1888

Reykjavik

FAEROES
(Denmark)
SHETLAND IS.

Nordenskiold

Russian America
until 1867

ALASKA

Ft. Yukon
KLONDIKE

Nome City
St. Michaels

Dawson

Ft. Selkick

DOMINION

OF

CANADA

Hudson
Bay

CAPE FAREWELL

ORKNEY IS.

SCOTLAND
Glasgow
IRELAND ENG
Dublin LAND
Londo

ST. LAW-
RENCE I.
(U.S.)

Skagway

Juneau

Sitka

Bering
Sea

(To Newfoundland)

LABRADOR

NEWFOUNDLAND

ALEUTIAN IS.
(U.S. 1867)

G. W. DeLong in Jeannette
1879

Vancouver

Seattle

Quebec
Montreal
Ottawa

Halifax

FRANC

Pacific

Chicago

Boston
New York
Washington

Atlantic

PORTUGAL SPAIN
Lisbon Madri
Gibraltar

SPAIN

Salt Lake City

San Francisco
UNITED STATES

AZORES
(Port.)

MIDWAY IS.
(U.S. after 1867)

Los Angeles

New Orleans

BERMUDA IS.
(Br.)

MADEIRA IS.
(Port.)

MOROCCO

CANARY IS.
(Sp.)

RIO DE ORO

HAWAIIAN IS.
(U.S. after 1898)

MEXICO

Gulf of Mexico

CUBA
(Sp. To 1898)

BAHAMA IS.(Br.)

Ocean

Mexico
City

Verä Cruz

JAMAICA

HAITI PUERTO RICO (U.S. 1898)
DANISH WEST INDIES
GUADELOUPE (Fr.)
MARTINIQUE (Fr.)
BARBADOS (Br.)
TRINIDAD (Br.)

CAPE VERDE IS.
(Port.)

PORT.
GUINEA

CLIPPERTON I.
(Fr.)

GUAT.
SALVADOR

BR.
HOND.

Caribbean Sea

NIC.

C.R.

Caracas
VENEZUELA

BR. DU. FR.
GUIANA

SIERRA LEONE
LIBERIA
GOLD COAS

REP. OF
Bogotá
COLOMBIA

Quito

ECUADOR

UNITED STATES

Ocea

MARQUESAS IS.
(Fr.)

Belem

Recife

ASCENSION
(Br.)

SAMOA IS.
(Ger. 1899)
(U.S. 1899)

SOCIETY IS.
(Fr. 1880)

TUAMOTU IS.
(Fr. 1881)

Callao
Lima

PERU

BOLIVIA

OF

BRAZIL

São Salvador

ST. HELENA
(Br.)

Mollendo

La Paz

São Paulo

Rio de Janeiro

TONGA OR FRIENDLY IS.
(Br. 1899)

Arica

Antofagasta

PARAGUAY

Santos

EASTER I.(Chile)

Asunción

Valparaiso

JUAN
FERN-
ANDEZ
IS.
(Chile)

Santiago

ARGENTINA

Montevideo

URUGUAY
Buenos Aires

TRISTAN DA CUNHA
(Br.)

THE WORLD ABOUT 1900

Showing the colonial empires,
showing also the more recent Arctic explorations

EQUATORIAL SCALE 1:131,472,000   2,075 STATUTE MILES TO ONE INCH

U.S. territory		Italian territory
British territory		Belgian territory
French territory		Netherlands territory
German territory		Portuguese territory
Russian territory		Spanish territory
Turkish territory		Japanese territory

FALKLAND IS.
(Br.)

TIERRA DEL FUEGO

CAPE HORN

6   7   8   9   10

20°   40°   60°   80°   100°   120°   140°   160°

Arctic Ocean

← Fridtjof Nansen in Fram 1893-1896

A

80°

FRANZ JOSEF LAND OR
FRIDTJOF NANSEN LAND
(Russia 1928)

NORTHERN LAND
(NICHOLAS II)

SPITSBERGEN
(Norway 1920)

Baron →
Adolf Erik

NEW SIBERIAN
ISLANDS

DE LONG IS.

B

DeLong 1879-1881 →

BEAR I.
(Nor.)

*Barents
Sea*

*Kara
Sea*

TAIMYR PENINSULA

Nordenskiöld 1878-1879

WRANGEL I.

De Long Strait

Vega →

Nansen 1893-1896

NORTH
CAPE

Hammerfest
IS.

Vardö

1879-1879

Nordenskiöld 1878-1879   In

C

Archangel

RUSSIAN   EMPIRE

Yakutsk

KDM.
OF
SWEDEN
AND
NORWAY

GR. DUCHY OF
FINLAND
Russian Tsar Grand
Duke since 1809

60°

Christiania

St. Petersburg

Göteborg   Stockholm

Moscow   Tobolsk

Tomsk

Krasnoyarsk

Kurgan

Omsk

Ufa   Trans-Siberian Railway

Irkutsk

Samara

*Lake
Baikal*

Blagovyeshchensk

SAKHALIN
(Russia 1875)

Petropavlovsk

*Sea of
Okhotsk*

DEN.

Hamburg

GER.   Berlin

Warsaw

Volga

MONGOLIA

Chita

MANCHURIA

Khabarovsk

Vienna

EMP.

AUS.
HUNG.   Budapest

Odessa

*Aral
Sea*

*Lake
Balkhash*

Urga

Harbin

Vladivostok

KURILE IS.

Nordenskiöld 1879

D

Marseille

Rome

SWITZ.
ITALY

SERB.
RUM.
BUL.

Black Sea

KULJA
(Russia 1871-188.)

EMPIRE

Moukden

Port Arthur
(Russia 1898)

KOREA

EMPIRE

Tokyo

40°

Naples

GREECE

TURKISH EMPIRE

Constantinople

MERV
(1885)

SINKIANG

Kashgar

OF

Peking

Weihaiwei
(Br. 1898)

OF

Yokohama

ALG.

TUNIS

MALTA
(Br.)

CRETE
(Gr. 1898)

CYPRUS
(Br. 1878)

Teheran

Kabul

TIBET

Lhasa

CHINA

Ching, Manchu
Dynasty since 1644

Tsing Tao
(Ger. 1897)

JAPAN

RYUKYU IS.
(Jap. 1879)

OGASAWARA IS.
(BONIN IS.)
(Jap. 1878)

MARCUS I.
(Jap. 1899)

TRIPOLI
(Turk.)

Bagdad

Alexandria

PERSIA

AFG.

BALU.

Delhi

NEPAL

BHUTAN

CHINA PROPER

Shanghai

Yangtze

FORMOSA
(Jap. since 1895)

WAKE I.
(U.S. 1898)

E

EGYPT

ARABIA

SUDAN

OMAN

Muscat

BRITISH INDIAN EMPIRE
also many semiautonomous
Indian states
INDIA

BURMA

Macao
(Port.)

Hong
Kong
(Br.)

Kwangchawwan
(Fr. 1898)

20°

Mecca

KURIA
MURIA IS.
(Br.)

GOA
(Port.)

Bombay

Calcutta

Mandalay

Rangoon

SIAM

INDO-
CHINA

PHILIPPINE
IS.
(U.S. 1899)

MARIANAS
(Ger. 1899)

GUAM
(U.S. 1898)

CAROLINES
(Ger. 1899)

MARSHALL IS.
(Ger. 1899)

ERIT.

ADEN

SOCOTRA
(Br. 1886)

LACCADIVE IS.
(Br.)

Mahé
(Fr.)

Madras

Pondichéry

ANDAMAN IS.
(Br.)

Bangkok

PELEW IS.
(Ger. 1899)

GILBERT IS.
(Br. 1899)

NIGERIA

KAMERUN

FR. SOM.
BR. SOM.
IT. SOM.

CEYLON

NICOBAR IS.
(Br.)

MALDIVE IS.
(Br.)

STRAITS
SETTLEMENTS

SARAWAK

BORNEO
(1888)

MOLUCCA

NEW GUINEA

Ocean

NEW MECKLENBURG

BISMARCK IS.
(Ger. 1884)

ELLICE IS.
(Br. 1892)

F

OGO-
AND

SP.
GUINEA

CONGO FREE
STATE
Ruled by
Leopold II of
Belgium

*Lake
Chad*

E. AFR.

GER.
E. AFR.

ZANZIBAR
(Br. 1890)

SEYCHELLES
(Br.)

Singapore

SUMATRA

BORNEO

CELEBES
(Port.)

TIMOR
(Neth.)

(Neth.
1901)

(Ger.
1884)

(Br.
1884)

NEW
POMERANIA

SOLOMON IS.
Div. between
Br. and Ger. 1899

FIJI IS.
(Br. 1874)

CABINDA
(Port.)

Loanda

COMORO IS.
(Fr.)

COCOS IS
(Br. 1876)

JAVA

Darwin

NORTHERN
TERRITORY

NEW
HEBRIDES

NEW
CALEDONIA
(Fr.)

LOYALTY IS.
(Fr. 1864)

ANGOLA

RHODESIA

GER.
E. AFR.

Mozambique

MADAGASCAR
(Fr. 1896)

MAURITIUS (Br.)

Indian

COMMONWEALTH OF AUSTRALIA
(including Tasmania formed in 1901)

QUEENSLAND

Brisbane

GER.
S.W.
AFR.

BECHUANA-
LAND

TRANS-
VAAL

Lourenço
Marques

REUNION (Fr.)

WESTERN
AUSTRALIA

SOUTH
AUSTRALIA

NEW
SOUTH
WALES

Sydney

ORANGE
FREE
STATE

CAPE
COLONY

NATAL

Capetown

Perth

Adelaide

Melbourne

Ocean

TASMANIA

Wellington

G

NEW
ZEALAND
Organized as a
Dominion in 1907

60°

H

20°   40°   60°   80°   100°   120°   140°

A-410041-29-1-1-1-1

Copyright by Rand McNally & Company, Made in U.S.A.

6   7   8   9   10

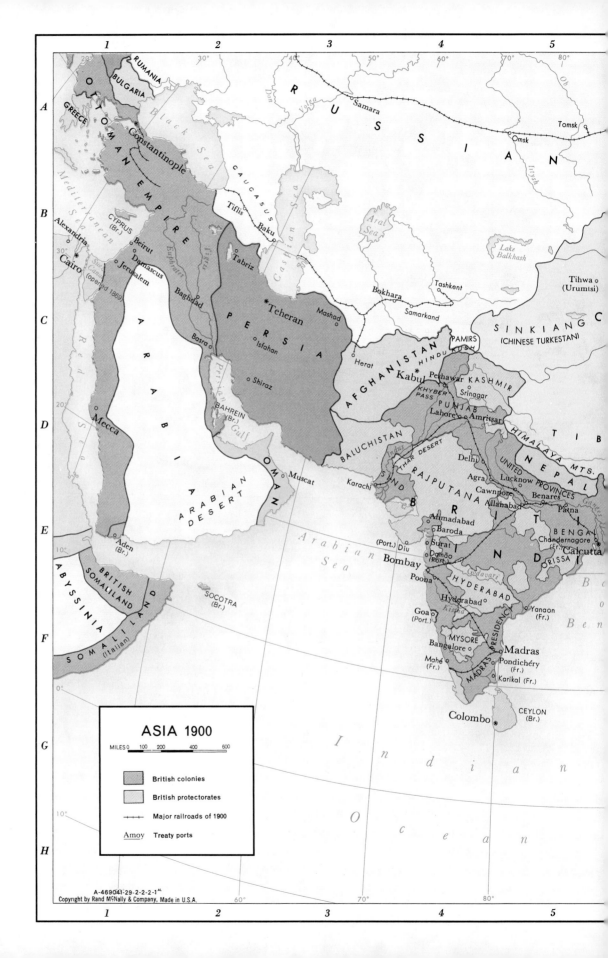

ASIA 1900

MILES 0 100 200 400 600

British colonies

British protectorates

Major railroads of 1900

Amoy Treaty ports

A-469041-29-2-2-1^{AL}
Copyright by Rand McNally & Company, Made in U.S.A.

Map labels:

RUMANIA
BULGARIA
GREECE
OTTOMAN EMPIRE
Constantinople
Black Sea
CAUCASUS
Tiflis
Baku
Caspian Sea
RUSSIAN
Samara
Omsk
Tomsk
Ob
Irtysh
Volga
Don
CYPRUS (Br.)
Alexandria
Beirut
Damascus
Jerusalem
Cairo
Suez Canal (opened 1869)
Mediterranean Sea
Euphrates
Tigris
Baghdad
Basra
Tabriz
PERSIA
*Teheran
Mashad
Isfahan
Shiraz
Herat
Bokhara
Samarkand
Tashkent
Aral Sea
Lake Balkhash
Tihwa (Urumtsi)
SINKIANG (CHINESE TURKESTAN)
PAMIRS
HINDU KUSH
AFGHANISTAN
Kabul
Peshawar
KASHMIR
Srinagar
KHYBER PASS
PUNJAB
Lahore
Amritsar
HIMALAYA MTS.
NEPAL
TIB
BALUCHISTAN
Karachi
SIND
THAR DESERT
Indus
Delhi
Agra
Lucknow
UNITED PROVINCES
Cawnpore
Allahabad
Benares
Patna
BRITISH
RAJPUTANA
Muscat
OMAN
Persian Gulf
BAHREIN (Br.)
ARABIA
ARABIAN DESERT
Mecca
Red Sea
Aden (Br.)
ABYSSINIA
BRITISH SOMALILAND
SOMALILAND (Italian)
SOCOTRA (Br.)
Arabian Sea
Ahmadabad
Baroda
(Port.) Diu
Surat
Damão (Port.)
Bombay
Poona
Goa (Port.)
HYDERABAD
Hyderabad
Godavari
Kistna
INDIA
BENGAL
Chandernagore (Fr.)
Calcutta
ORISSA
Yanaon (Fr.)
Ganges
B
Ben
MYSORE
Bangalore
Mahé (Fr.)
MADRAS PRESIDENCY
Madras
Pondichéry (Fr.)
Karikal (Fr.)
Colombo
CEYLON (Br.)
Indian Ocean

82

6   7   8   9   10

100°   110°   120°   130°   140°   150°   160°   40°

EMPIRE

A

SAKHALIN
(Russ.)
(Southern half
to Japan 1905)

CHISHIMA
(KURILS)
(Jap.)

Heilung (Amur)

Lake
Baikal

MANCHURIA

HOKKAIDO

Irkutsk   Chita

Hakodate

B

Sea
of
Japan

Urga

MONGOLIA

Kirin

Vladivostok

JAPAN

Tokyo

P

Mukden

Pyongyang   Wonsan

Niigata

30°

(Liaotung Peninsula
Russ. lease 1898,
transferred to Japan 1905)

Newchwang

Seoul   KOREA (Annexed by
Japan
1910)

Yokohama

(Treaty port status
abolished in Japan 1899)

GOBI DESERT

Chinwangtao

Port
Arthur

Dalny
(Dairen)

Chefoo

Chemulpo

HONSHU

Kyoto   Nagoya
Kobe   Osaka

Peking

SHIKOKU

C

OGASAWARA
(BONINS)
(Jap.)

CHINESE

EMPIRE

Tientsin

Tsinan   Tsingtao

Weihaiwei 1898
(Br. lease 1898)
Kiaochow Bay
(Ger. lease 1898,
Japan 1914)

Pusan

KYUSHU

Nagasaki

Lanchow

Kaifeng

Huang (Yellow)

Sian

Nanking   Chinkiang
Soochow

Shanghai

RYUKYU IS.
(Japan)

20°

D

Chengtu

Ichang   Hankow   Wuhu
Shasi   Wuchang
Yochow   Hangchow   Ningpo
Kiukiang

Lhasa

CHINA

Chungking

Nanchang   Wenchow

Changsha

Santuao
Foochow

Taihoku

Yangtze

Brahmaputra

ASSAM

Amoy
Swatow

TAIWAN
(FORMOSA)
(Japan)
(from China 1895)

Yünnanfu

Hsi (West)   Canton

Pacific

H

BURMA
(Br from 1885)

Mengtze

Szemao

Wuchow

Lungchow

Samshui

Hong Kong
(Br. 1842, Suppl.
lease 1898)

E

Mandalay
(Br. from 1852)

TONGKING
(Fr. prot.
from 1884)

Pakhoi

Hanoi

Macao
(Port.)

Kwangchowwan
(Fr. lease 1898)

Klungchow

PHILIPPINE

Ocean

Prome

Luang Prabang

FRENCH

HAINAN

LUZON

Manila

CAROLINE IS.
(Ger.)
(Purchased from
Spain 1898)

10°

Rangoon

LAOS
(To
Fr. 1907)

INDO-

Hué

South
China
Sea

(U.S. from
Spain 1898)

SIAM

ANNAM

CHINA

Iloilo   Cebu

ISLANDS

PALAU IS.
(Ger.)
(Purchased from
Spain 1898)

F

Bangkok

(To Fr. 1907)

CAMBODIA
(Fr. prot. from 1863)

Mekong

Saigon

Zamboanga

MINDANAO

ANDAMAN
IS.
(Br.)

Gulf
of
Siam

Phnom
Penh

COCHIN
CHINA
(Fr. prot.
1862-67)

0°

NICOBAR
IS.
(Br.)

NORTH
BORNEO

NEW
GUINEA

finally subdued
the Dutch, 1899

ACHEH

Penang

BRUNEI

G

FEDERATED
MALAY STATES
(from 1895)

SARAWAK

MOLUCCAS

SUMATRA

Malacca

BORNEO

CELEBES

Amboina

JOHORE

Singapore

BANKA

EAST   INDIES

10°

Palembang

BILLITON

H

DUTCH

TIMOR
(Port.)

Batavia   Semarang   Surabaya
JAVA
Jokjakarta   Solo   BALI

100°   110°   120°

6   7   8   9   10

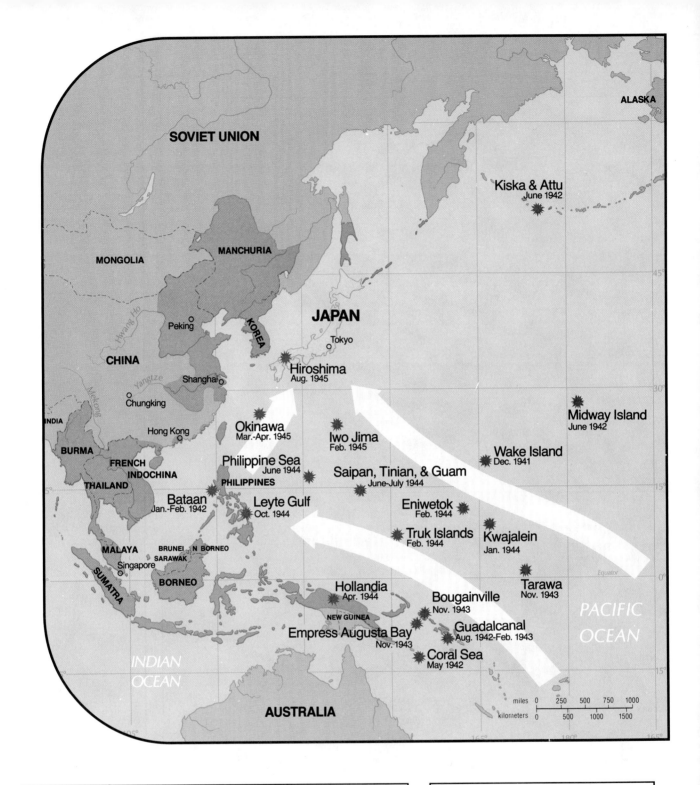

SOVIET UNION		ALASKA

Kiska & Attu
June 1942

MONGOLIA

MANCHURIA

Peking○

CHINA

JAPAN

Tokyo○

Shanghai○

Hiroshima
Aug. 1945

Chungking○

Midway Island
June 1942

INDIA

Hong Kong○

Okinawa
Mar.-Apr. 1945

Iwo Jima
Feb. 1945

Wake Island
Dec. 1941

BURMA

FRENCH
INDOCHINA

Philippine Sea
June 1944

Saipan, Tinian, & Guam
June-July 1944

THAILAND

PHILIPPINES

Bataan
Jan.-Feb. 1942

Leyte Gulf
Oct. 1944

Eniwetok
Feb. 1944

Truk Islands
Feb. 1944

Kwajalein
Jan. 1944

MALAYA

BRUNEI N BORNEO
SARAWAK

Singapore○

SUMATRA

BORNEO

Hollandia
Apr. 1944

NEW GUINEA

Empress Augusta Bay
Nov. 1943

Bougainville
Nov. 1943

Guadalcanal
Aug. 1942-Feb. 1943

Tarawa
Nov. 1943

Coral Sea
May 1942

PACIFIC
OCEAN

INDIAN
OCEAN

AUSTRALIA

miles 0 250 500 750 1000
kilometers 0 500 1000 1500

U. S. CASUALTIES IN SECOND WORLD WAR
1941-1946

Branch	Numbers engaged	Battle deaths	Other deaths	Total deaths	Wounds not mortal	Total casualties
Army*	11,260,000	234,874	83,400	318,274	565,861	884,135
Navy	4,183,466	36,950	25,664	62,614	37,778	100,392
Marines	669,100	19,773	4,778	24,511	67,207	91,718
Total	16,112,566	291,557	113,842	405,399	670,846	1,076,245

SECOND WORLD WAR CASUALTIES

Country	Battle Deaths	Wounded
Australia	26,976	180,684
China	1,324,516	1,762,006
India	32,121	64,354
Japan	1,270,000	140,000
New Zealand	11,625	17,000
United Kingdom	357,116	369,267
United States	291,557	670,846

*Includes Air Force

Source: Information Please Almanac (Boston: Houghton Mifflin Co., 1988)

Source: Information Please Almanac (Boston: Houghton Mifflin Co., 1988)

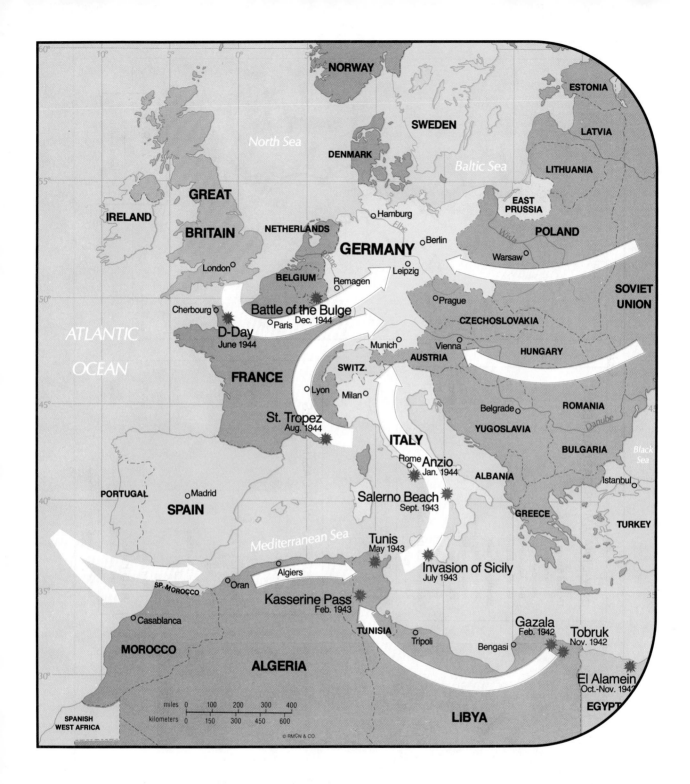

NORWAY

SWEDEN

DENMARK

North Sea

Baltic Sea

ESTONIA

LATVIA

LITHUANIA

EAST PRUSSIA

POLAND

○ Hamburg

○ Berlin

Warsaw ○

GERMANY

IRELAND

GREAT BRITAIN

NETHERLANDS

London ○

BELGIUM

Cherbourg ○

Remagen ○

○ Leipzig

Battle of the Bulge
Dec. 1944

○ Paris

D-Day
June 1944

SOVIET UNION

○ Prague

CZECHOSLOVAKIA

ATLANTIC

OCEAN

FRANCE

SWITZ.

○ Lyon

Munich ○

Vienna ○

AUSTRIA

HUNGARY

Milan ○

St. Tropez
Aug. 1944

Belgrade ○

ROMANIA

Danube

ITALY

Rome ○

Anzio
Jan. 1944

YUGOSLAVIA

BULGARIA

Black Sea

PORTUGAL

Madrid ○

SPAIN

Salerno Beach
Sept. 1943

ALBANIA

GREECE

Istanbul ○

TURKEY

Mediterranean Sea

Tunis
May 1943

Algiers ○

○ Oran

SP. MOROCCO

Kasserine Pass
Feb. 1943

Invasion of Sicily
July 1943

TUNISIA

○ Tripoli

Bengasi ○

Gazala
Feb. 1942

Tobruk
Nov. 1942

○ Casablanca

MOROCCO

ALGERIA

El Alamein
Oct.-Nov. 1942

EGYPT

miles 0 100 200 300 400

kilometers 0 150 300 450 600

LIBYA

SPANISH WEST AFRICA

© RMCN & CO.

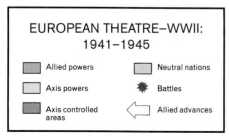

EUROPEAN THEATRE–WWII: 1941–1945

- ◼ Allied powers
- ◻ Axis powers
- ◼ Axis controlled areas
- ◻ Neutral nations
- ✸ Battles
- ◁ Allied advances

SECOND WORLD WAR CASUALTIES

Country	Battle Deaths	Wounded
Austria	280,000	350,117
Canada	32,714	53,145
France	201,568	400,000
Germany	3,250,000	7,250,000
Hungary	147,435	89,313
Italy	149,496	66,716
Poland	320,000	530,000
U.S.S.R.	6,115,000	14,012,000

Source: Information Please Almanac (Boston: Houghton Mifflin Co., 1988)

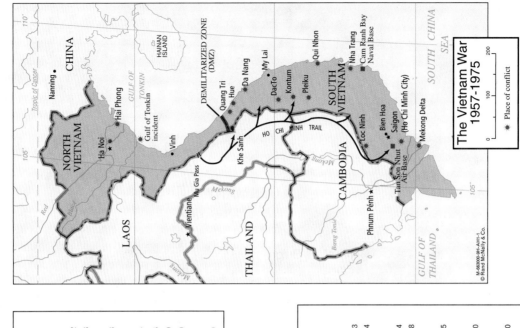

The Vietnam War
1957-1975

* Place of conflict

0   100   200

M-68000-9H-AH1-1.
© Rand McNally & Co.

CHINA
Nanning
NORTH VIETNAM
Ha Noi
Hai Phong
GULF OF TONKIN
HAINAN ISLAND
Gulf of Tonkin incident
Vinh
DEMILITARIZED ZONE (DMZ)
Quang Tri
Hue
Da Nang
My Lai
DacTo
Kontum
Pleiku
Qui Nhon
Nha Trang
Cam Ranh Bay Naval Base
SOUTH VIETNAM
Khe Sanh
HO CHI MINH TRAIL
Loc Ninh
Bien Hoa
Saigon (Ho Chi Minh City)
Tan Son Nhut Air Base
Mekong Delta
SOUTH CHINA SEA
Mu Gia Pass
LAOS
Vientiane
Mekong
THAILAND
CAMBODIA
Phnum Pénh
Beng Tonle
GULF OF THAILAND
Red
Black
Mekong
Tropic of Cancer

VIETNAM WAR CASUALTIES

United States

Battle deaths	47,382
Wounded	153,303
Died, non-combat	1,811
Missing, captured	10,753

South Vietnam

Military killed in action	110,357
Military wounded	499,026
Civilian killed	415,000
Civilian wounded	913,000

Communists Regulars and Guerillas

Killed in action	666,000

Source: U.S. Department of Defense

KOREAN WAR CASUALITIES

United States

Killed	36,913
Wounded	103,284

Republic of Korea

Killed	415,004
Wounded	482,568

United Nations

Killed and wounded	15,465

China

Killed and wounded	900,000

North Korea

Killed and wounded	520,000

Source: U.S. Department of Defense

KOREAN WAR
1950–1953

0   50   100 miles

MANCHURIA
CHINA
SEA OF JAPAN
NORTH KOREA
SOUTH KOREA
JAPAN
Chinese attack, Nov. 26, 1950
Pyongyang
Panmunjom
Kaesong
Inchon
Seoul
N. Korean invasion, June 25, 1950
Sept. 15, 1950
Limit of N. Korean advance, Aug. 1950
Pusan
YELLOW SEA
40°N.
38°N.
35°N.
125°E.
130°E.
© RMCN & CO.

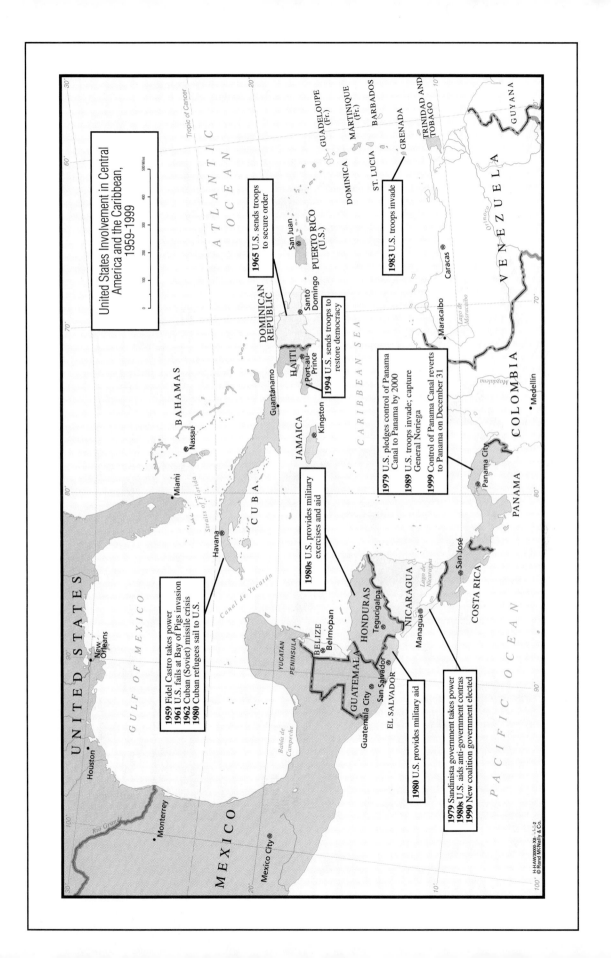

United States Involvement in Central America and the Caribbean, 1959–1999

1965 U.S. sends troops to secure order

1983 U.S. troops invade

1994 U.S. sends troops to restore democracy

1979 U.S. pledges control of Panama Canal to Panama by 2000
1989 U.S. troops invade; capture General Noriega
1999 Control of Panama Canal reverts to Panama on December 31

1980s U.S. provides military exercises and aid

1959 Fidel Castro takes power
1961 U.S. fails at Bay of Pigs invasion
1962 Cuban (Soviet) missile crisis
1980 Cuban refugees sail to U.S.

1980 U.S. provides military aid

1979 Sandinista government takes power
1980s U.S. aids anti-government contras
1990 New coalition government elected

ATLANTIC OCEAN

CARIBBEAN SEA

PACIFIC OCEAN

GULF OF MEXICO

UNITED STATES

MEXICO

BAHAMAS

CUBA

JAMAICA

HAITI

DOMINICAN REPUBLIC

PUERTO RICO (U.S.)

DOMINICA

MARTINIQUE (Fr.)

GUADELOUPE (Fr.)

ST. LUCIA

BARBADOS

GRENADA

TRINIDAD AND TOBAGO

GUYANA

VENEZUELA

COLOMBIA

PANAMA

COSTA RICA

NICARAGUA

HONDURAS

EL SALVADOR

GUATEMALA

BELIZE

YUCATAN PENINSULA

Houston

Monterrey

New Orleans

Mexico City

Miami

Nassau

Havana

Guantánamo

Kingston

Port-au-Prince

Santo Domingo

San Juan

Caracas

Maracaibo

Medellín

Panama City

San José

Managua

Tegucigalpa

San Salvador

Guatemala City

Belmopan

Rio Grande

Straits of Florida

Canal de Yucatán

Bahía de Campeche

Lago de Nicaragua

Lago de Maracaibo

Magdalena

Orinoco

Tropic of Cancer

0 100 200 300 400 500 Miles

H-HAW0000X-X8-_3-2-2
© Rand McNally & Co.

87

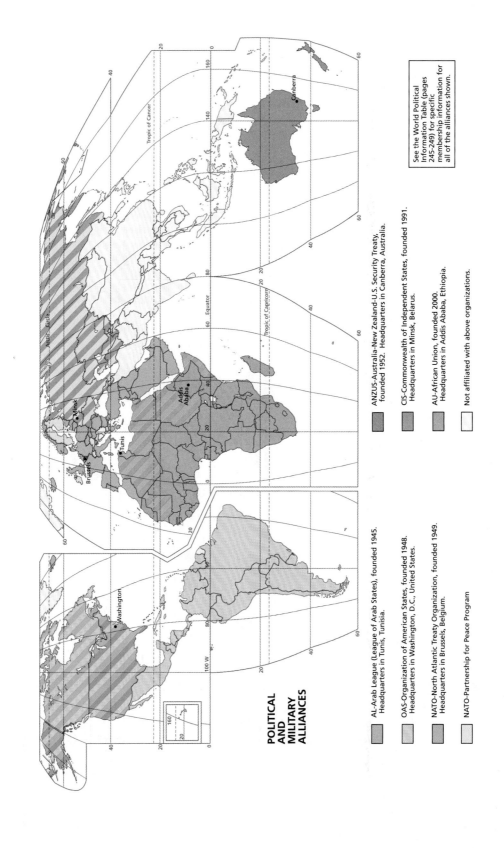

POLITICAL AND MILITARY ALLIANCES

AL-Arab League (League of Arab States), founded 1945. Headquarters in Tunis, Tunisia.

OAS-Organization of American States, founded 1948. Headquarters in Washington, D.C., United States.

NATO-North Atlantic Treaty Organization, founded 1949. Headquarters in Brussels, Belgium.

NATO-Partnership for Peace Program

ANZUS-Australia-New Zealand-U.S. Security Treaty, founded 1952. Headquarters in Canberra, Australia.

CIS-Commonwealth of Independent States, founded 1991. Headquarters in Minsk, Belarus.

AU-African Union, founded 2000. Headquarters in Addis Ababa, Ethiopia.

Not affiliated with above organizations.

See the World Political Information Table (pages 245-249) for specific membership information for all of the alliances shown.

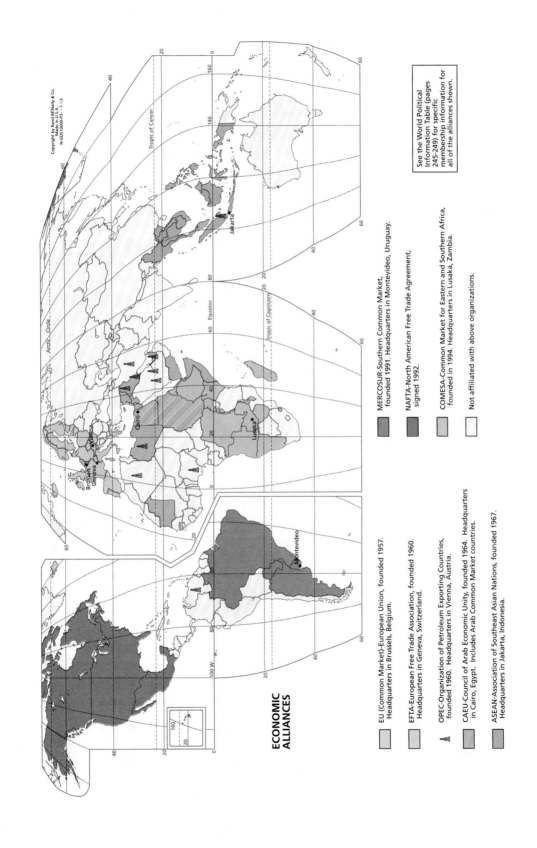

ECONOMIC ALLIANCES

EU (Common Market)-European Union, founded 1957. Headquarters in Brussels, Belgium.

EFTA-European Free Trade Association, founded 1960. Headquarters in Geneva, Switzerland.

OPEC-Organization of Petroleum Exporting Countries, founded 1960. Headquarters in Vienna, Austria.

CAEU-Council of Arab Economic Unity, founded 1964. Headquarters in Cairo, Egypt. Includes Arab Common Market countries.

ASEAN-Association of Southeast Asian Nations, founded 1967. Headquarters in Jakarta, Indonesia.

MERCOSUR-Southern Common Market, founded 1991. Headquarters in Montevideo, Uruguay.

NAFTA-North American Free Trade Agreement, signed 1992.

COMESA-Common Market for Eastern and Southern Africa, founded in 1994. Headquarters in Lusaka, Zambia.

Not affiliated with above organizations.

See the World Political Information Table (pages 245–249) for specific membership information for all of the alliances shown.

Copyright by Rand McNally & Co.
Made in U.S.A.
N-GD510000-P3 -3-3

89

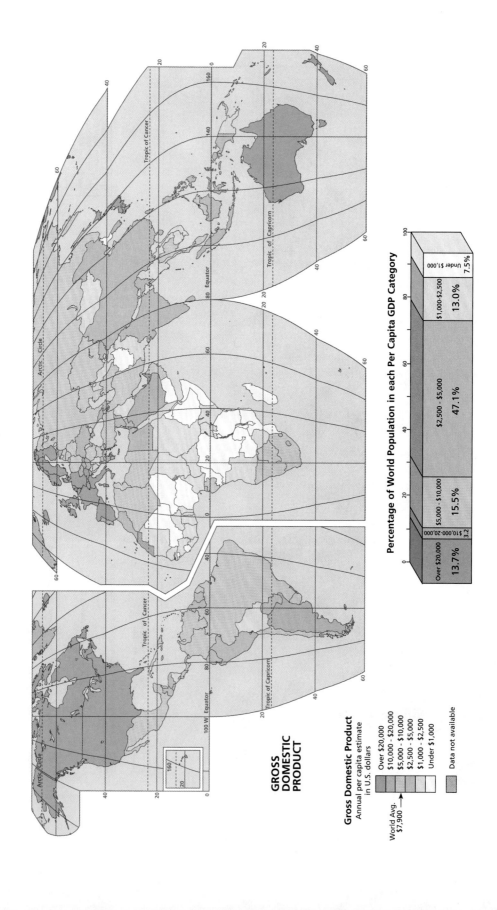

GROSS DOMESTIC PRODUCT

Gross Domestic Product
Annual per capita estimate
in U.S. dollars

World Avg.
$7,900

- Over $20,000
- $10,000 - $20,000
- $5,000 - $10,000
- $2,500 - $5,000
- $1,000 - $2,500
- Under $1,000
- Data not available

Percentage of World Population in each Per Capita GDP Category

Over $20,000 — 13.7%
$10,000-20,000 — 3.2
$5,000 - $10,000 — 15.5%
$2,500 - $5,000 — 47.1%
$1,000-$2,500 — 13.0%
Under $1,000 — 7.5%

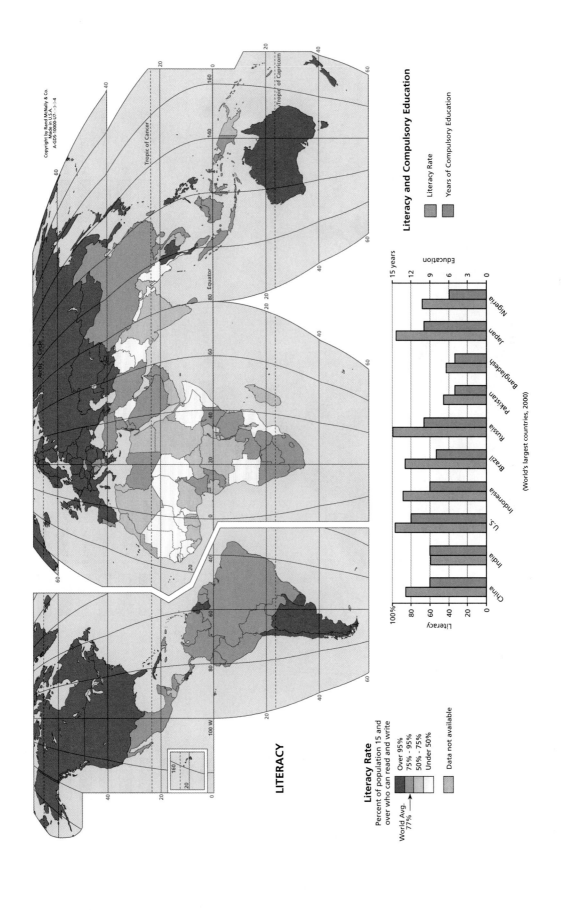

Copyright by Rand McNally & Co.
Made in U.S.A.
A-GDS-10000-U7-·-3--4

Literacy and Compulsory Education

Literacy Rate

Years of Compulsory Education

Education

15 years
12
9
6
3
0

Nigeria   Japan   Bangladesh   Pakistan   Russia   Brazil   Indonesia   U.S.   India   China

(World's largest countries, 2000)

Literacy
100%
80
60
40
20
0

LITERACY

Literacy Rate

Percent of population 15 and over who can read and write

World Avg.
77%

Over 95%
75% - 95%
50% - 75%
Under 50%

Data not available

160
20

60
40
20

Tropic of Cancer
Tropic of Capricorn

Arctic Circle
Equator

80
160
140

100 W
80

91

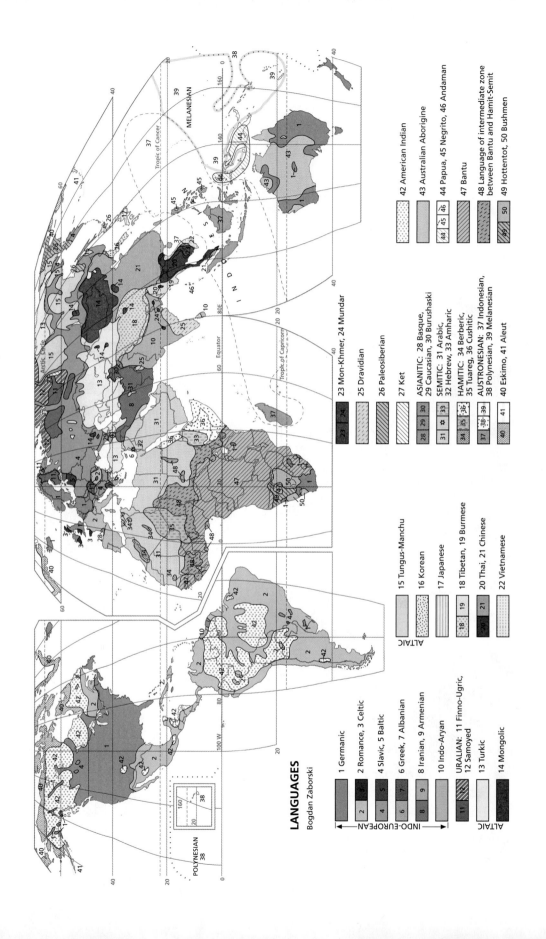

LANGUAGES
Bogdan Zaborski

INDO-EUROPEAN
1 Germanic
2 Romance, 3 Celtic
4 Slavic, 5 Baltic
6 Greek, 7 Albanian
8 Iranian, 9 Armenian
10 Indo-Aryan
URALIAN: 11 Finno-Ugric,
12 Samoyed

ALTAIC
13 Turkic
14 Mongolic

15 Tungus-Manchu
16 Korean
17 Japanese
18 Tibetan, 19 Burmese
20 Thai, 21 Chinese
22 Vietnamese

23 Mon-Khmer, 24 Mundar
25 Dravidian
26 Paleosiberian
27 Ket
ASIANITIC: 28 Basque,
29 Caucasian, 30 Burushaski
SEMITIC: 31 Arabic,
32 Hebrew, 33 Amharic
HAMITIC: 34 Berberic,
35 Tuareg, 36 Cushitic
AUSTRONESIAN: 37 Indonesian,
38 Polynesian, 39 Melanesian
40 Eskimo, 41 Aleut

42 American Indian
43 Australian Aborigine
44 Papua, 45 Negrito, 46 Andaman
47 Bantu
48 Language of intermediate zone
between Bantu and Hamit-Semit
49 Hottentot, 50 Bushmen

92

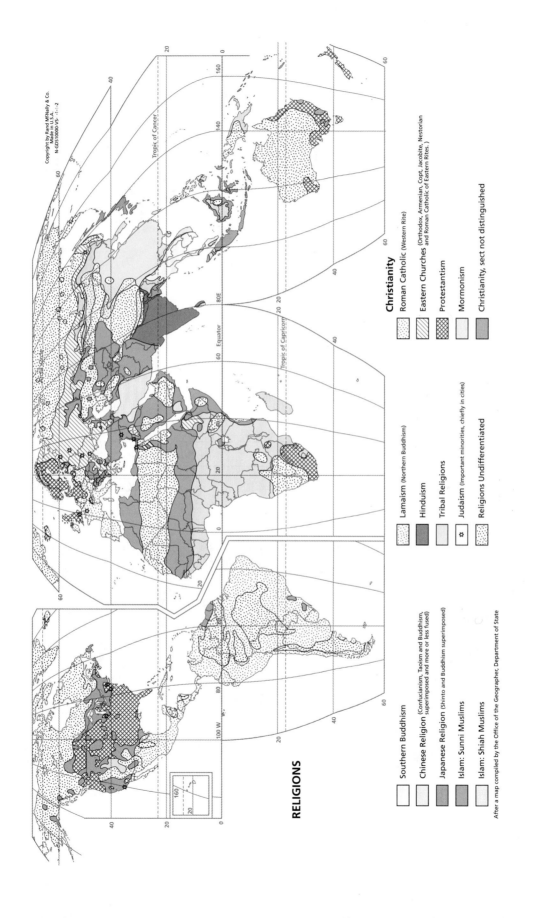

RELIGIONS

Southern Buddhism

Chinese Religion (Confucianism, Taoism and Buddhism, superimposed and more or less fused)

Japanese Religion (Shinto and Buddhism superimposed)

Islam: Sunni Muslims

Islam: Shiah Muslims

Lamaism (Northern Buddhism)

Hinduism

Tribal Religions

Judaism (Important minorities, chiefly in cities)

Religions Undifferentiated

Christianity

Roman Catholic (Western Rite)

Eastern Churches (Orthodox, Armenian, Copt, Jacobite, Nestorian and Roman Catholic of Eastern Rites.)

Protestantism

Mormonism

Christianity, sect not distinguished

After a map compiled by the Office of the Geographer, Department of State

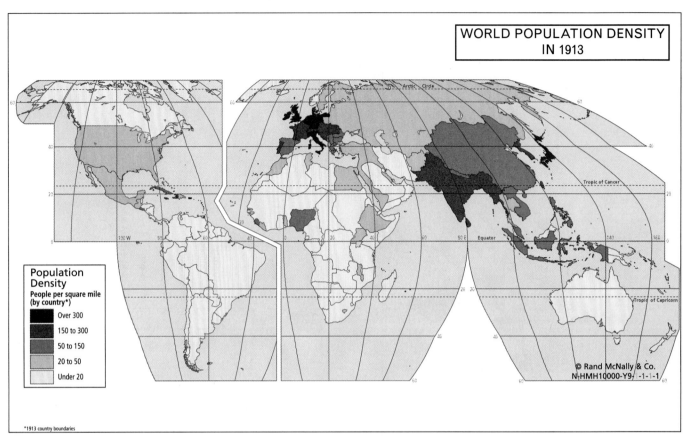

WORLD POPULATION DENSITY IN 1913

Population Density

People per square mile (by country*)

- Over 300
- 150 to 300
- 50 to 150
- 20 to 50
- Under 20

© Rand McNally & Co.
N-HMH10000-Y9- -1-1-1

*1913 country boundaries

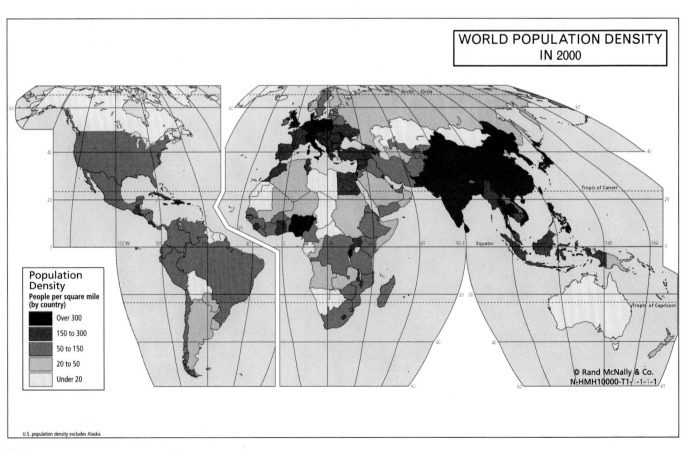

WORLD POPULATION DENSITY IN 2000

Population Density

People per square mile (by country)

- Over 300
- 150 to 300
- 50 to 150
- 20 to 50
- Under 20

© Rand McNally & Co.
N-HMH10000-T1- -1-1-1

U.S. population density excludes Alaska

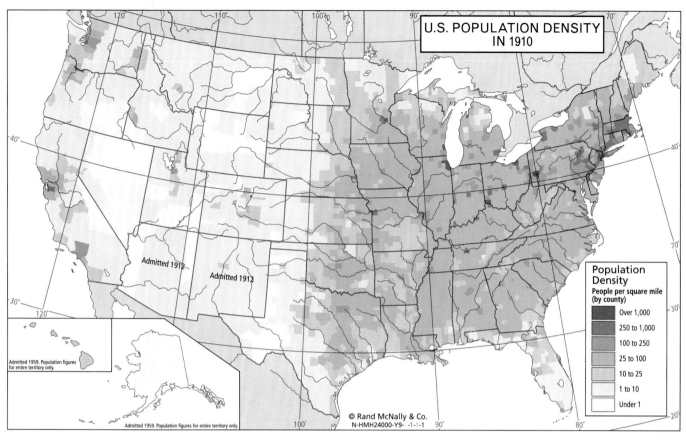

U.S. POPULATION DENSITY
IN 1910

Admitted 1912

Admitted 1912

Admitted 1959. Population figures for entire territory only.

Admitted 1959. Population figures for entire territory only.

Population Density
People per square mile (by county)

	Over 1,000
	250 to 1,000
	100 to 250
	25 to 100
	10 to 25
	1 to 10
	Under 1

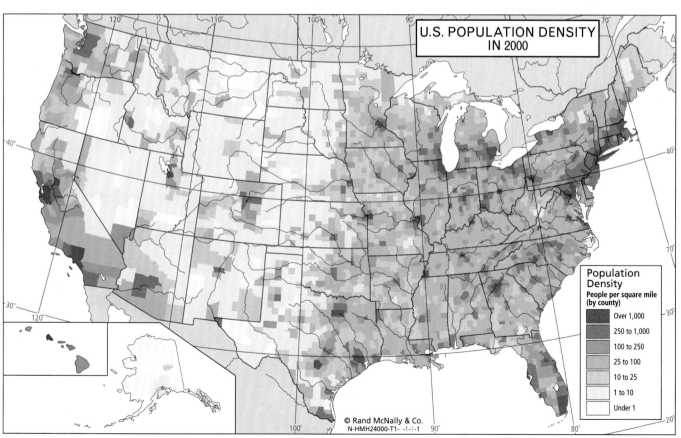

U.S. POPULATION DENSITY
IN 2000

Population Density
People per square mile (by county)

	Over 1,000
	250 to 1,000
	100 to 250
	25 to 100
	10 to 25
	1 to 10
	Under 1

WHITE POPULATION

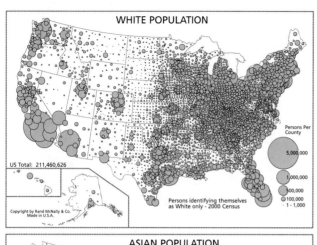

US Total: 211,460,626

Persons identifying themselves as White only - 2000 Census

Persons Per County

5,000,000
1,000,000
500,000
100,000
1 - 1,000

Copyright by Rand McNally & Co.
Made in U.S.A.

AFRICAN AMERICAN POPULATION

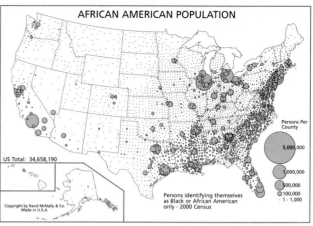

US Total: 34,658,190

Persons identifying themselves as Black or African American only - 2000 Census

Persons Per County

5,000,000
1,000,000
500,000
100,000
1 - 1,000

Copyright by Rand McNally & Co.
Made in U.S.A.

ASIAN POPULATION

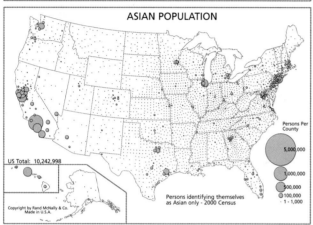

US Total: 10,242,998

Persons identifying themselves as Asian only - 2000 Census

Persons Per County

5,000,000
1,000,000
500,000
100,000
1 - 1,000

Copyright by Rand McNally & Co.
Made in U.S.A.

AMERICAN INDIAN AND ALASKA NATIVE POPULATION

US Total: 2,475,956

Persons identifying themselves as American Indian or Alaska Native only - 2000 Census

Persons Per County

5,000,000
1,000,000
500,000
100,000
1 - 1,000

Copyright by Rand McNally & Co.
Made in U.S.A.

NATIVE HAWAIIAN AND PACIFIC ISLANDER POPULATION

US Total: 398,835

Persons identifying themselves as Native Hawaiian or Other Pacific Islander only - 2000 Census

Persons Per County

5,000,000
1,000,000
500,000
100,000
1 - 1,000

Copyright by Rand McNally & Co.
Made in U.S.A.

SOME OTHER RACE

US Total: 15,359,073

Persons identifying themselves as belonging to some other race - 2000 Census

Persons Per County

5,000,000
1,000,000
500,000
100,000
1 - 1,000

Copyright by Rand McNally & Co.
Made in U.S.A.

TWO OR MORE RACES

US Total: 6,826,228

Persons identifying themselves as belonging to two or more races - 2000 Census

Persons Per County

5,000,000
1,000,000
500,000
100,000
1 - 1,000

Copyright by Rand McNally & Co.
Made in U.S.A.

HISPANIC POPULATION (ANY RACE)

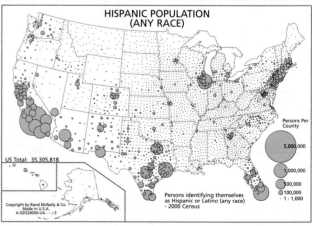

US Total: 35,305,818

Persons identifying themselves as Hispanic or Latino (any race) - 2000 Census

Persons Per County

5,000,000
1,000,000
500,000
100,000
1 - 1,000

Copyright by Rand McNally & Co.
Made in U.S.A.
A-GD524000-U4 - - >3

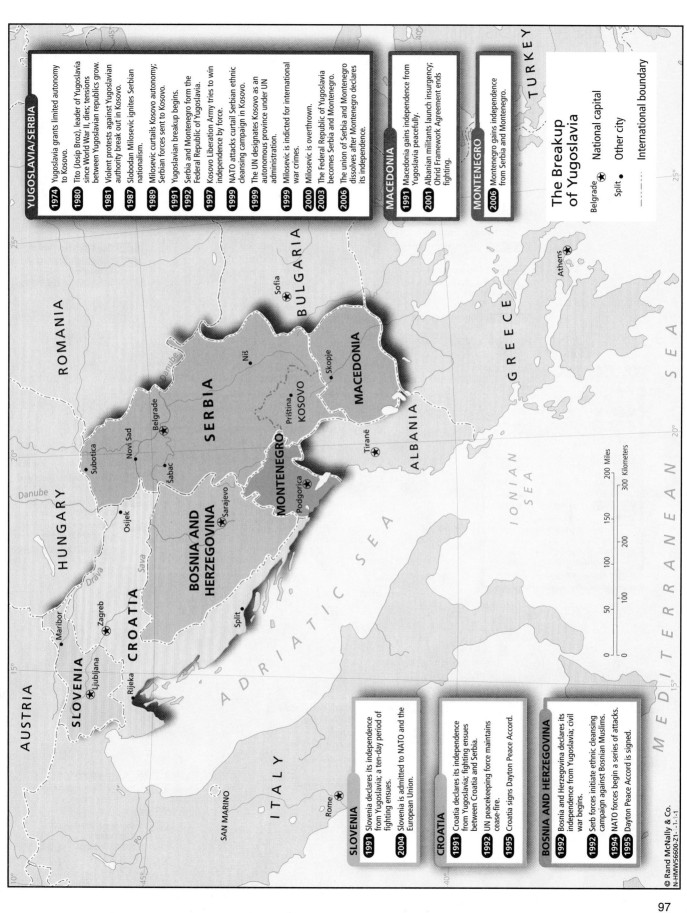

YUGOSLAVIA/SERBIA

1974 Yugoslavia grants limited autonomy to Kosovo.

1980 Tito (Josip Broz), leader of Yugoslavia since World War II, dies; tensions between Yugoslavian republics grow.

1981 Violent protests against Yugoslavian authority break out in Kosovo.

1987 Slobodan Milosevic ignites Serbian nationalism.

1989 Milosevic curtails Kosovo autonomy; Serbian forces sent to Kosovo.

1991 Yugoslavian breakup begins.

1992 Serbia and Montenegro form the Federal Republic of Yugoslavia.

1997 Kosovo Liberation Army tries to win independence by force.

1999 NATO attacks curtail Serbian ethnic cleansing campaign in Kosovo.

1999 The UN designates Kosovo as an autonomous province under UN administration.

1999 Milosevic is indicted for international war crimes.

2000 Milosevic is overthrown.

2003 The Federal Republic of Yugoslavia becomes Serbia and Montenegro.

2006 The union of Serbia and Montenegro dissolves after Montenegro declares its independence.

MACEDONIA

1991 Macedonia gains independence from Yugoslavia peacefully.

2001 Albanian militants launch insurgency; Ohrid Framework Agreement ends fighting.

MONTENEGRO

2006 Montenegro gains independence from Serbia and Montenegro.

The Breakup of Yugoslavia

Belgrade ✪ National capital

Split • Other city

‑ ‑ ‑ ‑ ‑ ‑ International boundary

SLOVENIA

1991 Slovenia declares its independence from Yugoslavia; a ten-day period of fighting ensues.

2004 Slovenia is admitted to NATO and the European Union.

CROATIA

1991 Croatia declares its independence from Yugoslavia; fighting ensues between Croatia and Serbia.

1992 UN peacekeeping force maintains cease-fire.

1995 Croatia signs Dayton Peace Accord.

BOSNIA AND HERZEGOVINA

1992 Bosnia and Herzegovina declares its independence from Yugoslavia; civil war begins.

1992 Serb forces initiate ethnic cleansing campaign against Bosnian Muslims.

1994 NATO forces begin a series of attacks.

1995 Dayton Peace Accord is signed.

© Rand McNally & Co.
N-HMW56600-Z1‑‑1‑-1-1

97

Middle East Events, 1945-2006

Beirut ⊛   National capital

Istanbul •   Other city

— · — · —   International boundary

░░░░░   Oil field

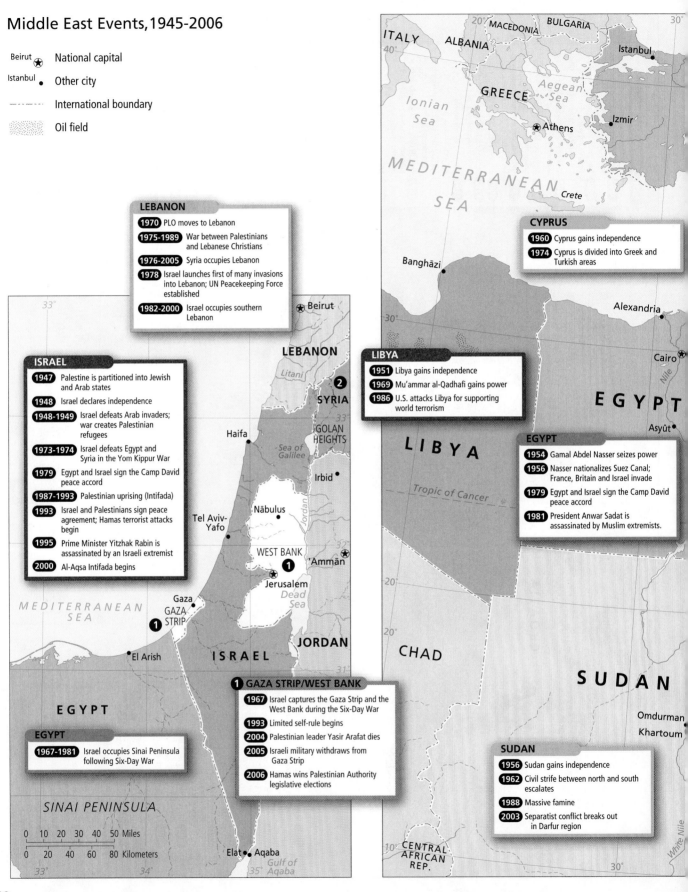

LEBANON

1970 PLO moves to Lebanon

1975-1989 War between Palestinians and Lebanese Christians

1976-2005 Syria occupies Lebanon

1978 Israel launches first of many invasions into Lebanon; UN Peacekeeping Force established

1982-2000 Israel occupies southern Lebanon

ISRAEL

1947 Palestine is partitioned into Jewish and Arab states

1948 Israel declares independence

1948-1949 Israel defeats Arab invaders; war creates Palestinian refugees

1973-1974 Israel defeats Egypt and Syria in the Yom Kippur War

1979 Egypt and Israel sign the Camp David peace accord

1987-1993 Palestinian uprising (Intifada)

1993 Israel and Palestinians sign peace agreement; Hamas terrorist attacks begin

1995 Prime Minister Yitzhak Rabin is assassinated by an Israeli extremist

2000 Al-Aqsa Intifada begins

EGYPT

1967-1981 Israel occupies Sinai Peninsula following Six-Day War

CYPRUS

1960 Cyprus gains independence

1974 Cyprus is divided into Greek and Turkish areas

LIBYA

1951 Libya gains independence

1969 Mu'ammar al-Qadhafi gains power

1986 U.S. attacks Libya for supporting world terrorism

EGYPT

1954 Gamal Abdel Nasser seizes power

1956 Nasser nationalizes Suez Canal; France, Britain and Israel invade

1979 Egypt and Israel sign the Camp David peace accord

1981 President Anwar Sadat is assassinated by Muslim extremists.

① GAZA STRIP/WEST BANK

1967 Israel captures the Gaza Strip and the West Bank during the Six-Day War

1993 Limited self-rule begins

2004 Palestinian leader Yasir Arafat dies

2005 Israeli military withdraws from Gaza Strip

2006 Hamas wins Palestinian Authority legislative elections

SUDAN

1956 Sudan gains independence

1962 Civil strife between north and south escalates

1988 Massive famine

2003 Separatist conflict breaks out in Darfur region

0 10 20 30 40 50 Miles

0 20 40 60 80 Kilometers

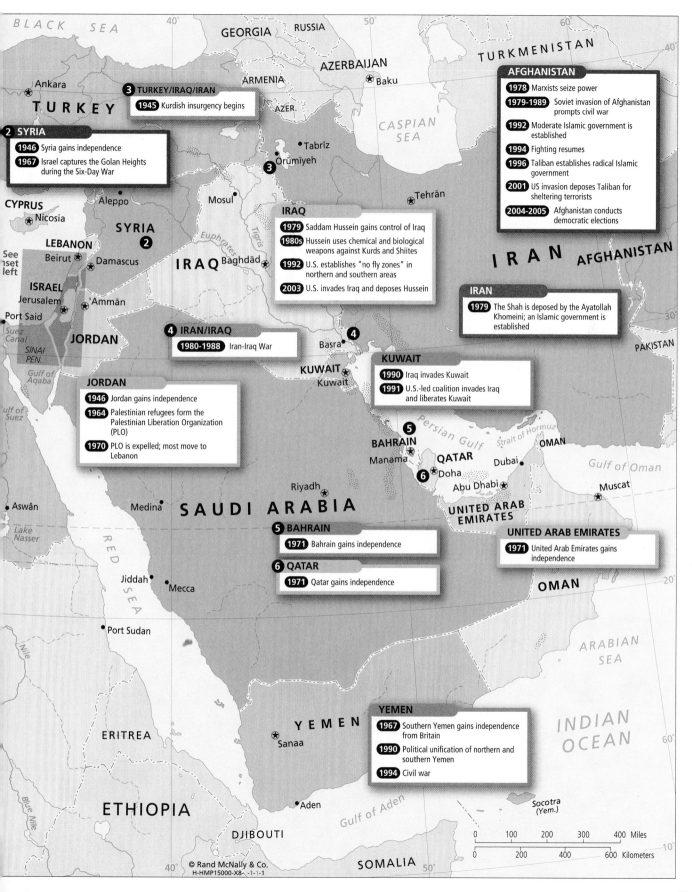

AFGHANISTAN
- **1978** Marxists seize power
- **1979-1989** Soviet invasion of Afghanistan prompts civil war
- **1992** Moderate Islamic government is established
- **1994** Fighting resumes
- **1996** Taliban establishes radical Islamic government
- **2001** US invasion deposes Taliban for sheltering terrorists
- **2004-2005** Afghanistan conducts democratic elections

3 TURKEY/IRAQ/IRAN
- **1945** Kurdish insurgency begins

2 SYRIA
- **1946** Syria gains independence
- **1967** Israel captures the Golan Heights during the Six-Day War

IRAQ
- **1979** Saddam Hussein gains control of Iraq
- **1980s** Hussein uses chemical and biological weapons against Kurds and Shiites
- **1992** U.S. establishes "no fly zones" in northern and southern areas
- **2003** U.S. invades Iraq and deposes Hussein

IRAN
- **1979** The Shah is deposed by the Ayatollah Khomeini; an Islamic government is established

4 IRAN/IRAQ
- **1980-1988** Iran-Iraq War

KUWAIT
- **1990** Iraq invades Kuwait
- **1991** U.S.-led coalition invades Iraq and liberates Kuwait

JORDAN
- **1946** Jordan gains independence
- **1964** Palestinian refugees form the Palestinian Liberation Organization (PLO)
- **1970** PLO is expelled; most move to Lebanon

5 BAHRAIN
- **1971** Bahrain gains independence

6 QATAR
- **1971** Qatar gains independence

UNITED ARAB EMIRATES
- **1971** United Arab Emirates gains independence

YEMEN
- **1967** Southern Yemen gains independence from Britain
- **1990** Political unification of northern and southern Yemen
- **1994** Civil war

© Rand McNally & Co.
H-HMP15000-X8-·-1-1-1

0   100   200   300   400 Miles
0   200   400   600 Kilometers

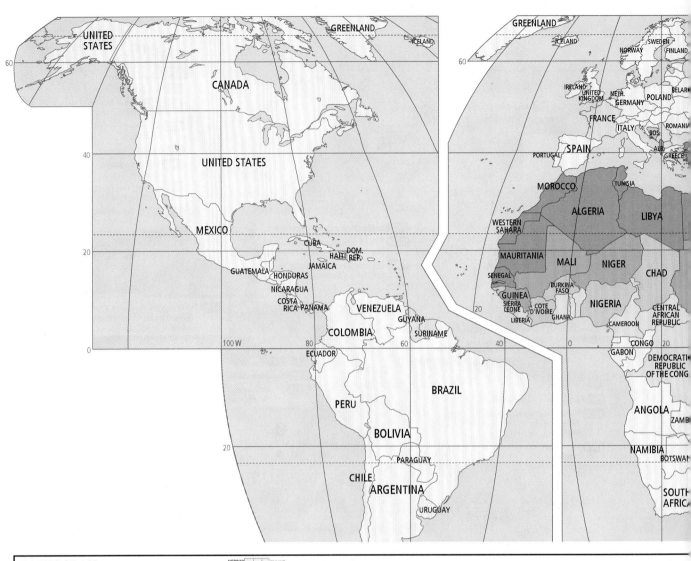

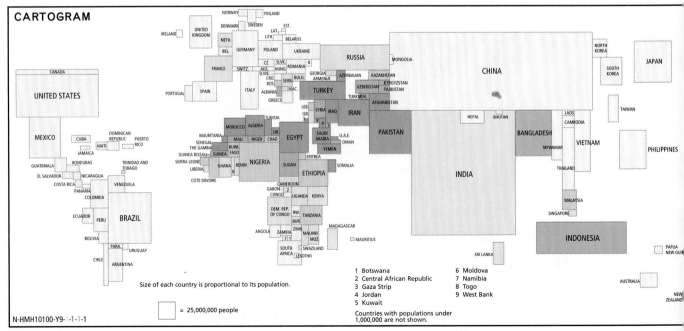

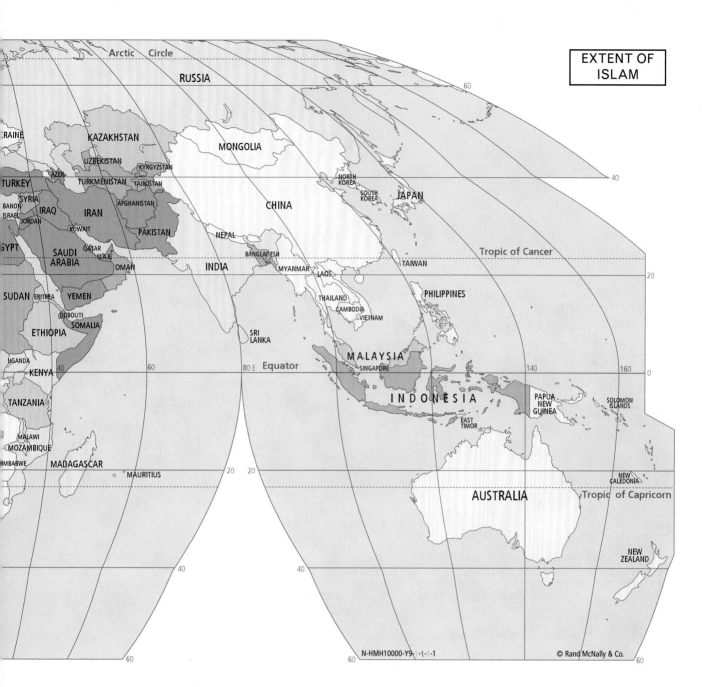

PERCENT MUSLIM

Muslim population as a percentage
of total population by country

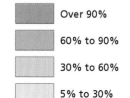

	Over 90%
	60% to 90%
	30% to 60%
	5% to 30%
	Under 5%

artograms

artograms deliberately distort map shapes to achieve specific effects. On this cartogram the
ze of each country is proportional to its population. Countries with large populations are
rger than countries with smaller populations, regardless of the actual size of these countries
the earth.

his cartogram depicts each country as a rectangle as opposed to other cartograms which
tempt to preserve some of the salient shape characteristics for each country. The advantage
the rectangle method is that size comparisons are easier when shapes are consistent.

he cartogram shows the same data as the map above it (Percent Muslim), but uses
pulation-based country shapes rather than actual country shapes. The cartogram allows
ap readers to make inferences about the relationship between population and Muslim
rcentage in each country.

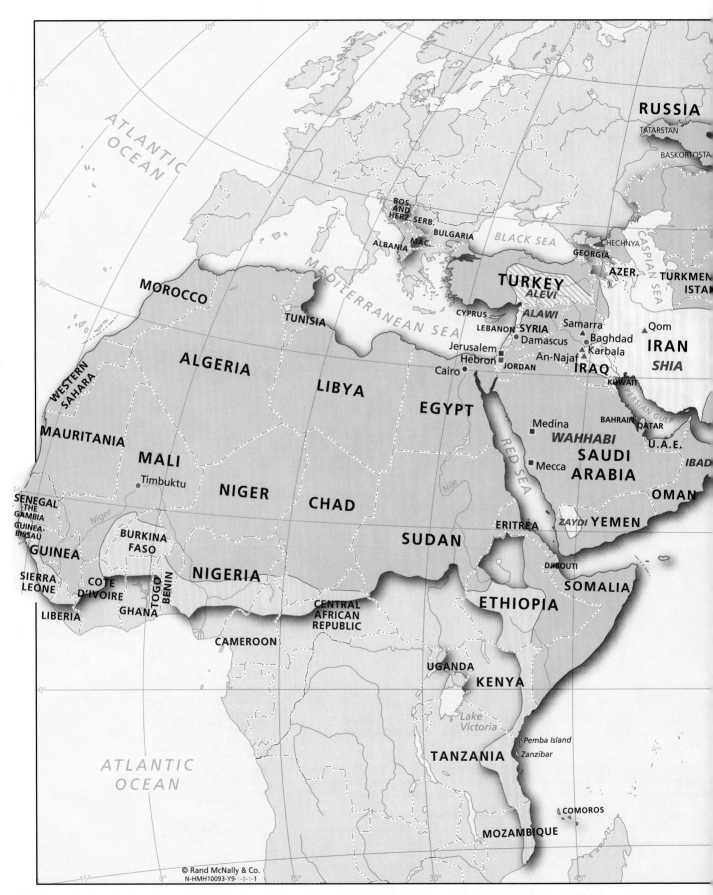

ATLANTIC OCEAN

RUSSIA

TATARSTAN

BASKORTOSTA

BOS. AND HERZ. SERB.

BULGARIA

BLACK SEA

ALBANIA

MAC.

CHECHNYA

GEORGIA

CASPIAN SEA

TURKEY

ALEVI

AZER.

TURKMEN

ISTA

CYPRUS

ALAWI

MEDITERRANEAN SEA

LEBANON

SYRIA

Samarra

Qom

IRAN

MOROCCO

TUNISIA

Jerusalem

Damascus

Baghdad

SHIA

Hebron

JORDAN

An-Najaf

Karbala

WESTERN SAHARA

ALGERIA

LIBYA

Cairo

IRAQ

KUWAIT

ALGERIA

EGYPT

PERSIAN GULF

MAURITANIA

Medina

BAHRAIN

QATAR

MALI

WAHHABI

SAUDI ARABIA

U.A.E.

IBAD

Timbuktu

NIGER

CHAD

RED SEA

Mecca

Nile

OMAN

SENEGAL

THE GAMBIA

Niger

SUDAN

ERITREA

ZAYDI

YEMEN

GUINEA-BISSAU

BURKINA FASO

GUINEA

NIGERIA

DJIBOUTI

SIERRA LEONE

COTE D'IVOIRE

TOGO BENIN

CENTRAL AFRICAN REPUBLIC

ETHIOPIA

SOMALIA

LIBERIA

GHANA

CAMEROON

UGANDA

KENYA

ATLANTIC OCEAN

Lake Victoria

Pemba Island

TANZANIA

Zanzibar

COMOROS

MOZAMBIQUE

© Rand McNally & Co.
N-HMH10093-Y9- -1-1-1

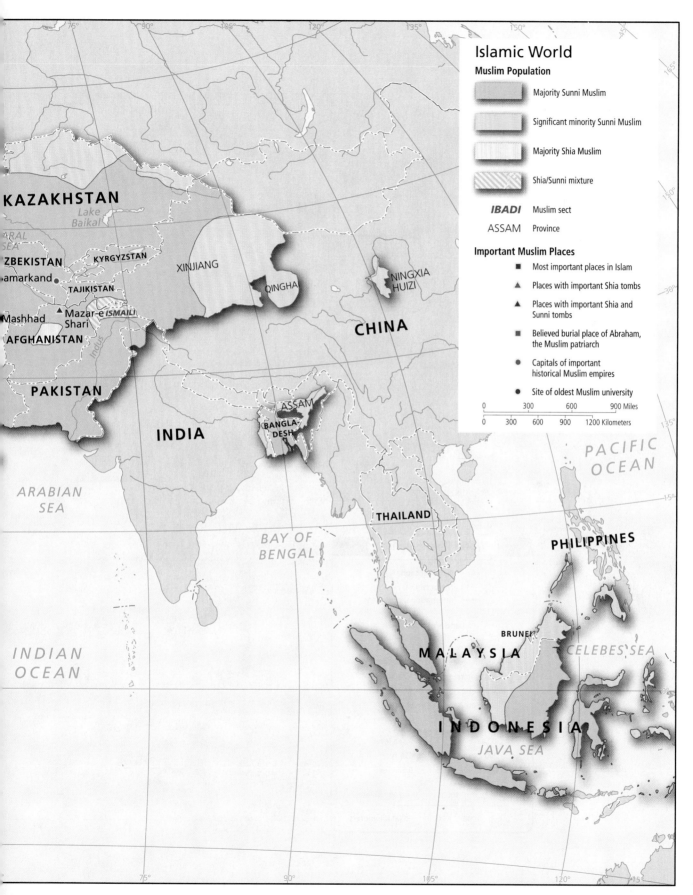

Islamic World

Muslim Population

Majority Sunni Muslim

Significant minority Sunni Muslim

Majority Shia Muslim

Shia/Sunni mixture

IBADI   Muslim sect

ASSAM   Province

Important Muslim Places

■ Most important places in Islam

▲ Places with important Shia tombs

▲ Places with important Shia and Sunni tombs

■ Believed burial place of Abraham, the Muslim patriarch

● Capitals of important historical Muslim empires

● Site of oldest Muslim university

| 0 | 300 | 600 | 900 Miles |
| 0 | 300 | 600 | 900 | 1200 Kilometers |

KAZAKHSTAN

Lake Baikal

ARAL SEA

ZBEKISTAN

KYRGYZSTAN

amarkand

TAJIKISTAN

XINJIANG

QINGHA

NINGXIA HUIZI

Mashhad

Mazar-e Shari   *ISMAILI*

CHINA

AFGHANISTAN

Indus

PAKISTAN

INDIA

ASSAM

BANGLA-DESH

ARABIAN SEA

BAY OF BENGAL

THAILAND

PACIFIC OCEAN

PHILIPPINES

INDIAN OCEAN

BRUNEI

MALAYSIA

CELEBES SEA

INDONESIA

JAVA SEA

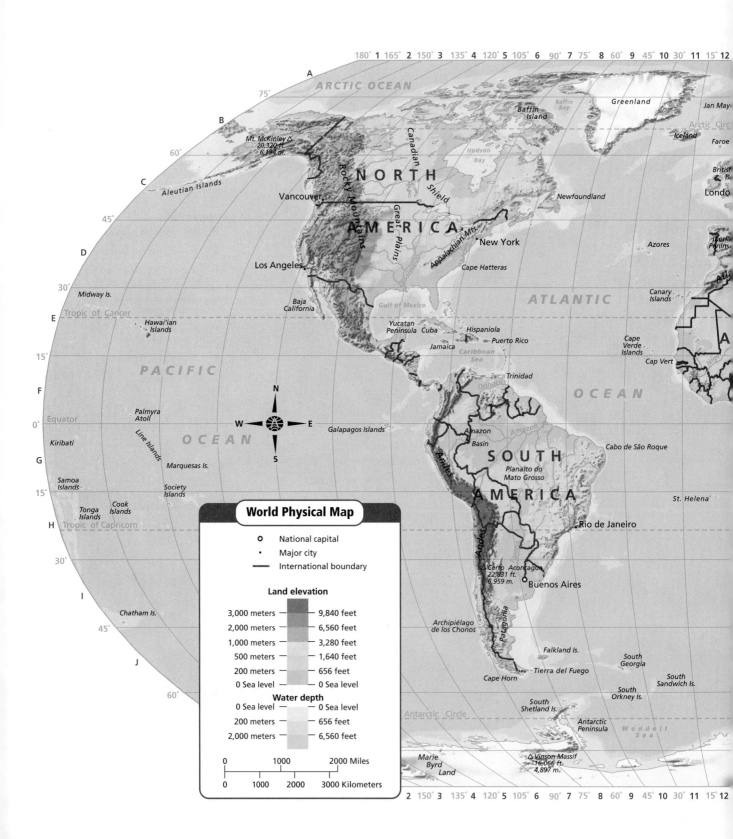

World Physical Map

○ National capital
• Major city
— International boundary

Land elevation

3,000 meters	9,840 feet
2,000 meters	6,560 feet
1,000 meters	3,280 feet
500 meters	1,640 feet
200 meters	656 feet
0 Sea level	0 Sea level

Water depth

0 Sea level	0 Sea level
200 meters	656 feet
2,000 meters	6,560 feet

0   1000   2000 Miles

0   1000   2000   3000 Kilometers

ARCTIC OCEAN

A

75°

Spitsbergen

Franz
Josef Land

Nordkapp

Novaya
Zemlya

B

60°

Scandinavia

Siberia

Bering
Sea

North
Sea

Volga

Ural Mts.

Ob'

Yenisey

C

Moscow

Sea of Okhotsk

Kamchatka
Peninsula

45°

Alps

Don

Aral Sea

A S I A

Sakhalin

Balkan
Peninsula

Black Sea

Caucasus

Sardinia

Gora El'brus
18,510 ft.
5,642 m.

Pamir

Hokkaidō

D

Sicily

Crete Cyprus

Zagros Mts.

Gobi Desert

Honshū

30°

Cairo

Plateau
of
Tibet

Beijing

Sea of Japan

Mts.

Sahara

Nile

Red Sea

Himalayas

Mt. Everest
29,028 ft.
8,848 m.

Kyūshū

East
China
Sea

PACIFIC

Tropic of Cancer

E

Arabian
Peninsula

Ganges

Taiwan

Mumbai
(Bombay)

Deccan

Arabian
Sea

Bay of
Bengal

Hainan Dao

Mariana
Islands

Wake
Island

15°

A F R I C A

Sahel

Socotra

Lakshadweep

South China
Sea

Luzon

Guam

O C E A N

Gulf of
Guinea

Congo

Ethiopian
Plateau

Sri Lanka

Mindanao

Palau
Islands

Caroline
Islands

Marshall
Islands

F

Maldive
Islands

Malay
Peninsula

Borneo

Equator

0°

Congo
Basin

Zambezi

Kilimanjaro
19,340 ft.
5,895 m.

Seychelles

Sumatra

Celebes

New Guinea

Solomon
Islands

G

Java

INDIAN

Cocos
Islands

15°

Madagascar

Coral Sea

New
Hebrides

Mauritius

Great
Sandy
Desert

New Caledonia

Fiji
Is.

Kalahari
Desert

Reunion

Darling

AUSTRALIA

Tropic of Capricorn

H

Johannesburg

OCEAN

Great Dividing Range

30°

Cape of Good Hope

Cape Leeuwin

Sydney

North Island

Aoraki
(Mt. Cook)
12,316 ft.
3,754 m.

I

Tasmania

South Island

45°

Îles Kerguélen

J

SOUTHERN

OCEAN

60°

Antarctic Circle

K

Queen Maud
Land

Enderby
Land

Wilkes Land

Victoria Land

75°

A N T A R C T I C A

© Rand McNally & Co.
Made in U.S.A.
N-CLA10000-A1- -5- -7

L

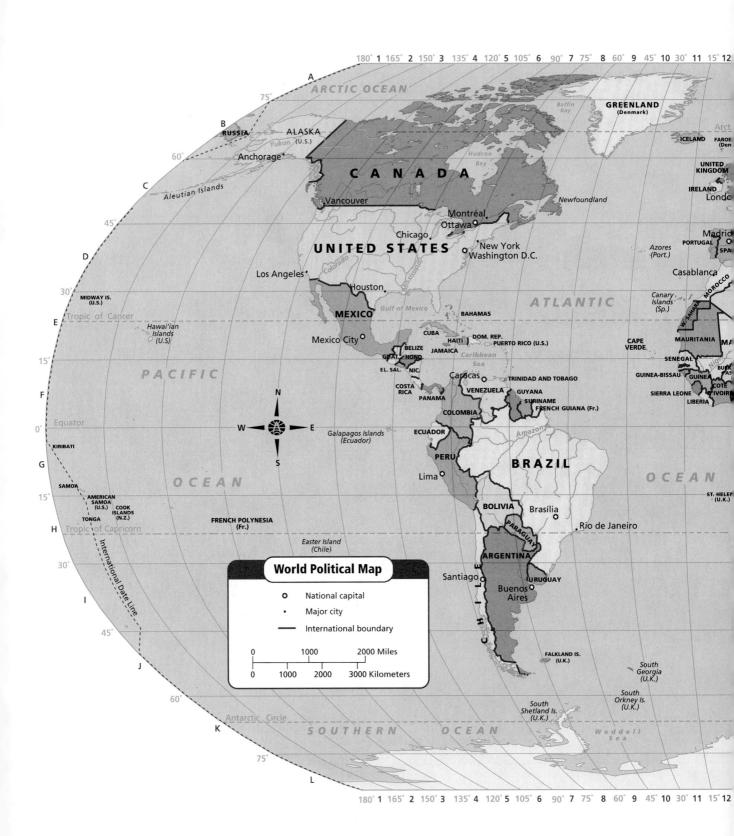

World Political Map

⊙ National capital

· Major city

— International boundary

0	1000	2000 Miles
0	1000	2000	3000 Kilometers

Labels on map

ARCTIC OCEAN

GREENLAND (Denmark)

Baffin Bay

Arct

ICELAND   FAROE (Den

RUSSIA   ALASKA (U.S.)

Yukon

Anchorage

UNITED KINGDOM

IRELAND   Londo

C A N A D A

Hudson Bay

Newfoundland

Aleutian Islands

Vancouver

Montréal
Ottawa

Chicago

Madrid

UNITED STATES

New York
Washington D.C.

PORTUGAL   SPA

Azores (Port.)

Los Angeles

Houston

Colorado

Casablanca

MOROCCO

MIDWAY IS. (U.S.)

Tropic of Cancer

Gulf of Mexico

ATLANTIC

Canary Islands (Sp.)

W. SAHARA

MEXICO

BAHAMAS

Hawai'ian Islands (U.S)

CUBA

Mexico City

BELIZE
GUAT. HOND.
EL. SAL. NIC.

HAITI   DOM. REP.
JAMAICA   PUERTO RICO (U.S.)

Caribbean Sea

CAPE VERDE

MAURITANIA   MA

SENEGAL

Niger

PACIFIC

COSTA RICA
PANAMA

Caracas

TRINIDAD AND TOBAGO

GUINEA-BISSAU   GUINEA

VENEZUELA   GUYANA
SURINAME
FRENCH GUIANA (Fr.)

SIERRA LEONE   COTE D'IVOIR
LIBERIA

COLOMBIA

N

Equator

Galapagos Islands (Ecuador)

ECUADOR

W   E

Amazon

KIRIBATI

PERU

BRAZIL

OCEAN

S

SAMOA

OCEAN

Lima

ST. HELE (U.K.)

AMERICAN SAMOA (U.S.)   COOK ISLANDS (N.Z.)

BOLIVIA

Brasília

TONGA

FRENCH POLYNESIA (Fr.)

Tropic of Capricorn

Rio de Janeiro

International Date Line

Easter Island (Chile)

PARAGUAY

ARGENTINA   URUGUAY

Santiago

Buenos Aires

CHILE

FALKLAND IS. (U.K.)

South Georgia (U.K.)

South Orkney Is. (U.K.)

South Shetland Is. (U.K.)

Antarctic Circle

SOUTHERN   OCEAN

Weddell Sea

13 15° **14** 30° **15** 45° **16** 60° **17** 75° **18** 90° **19** 105° **20** 120° **21** 135° **22** 150° **23** 165° **24** 180°

ARCTIC OCEAN

Franz Josef Land
75°
A

itsbergen
(Nor.)
Novaya
Zemlya

circle
B

Yenisey
Lena
60°
Bering

NORWAY
FINLAND

SWEDEN
EST.
LAT.
LITH.

R U S S I A

Sea of Okhotsk
C

north
Sea
DEN.
BELARUS

Volga
Moscow

Novosibirsk

NETH.
GERMANY
POLAND

45°

ANCE
CZ.
SLOV.
UKRAINE

AUS.
HUNG.
ROM.

KAZAKHSTAN

MONGOLIA

Sea of Japan

SWI.
BOS.
SERB.
MOLD.

NORTH
KOREA
D

ITALY
ALB.
MAC.
BUL.

Black Sea
GEO.
ARM. AZER.
UZBEKISTAN
KYRG.

Beijing
SOUTH
KOREA
Seoul
JAPAN

Rome
GREECE
TURKEY

TURKMENISTAN
TAJIK.

C H I N A

Tōkyō

Crete
CYPRUS
LEB.
SYRIA

TUNISIA
ISRAEL
IRAQ
IRAN
AFGHANISTAN

Tehrān

Shanghai
Yangtze
30°
PACIFIC
E

GERIA
JORDAN
KUWAIT

LIBYA
EGYPT
SAUDI
QATAR

PAKISTAN
Karāchi
NEPAL
Ganges

Tropic of Cancer

ARABIA
U.A.E.

BHU.
Kolkata
(Calcutta)
BNG.
TAIWAN
Hong Kong
NORTHERN
MARIANA ISLANDS
(U.S.)
WAKE ISLAND
(U.S.)

NIGER
CHAD
SUDAN

OMAN
Mumbai
(Bombay)
I N D I A

MYANMAR
LAOS
South China
15°

GUAM
(U.S.)

ERITREA
YEMEN

Arabian
Sea
Bay of
Bengal
THAILAND
VIETNAM
Sea
PHILIPPINES

Manila
F

NIGERIA
Addis
Ababa
DJIBOUTI

Bangkok
CAMBODIA

Lagos
CAMEROON
CENTRAL
AFRICAN
REPUBLIC
ETHIOPIA

SRI LANKA

BRUNEI

PALAU
FED. STATES OF
MICRONESIA

MARSHALL
ISLANDS

QUATORIAL
GUINEA

SOMALIA
MALAYSIA

GABON
RWANDA
UGANDA
KENYA
MALDIVES
SINGAPORE
Borneo
O C E A N

Congo
DEM. REP.
OF THE CONGO
BURUNDI

SEYCHELLES
Sumatra
New Guinea
Equator
0°

TANZANIA
Jakarta
I N D O N E S I A
PAPUA
NEW GUINEA

ANGOLA
ZAMBIA
MALAWI

I N D I A N
Java
EAST TIMOR
SOLOMON
ISLANDS
G

COMOROS
MADAGASCAR

ZIMBABWE
MAURITIUS
15°

VANUATU

NAMIBIA
MOZAMBIQUE
Coral Sea
NEW CALEDONIA
(Fr.)
FIJI

BOTSWANA
REUNION
(Fr.)
Tropic of Capricorn
H

Johannesburg
SWAZILAND
O C E A N

SOUTH
AFRICA
LESOTHO
AUSTRALIA
Brisbane

Perth
30°

Sydney

Melbourne
Auckland

NEW ZEALAND
I

Tasmania

Îles Kerguélen
(Fr.)
45°

J

60°
Antarctic Circle

S O U T H E R N   O C E A N
K

75°

A N T A R C T I C A
© Rand McNally & Co.
Made in U.S.A.
N-CLA10000-P1- -9-9-11
L

13 15° **14** 30° **15** 45° **16** 60° **17** 75° **18** 90° **19** 105° **20** 120° **21** 135° **22** 150° **23** 165° **24** 180°

107

Index

The following index lists important place names appearing on the maps in the *Historical Atlas of the World*. Countries and regions are indexed to the several maps which portray their areal and political development at successive periods. In general, each index entry includes a map reference key and the page number of the map. Alternate names and spellings are added in parentheses.

World Facts and Comparisons

General Information

Equatorial diameter of the earth, 7,926.38 miles (12,756.27 km.).

Polar diameter of the earth, 7,899.80 miles (12,713.50 km.).

Mean diameter of the earth, 7,917.52 miles (12,742.01 km.).

Equatorial circumference of the earth, 24,901.46 miles (40,075.02 km.).

Polar circumference of the earth, 24,855.34 miles (40,000.79 km.).

Mean distance from the earth to the sun, 93,020,000 miles (149,700,000 km.).

Mean distance from the earth to the moon, 238,857 miles (384,403 km.).

Total area of the earth, 197,000,000 sq. miles (510,100,000 sq. km.).

Highest elevation on the earth's surface, Mt. Everest, Asia, 29,028 ft. (8,848 m.).

Lowest elevation on the earth's land surface, shores of the Dead Sea, Asia, 1,339 ft. (408 m.) below sea level.

Greatest known depth of the ocean, southwest of Guam, Pacific Ocean, 35,810 ft. (10,915 m.).

Total land area of the earth (incl. inland water and Antarctica), 57,900,000 sq. miles (150,100,000 sq. km.).

Area of Africa, 11,700,000 sq. miles (30,300,000 sq. km.).

Area of Antarctica, 5,400,000 sq. miles (14,000,000 sq. km.).

Area of Asia, 17,300,000 sq. miles (44,900,000 sq. km.).

Area of Europe, 3,800,000 sq. miles (9,900,000 sq. km.).

Area of North America, 9,500,000 sq. miles (24,700,000 sq. km.).

Area of Oceania (incl. Australia) 3,300,000 sq. miles (8,500,000 sq. km.).

Area of South America, 6,900,000 sq. miles (17,800,000 sq. km.).

Population of the earth (est. 1/1/04), 6,339,505,000.

Principal Islands and Their Areas

ISLAND	Area (Sq. Mi.)	(Sq. Km)
Baffin I., Canada	195,928	507,451
Banks I., Canada	27,038	70,028
Borneo (Kalimantan), Asia	287,299	744,100
Bougainville, Papua New Guinea	3,591	9,300
Cape Breton I., Canada	3,981	10,311
Celebes (Sulawesi), Indonesia	73,057	189,216
Corsica, France	3,367	8,720
Crete, Greece	3,189	8,259
Cuba, N. America	42,780	110,800
Cyprus, Asia	3,572	9,251
Devon I., Canada	21,331	55,247
Ellesmere I., Canada	75,767	196,236
Great Britain, U.K.	88,795	229,978
Greenland, N. America	840,004	2,175,600
Hainan Dao, China	13,127	34,000
Hawaii, U.S.	4,021	10,414
Hispaniola, N. America	29,421	76,200
Hokkaidō, Japan	32,245	83,515
Honshū, Japan	89,176	239,966
Iceland, Europe	39,769	103,000
Ireland, Europe	32,587	84,400
Jamaica, N. America	4,247	11,000
Java (Jawa), Indonesia	51,038	132,187
Kodiak I., U.S.	3,670	9,505
Kyūshū, Japan	17,129	44,363
Long Island, U.S.	1,377	3,566
Luzon, Philippines	40,420	104,688
Madagascar, Africa	226,642	587,000
Melville I., Canada	16,274	42,149
Mindanao, Philippines	36,537	94,630
New Britain, Papua New Guinea	14,093	36,500
New Caledonia, Oceania	6,252	16,192
Newfoundland, Canada	42,031	108,860
New Guinea, Asia-Oceania	308,882	800,000
North I., New Zealand	44,333	114,821
Novaya Zemlya, Russia	31,892	82,600
Prince of Wales I., Canada	12,872	33,339
Puerto Rico, N. America	3,514	9,100
Sakhalin, Russia	29,498	76,400
Sardinia, Italy	9,301	24,090
Sicily, Italy	9,926	25,709
South I., New Zealand	57,708	149,463
Southampton I., Canada	15,913	41,214
Spitsbergen, Norway	15,260	39,523
Sri Lanka, Asia	24,942	64,600
Sumatra (Sumatera), Indonesia	182,860	473,606
Taiwan, Asia	13,900	36,000
Tasmania, Australia	26,178	67,800
Tierra del Fuego, S. America	18,600	48,174
Timor, Asia	5,743	14,874
Vancouver I., Canada	12,079	31,285
Victoria I., Canada	83,897	217,291

Principal Lakes, Oceans, Seas and Their Areas

LAKE Country	Area (Sq. Mi.)	(Sq. Km.)
Arabian Sea	1,492,000	3,863,000
Aral Sea, Kazakhstan-Uzbekistan	14,900	38,600
Arctic Ocean	5,400,000	14,000,000
Athabasca, L., Canada	3,064	7,935
Atlantic Ocean	29,600,000	76,800,000
Baikal, L. (Ozero Baykal), Russia	12,162	31,500
Balkash, L., Kazakhstan	7,066	18,301
Baltic Sea, Europe	163,000	422,000
Bering Sea, Asia-N.A.	876,000	2,270,000
Black Sea, Europe-Asia	178,000	461,000
Caribbean Sea, N.A.-S.A.	1,063,000	2,754,000
Caspian Sea, Asia-Europe	143,200	371,000
Chad, L., Cameroon-Chad-Nigeria	6,300	16,300
Erie, L., Canada-U.S.	9,910	25,667
Eyre, L., Australia	3,700	9,600
Great Bear Lake, Canada	12,095	31,326
Great Salt Lake, U.S.	1,680	4,351
Great Slave Lake, Canada	11,030	28,568
Hudson Bay, Canada	475,000	1,230,000
Huron, L., Canada-U.S.	23,000	59,600
Indian Ocean	26,500,000	68,600,000
Japan, Sea of, Asia	389,000	1,008,000
Ladozhskoye Ozero (L. Ladoga), Russia	6,800	17,700
Manitoba, L., Canada	1,785	4,624
Mediterranean Sea, Europe-Africa-Asia	967,000	2,505,000
Mexico, Gulf of, N. America	596,000	1,544,000
Michigan, L., U.S.	22,300	57,800
Nicaragua, Lago de, Nicaragua	3,150	8,158
North Sea, Europe	222,000	575,000
Nyasa, L., Malawi-Mozambique-Tanzania	11,150	28,878
Onezhskoye Ozero (L. Onega), Russia	3,753	9,720
Ontario, L., Canada-U.S.	7,540	19,529
Pacific Ocean	60,100,000	155,600,000
Red Sea, Africa-Asia	169,000	438,000
Rudolf, L., Ethiopia-Kenya	2,473	6,405
Southern Ocean	7,800,000	20,300,000
Superior, L., Canada-U.S.	31,700	82,100
Tanganyika, L., Africa	12,350	31,986
Titicaca, Lago, Bolivia-Peru	3,200	8,300
Torrens, L., Australia	2,278	5,900
Victoria, L., Kenya-Tanzania-Uganda	26,820	69,464
Winnipeg, L., Canada	9,416	24,387
Winnipegosis, L., Canada	2,075	5,374
Yellow Sea, China-Korea	480,000	1,240,000

Principal Mountains and Their Heights

MOUNTAIN Country	Elev. (Ft.)	(M.)
Aconcagua, Cerro, Argentina	22,831	6,959
Ağrı Dağı, Turkey	16,854	5,137
Annapurna, Nepal	26,545	8,091
Aoraki, New Zealand	12,316	3,754
Bia, Phou, Laos	9,252	2,820
Blanc, Mont (Monte Bianco), France-Italy	15,771	4,807
Bolívar, Pico, Venezuela	16,427	5,007
Borah Pk., Idaho, U.S.	12,662	3,859
Boundary Pk., Nevada, U.S.	13,143	4,006
Cameroon Mtn., Cameroon	13,451	4,100
Carrauntoohil, Ireland	3,406	1,038
Chaltel, Cerro (Monte Fitzroy), Argentina-Chile	10,958	3,340
Chimborazo, Ecuador	20,702	6,310
Chirripó, Cerro, Costa Rica	12,530	3,819
Cristóbal Colón, Pico, Colombia	18,947	5,775
Damāvand, Qolleh-ye, Iran	18,386	5,604
Duarte, Pico, Dominican Rep.	10,417	3,175
Dufourspitze (Monte Rosa), Italy-Switzerland	15,203	4,634
Elbert, Mt., Colorado, U.S.	14,433	4,399
El'brus, Gora, Russia	18,510	5,642
Etna, Mt., Italy	10,902	3,323
Everest, Mt., China-Nepal	29,028	8,848
Fairweather, Mt., Alaska-Canada	15,300	4,663
Fuji, Mt., Japan	12,388	3,776
Galdhøpiggen, Norway	8,100	2,469
Gannett Pk., Wyoming, U.S.	13,804	4,207
Gerlachovský štít, Slovakia	8,711	2,655
Giluwe, Mt., Papua New Guinea	14,331	4,368
Grand Teton, Wyoming, U.S.	13,770	4,197
Grossglockner, Austria	12,457	3,797
Haleakalā Crater, Hawaii, U.S.	10,032	3,058
Hood, Mt., Oregon, U.S.	11,239	3,426
Huascarán, Nevado, Peru	22,133	6,746
Illampu, Nevado, Bolivia	21,066	6,421
Illimani, Nevado de, Bolivia	21,184	6,457
Ismail Samani, pik, Tajikistan	24,590	7,495
Iztaccíhuatl, Mexico	17,159	5,230
Jaya, Puncak, Indonesia	16,503	5,030
Jungfrau, Switzerland	13,642	4,158
K2 (Godwin Austen), China-Pakistan	28,250	8,611
Kānchenjunga, India-Nepal	28,208	8,598
Kātrīnā, Jabal, Egypt	8,668	2,642
Kebnekaise, Sweden	6,926	2,111
Kilimanjaro, Tanzania	19,340	5,895
Kinabalu, Gunong, Malaysia	13,455	4,101
Kirinyaga (Mt. Kenya), Kenya	17,058	5,199
Klyuchevskaya Sopka, Vulkan, Russia	15,584	4,750
Kosciuszko, Mt., Australia	7,313	2,229
Koussi, Emi, Chad	11,204	3,415
Kula Kangri, Bhutan	24,784	7,554
Lassen Pk., California, U.S.	10,457	3,187
Llullaillaco, Volcán, Argentina-Chile	22,110	6,739
Logan, Mt., Canada	19,551	5,959
Margherita Peak, D.R.C. of the Congo-Uganda	16,763	5,109
Markham, Mt., Antarctica	14,049	4,282
Matterhorn, Italy-Switzerland	14,692	4,478
Mauna Loa, Hawaii, U.S.	13,677	4,169
Mayon Volcano, Philippines	8,077	2,462
McKinley, Mt., Alaska, U.S.	20,320	6,194
Mitchell, Mt., North Carolina, U.S.	6,684	2,037
Mulhacén, Spain (continental)	11,424	3,482
Musala, Bulgaria	9,596	2,925
Nabī Shu'ayb, Jabal an-, Yemen	12,008	3,660
Nanda Devi, India	25,645	7,817
Nānga Parbat, Pakistan	26,660	8,126
Narodnaya, Gora, Russia	6,214	1,894
Nevis, Ben, United Kingdom	4,406	1,343
Ojos del Salado, Nevado, Argentina-Chile	22,615	6,893
Ólimbos, Greece	9,570	2,917
Olympus, Mt., Washington, U.S.	7,969	2,429
Orizaba, Pico de, Mexico	18,406	5,610
Paektu San, North Korea-China	9,003	2,744
Paricutín, Mexico	9,186	2,800
Pelée, Montagne, Martinique	4,583	1,397
Pikes Pk., Colorado, U.S.	14,110	4,301
Pobedy, pik, China-Kyrgyzstan	24,406	7,439
Popocatépetl, Volcán, Mexico	17,930	5,465
Rainier, Mt., Washington, U.S.	14,411	4,392
Ras Dashen Terara, Ethiopia	15,158	4,620
Robson, Mt., Canada	12,972	3,954
Roraima, Mt., Brazil-Guyana-Venezuela	9,432	2,875
Ruapehu, Mt., New Zealand	9,177	2,797
Sajama, Nevado, Bolivia	21,463	6,542
Shasta, Mt., California, U.S.	14,162	4,317
Tahat, Algeria	9,541	2,908
Tajumulco, Volcán, Guatemala	13,845	4,220
Tirich Mīr, Pakistan	25,230	7,690
Toubkal, Jebel, Morocco	13,665	4,165
Turquino, Pico, Cuba	6,470	1,972
Uluru (Ayers Rock), Australia	2,831	863
Vesuvius, Italy	4,203	1,281
Victoria, Mt., Papua New Guinea	13,238	4,035
Vinson Massif, Antarctica	16,066	4,897
Washington, Mt., New Hampshire, U.S.	6,288	1,917
Whitney, Mt., California, U.S.	14,494	4,418
Wilhelm, Mt., Papua New Guinea	14,793	4,509
Wrangell, Mt., Alaska, U.S.	14,163	4,317
Yü Shan, Taiwan	13,114	3,997
Zugspitze, Austria-Germany	9,718	2,962

Principal Rivers and Their Lengths

RIVER Continent	Length (Mi.)	(Km.)
Aldan, Asia	1,412	2,273
Amazonas-Ucayali, S. America	3,900	6,276
Amu Darya, Asia	1,578	2,540
Amur, Asia	2,744	4,416
Araguaia, S. America	1,367	2,200
Arkansas, N. America	1,459	2,348
Athabasca, N. America	765	1,231
Ayeyarwady, Asia	1,300	2,092
Brahmaputra, Asia	1,770	2,849
Canadian, N. America	906	1,458
Churchill, N. America	1,000	1,609
Colorado, N. America (U.S.-Mexico)	1,450	2,334
Columbia, N. America	1,243	2,000
Congo (Zaïre), Africa	2,880	4,635
Danube, Europe	1,776	2,858
Darling, Australia	864	1,390
Dnieper, Europe	1,367	2,200
Dniester, Europe	840	1,352
Don, Europe	1,162	1,870
Elbe, Europe	720	1,159
Euphrates, Asia	1,510	2,430
Fraser, N. America	851	1,370
Ganges, Asia	1,560	2,511
Godāvari, Asia	930	1,497
Green, N. America	730	1,175
Huang (Yellow), Asia	3,395	5,464
Indus, Asia	1,800	2,897
Kama, Europe	1,122	1,805
Kasai, Africa	1,338	2,153
Kolyma, Asia	1,323	2,129
Lena, Asia	2,734	4,400
Limpopo, Africa	1,100	1,770
Mackenzie, N. America	2,635	4,241
Madeira, S. America	2,013	3,240
Marañón, S. America	1,000	1,609
Mekong, Asia	2,600	4,184
Mississippi, N. America	2,348	3,779
Missouri, N. America	2,315	3,726
Murray, Australia	1,566	2,520
Negro, S. America	1,305	2,100
Niger, Africa	2,600	4,184
Nile, Africa	4,145	6,671
North Platte, N. America	618	995
Ob'-Irtysh, Asia	3,362	5,411
Ohio, N. America	981	1,579
Orange, Africa	1,300	2,092
Orinoco, S. America	1,600	2,575
Ottawa, N. America	790	1,271
Paraguay, S. America	1,610	2,591
Paraná, S. America	2,796	4,500
Peace, N. America	1,195	1,923
Pechora, Europe	1,124	1,809
Pecos, N. America	735	1,183
Pilcomayo, S. America	1,550	2,494
Plata-Paraná, S. America	3,030	4,876
Purús, S. America	1,860	2,993
Red, N. America	1,270	2,044
Rhine, Europe	820	1,320
Rio Grande, N. America	1,885	3,034
St. Lawrence, N. America	800	1,287
Salween (Nu), Asia	1,750	2,816
São Francisco, S. America	1,988	3,199
Saskatchewan-Bow, N. America	1,205	1,939
Snake, N. America	1,038	1,670
Syr Darya, Asia	1,370	2,205
Tarim, Asia	1,328	2,137
Tigris, Asia	1,180	1,899
Tocantins, S. America	1,640	2,639
Ucayali, S. America	1,220	1,963
Ural, Asia	1,509	2,428
Uruguay, S. America	1,025	1,650
Verkhnyaya Tunguska (Angara), Asia	1,105	1,779
Vilyuy, Asia	1,647	2,650
Volga, Europe	2,194	3,531
Xingu, S. America	1,230	1,979
Yangtze (Chang), Asia	3,915	6,300
Yenisey, Asia	2,543	4,092
Yukon, N. America	1,979	3,185
Zambezi, Africa	1,700	2,736